Fostering Local Entrepreneurship in a Multinational Enterprise

Joe J. Amberg
and Sara L. McGaughey

Routledge
Taylor & Francis Group
LONDON AND NEW YORK

First published 2017 by Routledge

2 Park Square, Milton Park, Abingdon, Oxfordshire OX14 4RN
52 Vanderbilt Avenue, New York, NY 10017

Routledge is an imprint of the Taylor & Francis Group, an informa business

First issued in paperback 2019

British Library Cataloguing-in-Publication Data
A catalogue record for this book is available from the British Library

Library of Congress Cataloging-in-Publication Data
Names: Amberg, Joe J., author. | McGaughey, Sara L., 1968– author.
Title: Fostering local entrepreneurship in a multinational enterprise / by Joe J. Amberg and Sara L. McGaughey.
Description: Abingdon, Oxon ; New York, NY : Routledge, 2017. | Series: Routledge frontiers of business management ; 7 | Includes bibliographical references and index.
Identifiers: LCCN 2016040314 | ISBN 9781138913387 (hardback) | ISBN 9781315230702 (ebook)
Subjects: LCSH: International business enterprises—Management—Case studies. | Entrepreneurship—Case studies | New products—Case studies.
Classification: LCC HD62.4 .A4326 2017 | DDC 658.4/21—dc23
LC record available at https://lccn.loc.gov/2016040314

ISBN: 978-1-138-91338-7 (hbk)
ISBN: 978-0-367-35041-3 (pbk)

Typeset in Galliard
by Apex CoVantage, LLC

Fostering Local Entrepreneurship in a Multinational Enterprise

Corporate entrepreneurship involves new business creation within established companies, the strategic renewal of existing business, and, ultimately, the search for sustainable competitive advantage in an increasingly globalised economy. Yet it remains elusive for many firms.

In a collaboration between a practitioner and academic, Joe J. Amberg and Sara L. McGaughey explore corporate entrepreneuring within a large conglomerate multinational enterprise: Siemens AG. In early 2009, following a prolonged period of business stagnation and a huge bribery scandal, Siemens' top management identified a severe lack of entrepreneurship as a critical issue. The strengthening of 'local entrepreneurship' became a new priority in the strategic planning for 2010 to 2014. By examining three contrasting ventures in the Siemens business unit Fire Safety between 2008 and 2012, the authors identify key drivers and impediments that sustain inertia in corporate entrepreneuring within this global organisation.

This study offers an insightful contribution to our growing – yet still fledgling – understanding of corporate entrepreneurship in global corporations, highlighting the importance of context, interdependencies between critical factors, and the false promise of universal best practice.

Joe J. Amberg holds a DBA from Strathclyde University, UK, an MBA from University of St.Gallen and a Bachelor of Science from University of Rapperswil (CH). He is currently engaged in global portfolio project management and is project lead of critical innovation projects for V-ZUG AG, a Swiss household appliances corporation. From 1999 to 2012 Joe was employed in the Siemens Business Technologies Division, Fire Safety Unit, or its predecessors. His various roles included Head of R&D Fire Systems, Project Portfolio Manager Fire Systems, Global R&D Coordinator and Innovation Manager, Integration Manager for a Korean acquisition, and Business Development and Strategy for the global fire safety business.

Sara L. McGaughey is Professor of International Business at Griffith University, Australia. She holds a PhD (Management) from University of Queensland, and an MBA (International Business) and a Bachelor of Arts (Japanese) from Monash University, Australia. Sara's research interests include international new venturing, corporate entrepreneuring in global firms, headquarter-subsidiary relations, institutional entrepreneurship and global standards, foreign direct investment and knowledge spillovers, and qualitative research methods. She has published in *Academy of Management Review*, *Journal of Management Studies*, and *Journal of World Business*, among others, and has authored a research monograph on portfolio entrepreneurship and internationalisation.

Routledge Frontiers of Business Management

For a full list of titles in this series, please visit www.routledge.com/series/rfbm

1 **Managing Innovation and Cultural Management in the Digital Era**
The case of the National Palace Museum
Edited by Rua-Huan Tsaih and Tzu-Shian Han

2 **Managing Convergence in Innovation**
The new paradigm of technological innovation
Edited by Kong-rae Lee

3 **Corporate Sustainability Assessments**
Sustainability practices of multinational enterprises in Thailand
Edited by Jerome D. Donovan, Cheree Topple, Eryadi K. Masli, and Teerin Vanichseni

4 **Knowledge Spillover-based Strategic Entrepreneurship**
Edited by João J. Ferreira, Leo-Paul Dana, and Vanessa Ratten

5 **Japanese Management**
International perspectives
Hitoshi Iwashita

6 **Strategic Human Resource Management in China**
A Multiple Perspective
Min Min, Mary Bambacas, and Ying Zhu

7 **Fostering Local Entrepreneurship in a Multinational Enterprise**
Joe J. Amberg and Sara L. McGaughey

Contents

Figures

Tables

Acknowledgements

This study was made possible by the practitioners who shared their insights and experiences, the willingness of Siemens to grant organisational access for such research, and the resultant richness of the empirical data made available. We are particularly thankful for the generosity of all our interview partners at Siemens AG, who despite busy schedules gave freely of their time, knowledge, and experiences. Our study was also enriched and our understandings sharpened by numerous discussions with friends, colleagues, and seminar participants, and by the insights of manuscript reviewers. The Griffith Asia Institute, Griffith University kindly provided financial resources that helped bring this book to fruition; Yongling Lam and Samantha Phua at Routledge gave us swift and patient guidance; and Liveworm Studios at the Queensland College of Art made our clumsy artwork look almost divine. Finally, our heartfelt thanks go to our families for their steadfast encouragement, support, and patience throughout the entire project.

1 What is this book about?

Introduction

When looking at corporations from a life cycle perspective, most firms are born, grow up to maturity, but sooner or later stagnate in their activities and, more often than not, finally decline and die (Hoy, 2006). From a macroeconomic point of view, these cycles of birth and death of companies can be seen as an ever ongoing, and even necessary, process of rejuvenation. But for the stakeholders of a specific firm, such a stagnation, decline, and death could mean a partial or complete loss of one's stakes or even livelihood. Entrepreneurship theory and practice was initially focussed on identifying and explaining the nature of and mechanisms primarily related to the birth and growth of new firms. Most research in entrepreneurship remains predominantly occupied with the nascent, independent entrepreneur starting a new business. More recently, the field of *corporate entrepreneurship* is attracting both practitioner and scholarly attention.

Corporate entrepreneurship (CE) is "the process whereby an individual or a group of individuals, in association with an existing organisation, create a new organisation or instigate renewal or innovation within that organisation" (Sharma and Chrisman, 1999). Within the context of an existing organisation, CE can be understood as the successful search for and exploitation of entrepreneurial opportunities arising from information and knowledge asymmetries related to markets or technologies (Ireland, Covin, and Kuratko, 2009). Entrepreneurial behavior within established firms is perhaps more aptly termed '*corporate entrepreneuring*': it is an ongoing accomplishment involving constant search, creation, renewal, and innovation. That is, we inscribe entrepreneurship into a social ontology of *becoming* rather than simply *being*. There is no end point, but only moments in time.

While corporate entrepreneuring is increasingly seen as essential to long-term growth and sustainability – staving off stagnation, decline, and death – it remains elusive for many firms. Similarly, as a field of scholarly inquiry CE is still somewhat in its infancy. Corporate entrepreneuring, its antecedents, and its outcomes are heterogeneous, and we need to know more about this variety (Phan, Wright, Ucbasaran, and Tan, 2009; Hayton, Hornsby, and Bloodgood, 2013; Kuratko, Hornsby, and Hayton, 2015; Nason, McKelvie, and Lumpkin, 2015). Rather than building abstract, integrative frameworks based on prior studies with the expectation that they have relevance across a wide range of contexts, as has been the trend in recent years, these observations point to the need for more richly contextualised studies that acknowledge heterogeneity and allow for emergent, unanticipated insights across different contexts (Chadwick and Dabu, 2009; Hayton et al., 2013).

The research presented in this monograph responds directly to this need through an in-depth qualitative case study of corporate entrepreneurship and entrepreneuring within the Fire Safety business unit of Siemens AG – one of the oldest companies among the top global players. At the time of our study, the first author, Joe Amberg, had been working for the Fire Safety business unit of Siemens for over a decade, and a decade more in its predecessor. This long employment with Siemens Fire Safety, concurrent with field research (between September 2007 and October 2010, augmented by further documentary analysis in 2011 and 2012), led to a deep intimacy with the company's organisational history, strategy, processes, and practices, and afforded access to extensive internal networks and information. This valuable 'insider's perspective' was balanced by the critical 'outsider perspective' of the second author and university academic, Sara L. McGaughey – a scholar of international business and management, with special interests in entrepreneurship, organisation, and strategy. Hence, this research partnership sought to, in part, overcome the often lamented gap between academic research and managerial practice (Simon, 1967; Weick, 2001; Gulati, 2007; Rynes, Bartunek, and Daft, 2001; Frank and Landström, 2016).

In the remainder of this chapter we first elaborate the context and aims of our case study research. Mindful of a diverse audience for knowledge and examples of corporate entrepreneurship, we then reflect on the value of case study research and share our thoughts on how readers such as you might approach reading this book. This is followed by a short overview of the extant literature. We conclude with a guide to subsequent chapters, and in so doing foreshadow some of the main findings of our study.

Study context, aims, and readership

Context

Siemens AG was founded in 1847 as Siemens & Halske AG by Werner von Siemens, and was ranked 40th in the Global 500 Fortune list in 2010 (and ranked 71 in 2016).[1] As one of the world's largest multinational enterprises (MNEs), Siemens is running a tremendous number of businesses, with product and industry lifecycles related to its diverse operations representing all levels of maturity. Widely considered an industrial conglomerate, Siemens was active in three specific business fields at the time of our study: the generation, transmission, and distribution of electrical energy; diagnostic and therapeutic products and solutions in healthcare; and industrial manufacturing, transportation, building automation, and lighting systems. The MNE was perceived as significantly innovative when measured by new patents filed per year and the successful launch of product innovations in existing business fields. In FY 2010, for example, Siemens announced 8,800 new inventions and listed 4,300 new patents. At the end of 2009, Siemens patent ranking was ranked #2 at the European Trademark Office and #13 at the US Patent & Trademark Office.[2] Nonetheless, Siemens is usually not known as specifically entrepreneurial with regards to new business venturing endeavours or strategic renewal.

In the five years prior to data collection, Siemens AG showed significant symptoms of business stagnation by weak business performance. When comparing share price developments between 2003 and 2008 (end of year), for example, Siemens share price declined by 17.7 per cent, while comparable firms such as ABB (+148 per cent), Alstom (+153 per cent), Emerson (+13 per cent), or Schneider (+2 per cent) performed significantly better. The German stock index DAX increased by 19.7 per cent over the same period. A huge bribery scandal in relation to Siemens using a slush fund of more than €1.3bn to win overseas contracts in telecom and power business from 2001 to 2007 indicated severe shortcomings in company guidance. As a consequence, key company managers, including the chairman and the CEO, were replaced in 2007. A similar development of turnover stagnation, decreased profitability, and repeated top management turnover took place in the Siemens business unit Fire Safety,[3] in which the first author, Joe Amberg, had been working since 1988.

In this climate of crisis and change, Joe Amberg was appointed integration manager for the newly acquired and then highly entrepreneurial Shinwha Electronics[4] in South Korea following its takeover of 1 May 2008. In parallel, the acquisition and integration into the Siemens conglomerate of two similar companies[5] – also privately owned before and perceived as highly entrepreneurial and profitable – was judged as failures by the managers who were involved at the time. This constellation of business stagnation at Siemens, failed integrations of acquired companies, and the imminent endeavour of undertaking another comparable firm integration following the acquisition of Shinwha led to the first author seeking to better understand the performance levers operating in Siemens. A pilot study based on the Shinwha integration was thus undertaken while Joe Amberg was employed as the integration manager. This initial research highlighted the relevance of entrepreneurial activity for achieving firm performance in the Fire Safety business unit and, especially, a significant gap of such activity when comparing the involved Siemens entities with the pre-acquisition version of Shinwha Electronics.

Independent from but in parallel to the pilot study research, the Siemens top management identified at the start of 2009 a severe lack of entrepreneurship in the company as an important issue, and defined the strengthening of 'local entrepreneurship' as a new key action item in the strategic planning of Siemens AG for 2010 to 2014. The initiative was combined with a decentralisation of global headquarter functions of businesses, residing then almost exclusively in Germany. This strengthened the focus on 'local' entrepreneurship, even if the concrete business responsibility may remain global.

Aims

Against this backdrop of current events, corporate history, and professional interests, our aim was to explore the real-world complexity in the challenges and opportunities for corporate entrepreneuring within a large conglomerate MNE, with a view to better understand the extended periods of business stagnation and to identify ways to foster entrepreneurial behaviour. We chose to focus on the Fire Safety business unit, looking at three distinct initiatives within it – a China subsidiary within Fire Safety that became part of the Siemens-wide SMART initiative intended to foster local entrepreneurship; the acquisition of the entrepreneurial Korean firm, Shinwha Electronics; and the carve-out of a failed business with efforts to create a more entrepreneurial firm – the SP new setup – in preparation for its sale.

Our research was thus guided by questions such as, *What explains the continuing apparent low level of, or lack of success in, corporate entrepreneuring in Siemens Fire Safety? Does corporate entrpreneuring manifest differently across the three case studies, and if so, why and with what consequences? How might 'local entrepreneurship' be strengthened in the organisational and industry context of Siemens Fire Safety?* We approached these questions not only with extensive corporate history and contextual knowledge but also with a 'theoretical sensitivity' based on the young but rapidly growing body of literature on corporate entrepreneurship. In writing, we were also mindful of those who might wish to read this book.

The readers' role in constructing meaning

We anticipate – or hope – that the readership or audience of this book will be diverse. You could be, for example, an academic engaged in the study of corporate entrepreneuring; an executive within a large multinational enterprise or smaller firm seeking insights or ideas that may inform your own business practice; a student studying business or entrepreneurship; a policy maker considering how better to foster corporate entrepreneurship; or perhaps just a curious individual. It is our view as authors that 'academic' writing should be accessible to all such audiences. Qualitative case studies of firms can convey meaning to such a diverse readership in a way that other forms of scientific research and writing are less capable (McGaughey, 2004, 2006; Amberg and McGaughey, 2016). They can facilitate in-depth understanding of complex dynamics and subtle nuances, thereby contributing to theory and model development or refinement. Published case studies have also long been acknowledged as one of the best ways for aspiring or practicing managers to develop judgement and analytical skills, including the evaluation of circumstances from multiple perspectives (Weil, Oyelere and Rainsburg, 2004; Culpin and Scott, 2012). They expose people to real-world complexity in relation to, for example, decision-making (Gill, 2014), and are valued in management education for pulling together theory and practice (Weil, Oyelere, Yeoh, and Firer, 2001). Yet what each of you as a reader takes away from this book may well be very different.

The fields of entrepreneurship and international business – in which this monograph is situated – remain dominated by normative discourses. In such discourses, the implied reader (i.e. the prototypical reader) is assumed to be a largely passive recipient of ideas, provided they are cloaked in the rhetoric of 'objectivity' and 'truth'. This view of reading assumes that a text (e.g. story, journal article, quote, interview transcript) carries with it a message devised by the authors that is merely paraphrased in the reading of it (Monin, Barry, and Monin, 2003; McGaughey, 2006). Instead, influenced by schools of thought that include reader-response criticism (e.g. Fish, 1990) and reception aesthetics (e.g. Iser, 1978, 1980), we see you, the reader, as an active agent in the *construction* of meaning, and not merely a consumer of the written word (see McGaughey, 2006). This does not dismiss an author's intention – including ours – to produce a certain 'reading experience' by guiding the reader to the desired conclusion. Yet the reader – or reading community in which there is a shared approach to interpretation among members – may not fully conform to this authorial intent. With any text, there is always missing information, gaps to be filled in, assumptions to be made, or new possible interpretations to be considered. Each new reading of a narrative or case study may lead to new meanings for you, the reader, as you draw upon your past experience and stocks of knowledge, your present emotions and personality, and your expectations for the future (Polkinghorne, 1988). This makes reading an 'event in time' (Rosenblatt, 1978).

Recognising the role of the reader as an active agent in the construction of meaning lends itself to a particular type of generalisability of the research findings. While case studies of a limited number of firms – or, indeed, single firm – have been criticised as not leading to empirical generalisations, we do not seek to generalise to populations of firms. Our intimate connection with the empirical (socially constructed) reality through extended fieldwork and documentary analysis enabled us to discern *patterns* from richly contextualised *instances* and, hence, to make generalisations (Wolcott, 1999). These generalisations are not, however, to populations. Rather, generalisability is to similar cases and theory (Wolcott, 1999; Garud, Jain and Kumaraswamy, 2002), but at the same time are very much dependent on the reading community. The verisimilitude – or life-likeness – possible through a richly contextualised case study approach and verbatim quotes used in subsequent chapters facilitates 'naturalistic generalisations' (Stake, 1978) which are "arrived at by [the reader] recognising the similarities of objects and issues in and out of context and sensing the natural covariations of happening" (Stake, 1978, p. 6). Naturalistic generalisations thus draw upon the unique biography of each reader and the interpretive strategies shared by communities of readers. Each of you will also bring your own prior understandings as you read the overview of prior literature that follows.

Existing knowledge of corporate entrepreneurship

What is corporate entrepreneurship?

Burgelman (1983, 1984, 1985a, 1985b) is often credited as the founder of the research stream on corporate entrepreneurship (CE), defining entrepreneurial activity as a natural and integral part of the strategic process in large, established firms "[. . .] by extending the firm's domain of competence and corresponding opportunity set through internally generated new resource combinations" (1984, p. 154). Zahra proposed an expansion of this definition by including the aspect of strategic renewal: "Corporate entrepreneurship refers to formal and informal activities aimed at creating new business in established companies through product and process innovations and market developments. [. . .] Corporate entrepreneurship also entails the strategic renewal of an existing business" (1991, p. 262). Thus, CE may take place at the corporate, division, functional, and project levels. The even more inclusive definition of CE by Sharma and Chrisman (1999, p. 16) is adopted in our study: "Corporate entrepreneurship is the process whereby an individual or a group of individuals, in association with an existing organisation, create a new organisation or instigate renewal or innovation within that organisation". It thus comprises all activities of corporate venturing, strategic renewal, and innovation, which themselves overlap. Corporate venturing may involve the creation of an entirely new business (Govindarajan and Trimble, 2005; Kuratko and Audretsch, 2009) or investment in early growth-stage businesses created by external parties (external CV) and corporate venture capital (CVC) transactions (Phan et al., 2009). Strategic renewal refers to the refreshment or replacement of attributes of an organisation that have the potential to substantially affect its long-term prospects and to provide a foundation for future growth or development (Agarwal and Helfat, 2009). Innovation involves new or significantly improved products (goods or services) or processes, new marketing methods, and new organisational methods in business practices, workplace organisation, or external relations (OECD and Eurostat, 2005). Importantly, corporate entrepreneuring not only manifests in large organisations, but also in small- and medium-sized firms (e.g. McGaughey, 2007a, 2007b).

Nonetheless, authors still use a variety of other terms to refer to specific entrepreneurial activities, and there remain many definitional ambiguities (Sharma and Chrisman, 1999; Grégoire, Noel, Dery, and Bechard, 2006; Phan et al., 2009). Intrapreneurship, for example, seems to be a synonym for CE. Even if studies labelled with 'intrapreneurship' do not show up significantly within entrepreneurship research in recent meta studies (Cornelius, Landström and Persson, 2006; Grégoire et al., 2006; Reader and Watkins, 2006; Schildt, Zahra, and Sillanpää, 2006; Keupp and Gassmann, 2009), scores of articles and books using the label have been published over the last 40 years (e.g. Geneen, 1985; Pinchot, 1985; Duncan, Ginter, Rucks, and Jacobs, 1988; Hisrich, 1990; Carrier, 1994; Coulson-Thomas, 2000; Koen, 2000; Bostjan, 2007; Ebner, Korunka, Frank, and Lueger, 2008). Typically, articles on intrapreneurship are not published in top-tier academic journals, but show tendencies towards a practitioner-oriented research focus. Even studies using the concepts of CE, strategic renewal, corporate venturing, and innovation use them differently. Narayanan, Yang, and Zahra (2009), for example, develop a framework that integrates CE or intrapreneurship as *part of* corporate venturing. Looking at the 'common denominators' of published CE studies, Burgers and Jansen (2008) found the three prevailing key dimensions of innovation, venturing, and strategic renewal. Nonetheless, across all CE articles, only the aspect of innovation seems to be shared constantly (Covin and Miles, 1999, p. 47). Indeed, defining the concept of CE – or achieving consensus in the boundaries of its domain – remains a significant and continuing challenge (Kuratko et al., 2015).

Strategic entrepreneurship and CE

A particularly relevant and recent development in the CE literature from our perspective, and consistent with a depiction of CE as an integral part of the strategic processes of a firm (Burgelman, 1984, p. 154), is the emerging research stream on 'strategic entrepreneurship' (Ireland, Hitt, and Sirmon, 2003; Covin and Miles, 2007; Ireland and Webb, 2007; Audretsch, Lehmann, and Plummer, 2009; Ireland et al., 2009; Hitt, Ireland, Sirmon, and Trahms, 2011; Kuratko and Audretsch, 2009). For example, Covin and Miles (1999) proposed entrepreneurial relevance for four distinct strategic activities: (1) the sustained regeneration of the firm by continually introducing new products and services or entering new markets; (2) organisational rejuvenation by improving the competitive standing through altering internal processes, structures, and capabilities; (3) strategic renewals by fundamentally altering how to compete in a specific industry regarding the markets and competitors; and (4) a domain redefinition by creating new product-market arenas not previously established. All four elements are seen as closely linked to concepts related to competitive advantage, such as differentiation, cost leadership, and quick response (Porter, 1980, 1985). Related, Ireland et al. (2009, p. 21) define an entrepreneurial strategy of a firm "as a vision directed, organisation-wide reliance on entrepreneurial behaviour that purposefully and continuously rejuvenates the organisation and shapes the scope of its operations through the recognition and exploitation of entrepreneurial opportunity".

The exploration of entrepreneurial opportunities, and the exploitation of those opportunities selected, has long been recognised as important in the quest for both entrepreneurial and Ricardian rents (Chadwick and Dabu, 2009). Entrepreneurial rents flow from the unique abilities of individuals and firms to anticipate, exploit, and create market disequilibria, such as emerging opportunities to market products or services. In contrast, Ricardian rents accrue from owning an economically valuable factor of production that has inelastic supply (Teece, Pisano, and Shuen, 1997), such as differences in the quality of human resources. They can also arise from heterogeneity that is not intrinsic to the strategic factor, but that evolves over time – such as complex and causally ambiguous social relations that underpin effective teamwork (McGaughey and Liesch, 2002; Chadwick and Dabu, 2009). Figure 1.1 captures core elements in the entrepreneurial process.

A mandatory prerequisite for entrepreneurship is the potential existence of entrepreneurial opportunities, defined as the situations in which new goods, services, raw material, and organisation can be introduced and sold at greater than their cost of production (Casson, 1982; Venkataraman, 1997). Creation and recognition are both sources of such opportunities and mutually influence each other (Hills, Lumpkin, and Singh, 1997; Alvarez and Barney, 2007). Decision-making

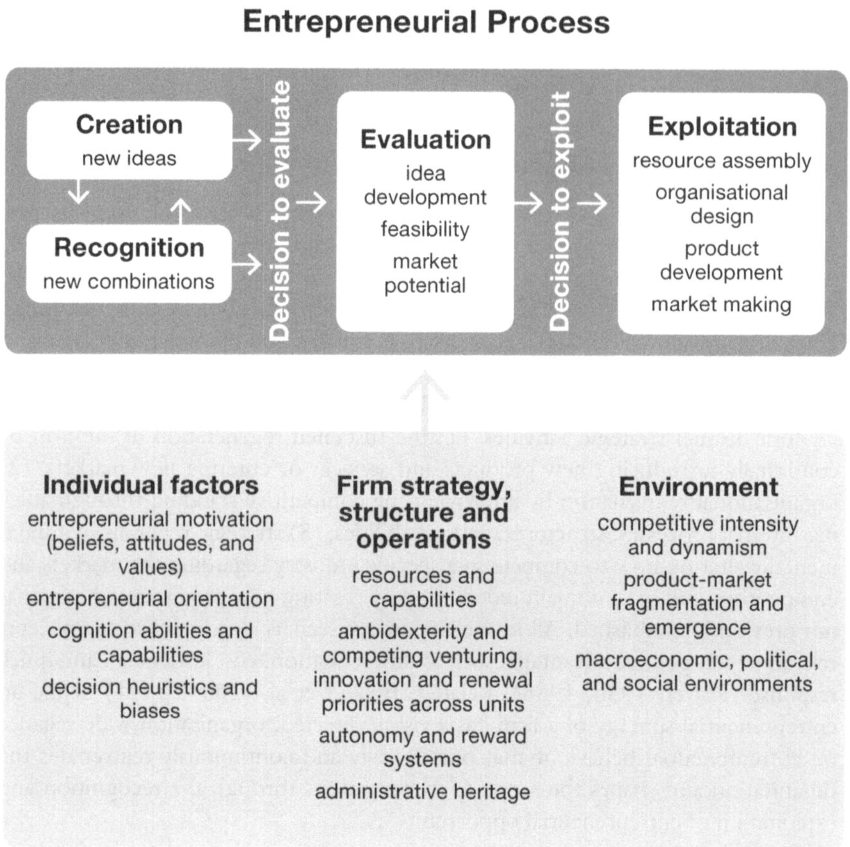

Figure 1.1 Core aspects of the entrepreneurial process

is pivotal in the entrepreneurial process (Shepherd, Williams, and Patzelt, 2015): normally a fraction of initial opportunity ideas are chosen for further development and evaluated on feasibility and market potential.

When comparing generic models of corporate entrepreneurship integrating key aspects of a firm, including its subsidiaries (e.g. Guth and Ginsberg, 1990; Covin and Slevin, 1991; Lumpkin and Dess, 1996a; Birkinshaw and Hood, 1998; Covin and Miles, 1999; Paterson and Brock, 2002; Kuratko, Hornsby, and Goldsby, 2004; Narayanan et al., 2009), there is no common set of proposed single elements. Nonetheless, there are common clusters: (1) external factors of the firm environment, (2) firm mission and strategy, (3) structural arrangements in organisation and processes, and (4) people-related aspects comprising elements of values, philosophy and culture, motivation and rewards, decision heuristics or biases, and granted autonomy and support. Indeed, the extent to which perceived opportunities subsequently are exploited is strongly linked with the attitude toward risk and uncertainty of a potential entrepreneur (Shane, 2003, p. 61; Acs and Audretsch, 2005, p. 37), the beliefs of managers regarding the possibility of successful new resource combinations, and decision heuristics and biases (Guth and Ginsberg, 1990; Barr, Stimpert, and Huff, 1992; Shepherd et al., 2015) – all of which are rooted in individual entrepreneurial values and prior experience (Ireland et al., 2009). Unfortunately, most of the relevant studies on individual-level factors have been carried out in the context of independent entrepreneurs, with little field research in the context of corporate entrepreneurship (Corbett and Hmieleski, 2007).

In considering entrepreneurial processes such as those depicted in Figure 1.1, the concept of an 'entrepreneurial orientation' (Lumpkin and Dess, 1996a, 1996b) comes to the fore. An 'entrepreneurial orientation' refers to the processes, practices, and decision-making activities that lead to new entry – whether this new entry be the act of launching a new venture independently or within an existing corporation, or entering new or existing markets with new or existing product and services. The significance of this concept of entrepreneurial orientation (EO) as a discrete and fundamental research stream has been confirmed by the vastness of studies applying it to date (e.g. Miller, 1983; Covin and Slevin, 1986; Covin and Slevin, 1989; Covin and Slevin, 1991; Lumpkin and Dess, 1996a, 1996b; Jantunen, Puumalainen, Saarenketo, and Kylaheiko, 2005; Covin, Green, and Slevin, 2006; Lee and Williams, 2007; Lumpkin, Cogliser, and Schneider, 2009). Miller (1983, p. 771) suggested that an entrepreneurial firm "engages in product market innovation, undertakes somewhat risky ventures and is first to come up with 'proactive' innovations, beating competitors to the punch" (1983, p. 770). Over time these three dimensions of an entrepreneurial orientation – being innovative, risk taking, and being proactive in anticipating and acting on future opportunities – were augmented with a propensity to act autonomously, and to directly and intensely challenge competitors to achieve entry or to improve market positions. Lumpkin and Dess described the EO construct with these five dimensions – autonomy, innovativeness, risk-taking, proactiveness, and competitive aggressiveness – as "useful for characterising and distinguishing key entrepreneurial processes" (1996a, p. 136), and saw it "answer the question of how new ventures are undertaken, whereas the term entrepreneurship refers to the content of entrepreneurial decisions by addressing what is undertaken" (1997, p. 1).

The entrepreneurial process depicted in Figure 1.1 raises an important issue for established firms, known as "the productivity dilemma" (Abernathy, 1978; Benner and Tushman, 2003). That is, how can a firm most effectively exploit mature businesses where efficiency, control, and incremental improvements are prized, and at the same time compete in new markets and technologies where autonomy, flexibility, and experimentation are needed? (see O'Reilly and Tushman, 2013). As Garvin (2004) observed, new ventures flourish best in open, exploratory environments, but most corporations are geared toward mature business and efficient, predictable operations. The need for ambidexterity has thus gained considerable attention in recent years (Birkinshaw and Gibson, 2004; Gilbert, 2006; Burgers and Jansen, 2008; Im and Rai, 2008; Andriopoulos and Lewis, 2009; Cao, Gedajlovic, and Zhang, 2009; Jansen, Tempelaar, van den Bosch, and Volberda,

2009; Mom, van den Bosch, and Volberda, 2009; Raisch, Birkinshaw, Probst, and Tushman, 2009; Taylor and Helfat, 2009), with comprehensive reviews of the field and reflective commentary on its advances (e.g. Raisch and Birkinshaw, 2008; Birkinshaw and Gupta, 2013; O'Reilly and Tushman, 2013). From a strategic perspective, the question of whether pursuing such a hybrid strategy really pays arises: recent research seems to confirm the superior performance of pursuing pure strategies (Thornhill and White, 2007). However, for multinational corporations operating many businesses in parallel and in different states of maturity of product life cycles, the ambidexterity required in managing exploitation and exploration at the same time is somewhat unavoidable. It is therefore important to understand the relevant elements (e.g. processes, organisational structures, and involved culture), the levels to be taken into account (e.g. whole firm, divisions, business units, teams, and individuals), and promising approaches (e.g. internalisation versus externalisation) to achieve ambidexterity (Raisch and Birkinshaw, 2008; Raisch et al., 2009).

Corporate entrepreneuring in MNEs

Traditionally, it was assumed that the headquarters of the multinational enterprise (MNE) was the main driver of innovation and entrepreneurship (Vernon, 1966). MNEs are, however, increasingly seen as differentiated networks in which the roles of individual subsidiaries (also referred to as "branches" in Siemens) vary according to their specific capabilities, their internal and external networks, and the environment in which they are embedded (Doz and Prahalad, 1984; Hedlund, 1986; Ghoshal and Bartlett, 1989, 1990; Nohria and Ghoshal, 1994; Birkinshaw and Hood, 2001; Andersson, Forsgren, and Holm, 2007; Alfoldi, Clegg, and McGaughey, 2012). MNEs can profit from the dissimilarities of the multiple local environments in which they are embedded, gaining access to a diversity of new ideas and information that is fundamental to opportunity recognition and novel recombinations (Kogut and Zander, 1993; Hoenen, Nell and Ambos, 2014; McGaughey, Kumaraswarmy, and Liesch, 2016).

Several subsidiary typologies have been proposed to depict their role in the MNE and in corporate entrepreneuring. Perhaps the most cited typology is that of Bartlett and Ghoshal (2002), who use the two dimensions "Strategic Importance of Local Environment" and "Level of Local Resources and Capabilities" to create four basic types of subsidiary positioning: (1) strategic leader, (2) contributor, (3) implementer, and (4) black hole. A strategic leader represents high internal competence, is located in a strategically important country, and is treated by headquarters as a legitimate partner in defining and implementing firm strategy. A contributor "captures the benefits of certain local facilities or capabilities and applies them to the broader worldwide operations" (Bartlett and Ghoshal, 2002, p. 123). Most of the subsidiaries are seen as simply having sufficient competence to maintain their local operations in a market that is nonstrategic, and thus play the role of implementers. Finally, a national organisation is considered a black hole if it *should* play the role of a strategic leader but lacks the competence to do so. Hence, the tendency has been to focus on relative resource superiority and subsidiary specific advantages, not only relative to external competitors but also relative to rivals within the MNE. That is, the various MNE units compete with each other for scarce resources (e.g. investment funds) and for the award of mandates from superior entities within the MNE. More recently, Rugman, Verbeke, and Yuan (2011) have 'unbundled' subsidiary roles to consider different elements of the value chain (e.g. innovation, production, sales, and administrative support), and have highlighted how subsidiaries may take on different roles in each. Similarly, host country location characteristics differ. An important observation is that the location advantages instrumental to subsidiary creation and development, and the requisite capabilities, are unlikely to be identical across all value chain activity sets in any given country.

Birkinshaw and Morrison (1995) proposed a distinction of three quite similar role types for subsidiaries based on a review of research literature on role types and their own empirical research: world mandate, specialised contributor, and local implementer. The world mandate represents here 'decentralised centralisation', whereby the subsidiary has a worldwide (or at least regional) responsibility for a specific product line, and the entire value chain is delegated to a subsidiary. The roles of specialised contributor and local implementer are comparable to the definitions of Bartlett and Ghoshal (2002). Three modes by which a world mandate of a subsidiary emerges were identified: (1) 'born' in the subsidiary by growing the subsidiary organically by the parent company; (2) 'thrust upon' the subsidiary when bought (acquisition) from the parent; and (3) 'achieved' by the subsidiary through their own initiatives. Subsidiary initiatives constitute a form of corporate entrepreneurship, incorporating proactive and risk-taking behaviour, the use of resources beyond the control of the subsidiary, and the acquisition and use of power and influence (Birkinshaw, Hood, and Young, 2005; Lu, Chen, and Lee, 2007). In a study of 24 subsidiaries of MNEs in Scotland, Birkinshaw and colleagues (2005, p. 246) found evidence that if the subsidiary is able to develop some autonomy, it is much better positioned to start developing local suppliers and customers of its own, which in turn may lead to a broader value-added scope. The authors concluded that further investigations on autonomy, motivation, and culture as antecedents of entrepreneurial orientation would be required, especially in parent–subsidiary relationships (Birkinshaw et al. 2005). More recently, evidence is emerging that it is not only within parents or subsidiaries that corporate entrepreneuring may reside, but also in 'intermediary units'. These include operating units assigned regional management mandates (Alfoldi et al., 2012) and regional headquarters in the MNE (Hoenen et al., 2014), which may be particularly adept in sensing opportunities beyond their home markets and initiating their exploitation.

Fostering CE through managerial entrepreneurship

Research seeking to identify factors that foster entrepreneurship in established companies identify a number of recurrent themes. Many of these are captured by what Chadwick and Dabu (2009) term 'managerial entrepreneurship': the system of firm-specific managerial processes that enhances knowledge generation, coordination, and exploitation within firms. While their focus is specifically on human resource management processes and activities, a range of systems, structures, and processes (e.g. planning systems, reporting structures, and team-building initiatives) may also form part of managerial entrepreneurship. A distinction is drawn between formal and informal managerial entrepreneurship. Formal managerial entrepreneurship is directed by decision makers through, for example, HRM systems. In contrast, informal managerial entrepreneurship arises from workers' discretionary efforts. The two are, however, related: deliberate actions of managers may help build up intra-organisational contexts favourable to coordinating and utilising the dispersed knowledge held by employees for corporate entrepreneurship, and thus also influence informal managerial entrepreneurship.

Widely considered essential for successful corporate entrepreneuring is an "entrepreneurial strategic vision", described as "a commitment to innovation and entrepreneurial processes and behaviour that is expressed as the organisation's philosophical modus operandi" (Ireland et al., 2009, p. 26). The strategic vision is the mechanisms by which top management paint the picture of the type of organisation they intend to lead: one that is focussed on innovation and opportunities for new ventures, and that is self-renewing. The crafting and successful communication of a strong entrepreneurial vision is seen as being of key importance to motivate employees towards entrepreneurial endeavours (Guth and Ginsberg, 1990; Covin and Miles, 1999). Essential in this vision is a 'long-term orientation', which is reflected in a tendency to prioritise the long-range implications and impacts of decisions and actions that show results after an extended time period (Morris, Kuratko, and Covin, 2008; Kuratko and Audretsch, 2009; Lumpkin, Bringham, and Moss, 2010). On the level of firm management, this long-term orientation manifests where "top executives have the motivation and wherewithal to pursue the interests of the business in a far sighted and inclusive way" (Le Breton-Miller and Miller, 2006, p. 741).

The key role of entrepreneurial strategy and the MNE subsidiary CEO was confirmed by three explorative case studies in German-owned subsidiaries in France (Dörrenbächer and Geppert, 2008). Here the authors found a considerable impact of the subsidiary managers' personal interests on the subsidiaries' initiatives (and thus on the parent–subsidiary relationships), strongly linked with the managers' socio-political and biographical backgrounds, as well as their former career paths and current career interests. Similarly, Boojihawon, Dimitratos, and Young (2007) observed the significance for a "dispersed corporate entrepreneurship" (Covin and Slevin, 1991) among MNE units based on a shared global vision, entrepreneurial orientation consisting of cross-border innovative, proactive, and risk-seeking behaviour, and an entrepreneurial MNE network management (Ghoshal and Bartlett, 1990). The authors conclude that "it pays to be an energetic multinational subsidiary manager with a strong global vision; to attempt to nurture a subsidiary with an active entrepreneurial orientation; and to seek to cultivate an ability to manage the MNC network successfully with the objective of building team working and pursuing critical resources and learning" (Boojihawon et al., 2007, p. 569).

Related to strategy, an organisational structure or architecture that includes loose intra-organisational boundaries (Antoncic and Hisrich, 2001), a reduction in bureaucratic barriers, and flexible policies and procedures of companies (Kuratko, Montagno, and Hornsby, 1990), and that fosters external knowledge exchange (Dimitratos, Liouka, and Young, 2009; Hoenen et al., 2014) is also widely advocated to foster CE and is a part of managerial entrepreneurship. For example, four distinct structural configurations have been proposed as specifically relevant for explaining corporate entrepreneurship (Miller, 1986, 1996; Morris et al., 2008): a highly informal, 'simple' firm structure with power centralisation at the top and low bureaucratisation; a 'machine bureaucracy' based on many formal rules, policies, and procedures; a highly flexible 'organic' structure with limited hierarchy and power decentralisation and prevailing in highly dynamic environments; and, finally, a 'divisionalised' structure when looking at large conglomerates like Siemens. While a divisional structure is described as behaving in a highly bureaucratic manner as a whole, single divisions and subunits may resemble many different structural types again (Morris et al., 2008). The configuration providing fewest stimuli for entrepreneurial activity seems to be the 'machine bureaucracy' that follows primarily formal guidelines and plans, focuses on well-established and controlled internal processes rather than on market developments, and concentrates power among top executives and process designers (Morris et al., 2008, p. 226). That is, organisational structures help shape – for good or bad – the behaviour of human resources and hence the generation, coordination, and exploitation of knowledge in corporate entrepreneuring.

Hayton and colleagues (2005, 2013) provide two of the most comprehensive reviews of the relationship between corporate entrepreneurship and HRM to date based on assumptions of the centrality of knowledge and learning. Like Chadwick and Dabu (2009), their model assumes that internal and external knowledge exchange is essential to opportunity exploration and that exploitation is underpinned by social capital and trust, as is the risk-taking behaviour necessary in high-uncertainty contexts (Brockhaus, 1980; Petrakis, 2005; Ling, Simsek, Lubatkin, and Veiga, 2008). Synthesising a large body of literature, Hayton (2005) identified the importance of socialisation and team-oriented training involving members from different functional areas; job designs that allow for autonomy and discretionary behaviours; high levels of perceived support from top management that often manifest in the form of resource availability and 'slack' in human resources, sponsorship, and coaching; and appropriate (often intrinsic) rewards, recognition, and incentives (see also Fry, 1987; Brazeal, 1993; Hayton, 2005; Verbeke and Yuan, 2013; Tang, Wei, Snape, and Ng, 2015). A long-term career orientation that favours retention has also been identified as important, as well as rewards systems that consider the longer term (Schuler, 1986), foster acceptance and management of risk (Fry, 1987), and reward outcomes rather than conformity to pre-defined plans (Chadwick and Dabu, 2009).

An organisational culture that promotes discretionary, informal behaviours that lie at the heart of corporate entrepreneuring and that eschew excessive controls and bureaucracy (Dess et al., 2003) was also found to be relevant. Formal HRM practices play a key role in sustaining such cultures conducive to CE, including firm cultures incorporating a willingness for change, shared goals of innovation, trust, freedom granted for entrepreneurial action, forgiveness for failures, and management proactivity towards innovation (Hayton, 2005; Menzel, Aaltio, and Ulijn, 2007). Such social climate or cultural elements lead to greater knowledge exchange and recombinations, which result in higher performance. HRM systems and practices thereby promote both formal and informal managerial entrepreneurship (Hayton, 2005; Chadwick and Dabu, 2009; Hayton et al., 2013) and function as part of the firm's strategic infrastructure for generating and leveraging the entrepreneurial knowledge needed to sustain a firm's competitive advantage over time (Chadwick and Dabu, 2009).

Overarching, integrative frameworks of the role HRM may play in fostering CE, while invaluable for synthesising a growing body of literature, have typically overlooked the potentially important distinction between exploration and exploitation and the specific human capital involved or required. For example, teamwork and a tolerance for risk are advocated, but does this apply equally to all engaged across the various roles undertaken in corporate entrepreneurship? More nuanced and focussed investigations are, however, emerging. For example, Hayton and Kelly (2006) advocate a competency-based framework for CE, identifying four key competences – innovating, brokering, championing, and sponsoring – and the specific human capital characteristics underpinning each. Each competence may be aligned with one or more different roles associated with success of CE, typically residing at different levels in the organisation. Similarly, Hornsby, Kuratko, Shepherd, and Bott (2009) identify heterogeneity in the motivation for entrepreneurial action across managerial levels. There remains, however, considerable scope to recognise the complexity and to revisit the 'human' in strategic HRM (Wright and McMahon, 2011, p. 102) and its role in CE.

Integrating a variety of elements from this discussion, Ireland et al. (2009) present perhaps the most comprehensive CE-strategy model to date, derived from the review of nine prior CE models linked to firm strategy (Burgelman, 1983b, Guth and Ginsberg, 1990; Covin and Slevin, 1991; Hornsby, Naffziger, Kuratko, and Montagno, 1993; Lumpkin and Dess, 1996a; Floyd and Lane, 2000; Kuratko et al., 2004; Kuratko et al., 2005). Antecedents, elements of corporate entrepreneurship strategy, and outcomes of using a CE strategy at multiple levels of analysis – organisation, top management, and other organisational members employees – are combined in a recursively interacting network model. That is, they highlight the multi-level and interconnected nature of entrepreneurial strategic vision, organisational architecture, and entrepreneurial processes and behaviour throughout the organisations. The authors suggested that "a bundle of 'fits' [. . .] are necessary for CE success" (2009, p. 39). Such 'bundles' of complementary elements leading to success may well vary according to the specific types of corporate entrepreneurship (i.e. firm innovation, venturing, and strategic renewal) sought (Verbeke, Chrisman, and Yuan, 2007). Conceivably, complementary bundles of elements may also reinforce ongoing failure in corporate entrepreneuring.

A guide to subsequent chapters

Much case-based research in corporate entrepreneurship is oriented towards studying success and offering generic prescriptions for its realisation. Instead, we identify a pattern of critical, interdependent factors residing at multiple levels within the Siemens Fire Safety business unit that mutually reinforce each other and sustain inertia in *low* levels of corporate entrepreneurship. At the same time, we acknowledge emerging initiatives to foster corporate entrepreneurship – including innovations, corporate venturing, and efforts at strategic renewal. This study thus offers a rare contribution to our growing – yet still fledgling – understanding of corporate entrepreneuring in global corporations, and highlights the importance of understanding the specific corporate context for any entrepreneurial endeavour.

As a way to structure our findings, we draw on Kuratko et al.'s (2004) model of the critical elements needed for sustained corporate entrepreneurship, as summarised in Figure 1.2. Their model comprises five building blocks: external transformation triggers, the corporate entrepreneurial strategy of the firm, organisational antecedents, individual entrepreneurial behaviour, and entrepreneurial outcomes. Importantly, this model emphasises the importance of perceived outcomes for both individuals (e.g. intrinsic and extrinsic rewards) and the organisation (e.g. reaching growth targets) arising from the implementation of the entrepreneurial strategy, and the subsequent motivation to further engage in corporate entrepreneuring and the shape of future CE strategies.

Chapter 2 explores the organisational milieu and triggers for change experienced by Siemens Fire Safety managers. More explicitly, we provide the organisational and industry context for our study of apparent inertia in low levels of corporate entrepreneuring and business stagnation within the Fire Safety business unit of the Building Technologies division of Siemens AG. We describe the three

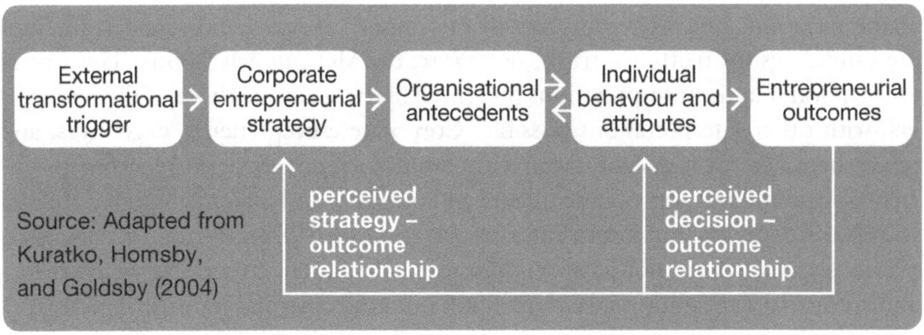

Figure 1.2 Critical elements for sustained corporate entrepreneurship

embedded cases within Fire Safety – each highlighting different aspects of corporate entrepreneurship – and conclude by briefly describing our research method and, in particular, the research process and key sources of data.

We begin presenting findings from our case study research in Chapter 3, where we explore what it *means* to those working within Siemens Fire Safety to be an entrepreneur or to act entrepreneurially, and to what extent entrepreneurial behaviour is perceived to manifest in the Fire Safety business unit at the time of, and prior to, our study. Chapters 4, 5, and 6 explore three broad characteristics of the organisation and their effect on entrepreneurial behaviour. More specifically, Chapter 4 describes the dominant 'process orientation' in Siemens' organisational architecture, exploring how it manifests across the three case studies. We reflect on both the enabling and detrimental attributes of Siemens' process orientation in relation to corporate entrepreneuring, and ways in which negative aspects can or are being addressed. Chapter 5 considers the nature and strategic context of subsidiary mandates and organisational factors that affect the pursuit of, and change in, mandates, including subsidiary and individual initiatives. Notably, each of the three studied entities is subject to very different mandates and commensurately different opportunities for and impediments to entrepreneurial behaviour. Although Chapters 4 and 5 touch upon 'people-related' aspects of corporate entrepreneuring, Chapter 6 more explicitly focuses on the management of people within Siemens Fire Safety. Here we explore how formal and informal human resource management policies and practices contribute to (or undermine) managerial entrepreneurship and, as a corollary, corporate entrepreneuring.

We conclude in Chapter 7 by drawing our findings together and highlighting how a particular configuration of elements – the external environment and transformational triggers, corporate entrepreneurial strategy, organisational antecedents, individual entrepreneurial behaviours, and related outcomes – create recursive relationships that sustain low levels of corporate entrepreneuring in Siemens Fire Safety. We reflect on these conclusions with reference to events in Siemens subsequent to our data collection and the implications for large conglomerate MNEs such as Siemens seeking to foster corporate entrepreneurship, and offer suggestions for future research and practice.

The analysis that unfolds is not the 'one truth', but possible ways of looking at the situation. Any story can be told in a variety of ways, and research findings are candidates for truth – *a* truth, not *the* truth (McGaughey, 2006). This brings recognition that the interpretations presented in the study are those of the researchers, with other interpretations possible. Corporate entrepreneurs, executives, and researchers alike are inevitably faced with 'bounded rationality': problems of insufficient information of appropriate quality and quantity, and limited cognitive abilities to process complex bundles of information (Simon, 1982). Further, as discussed previously, readers are not passive consumers of research. In reading we construct and reconstruct meaning as we draw upon our collective and individual past experience and stocks of knowledge, our present emotions and personality, and our expectations for the future. As Czarniawaka (1999, p. 25) observes, "[t]o read is always to write, even if sometimes without the material traces". What follows is just one telling of the story among many. It may well invite multiple readings.

Notes

1 Ranking is done by turnovers (see http://beta.fortune.com/global500/list). A more detailed description of Siemens is provided in Chapter 2.
2 Source: http://www.siemens.com/innovation/en/about_fande/patents/index.htm, last accessed 2011-02-02.
3 See Chapter 2 for a detailed description of Siemens' organisational structure, business focus, and history.
4 As described in detail in Chapter 2.
5 Bewator Ltd. (Sweden, 2005) and iMetrex Ltd., India and Ireland, 2007.

References

Abernathy, W. J. (1978). *The productivity dilemma*. Baltimore: Johns Hopkins University Press.

Acs, Z. J. and Audretsch, D. B. (Eds.). (2005). *Handbook of entrepreneurship research: An interdisciplinary survey and introduction*. New York: Springer.

Agarwal, R. and Helfat, C. E. (2009). Strategic renewal of organisations. *Organisation Science, 20*(2), 281–293.

Alfoldi, E., Clegg, J. and McGaughey, S. L. (2012). Coordination at the edge of the empire: Subsidiary regional management mandates in the multinational enterprise. *Journal of International Management, 18*, 276–292.

Alvarez, S. A. and Barney, J. B. (2007). Discovery and creation: Alternative theories of entrepreneurial action. *Strategic Entrepreneurship Journal, 1*(1–2), 11–26.

Amberg, J. J. and McGaughey, S. L. (2016). Human resource activities and corporate entrepreneurship in a multinational enterprise. *The International Journal of Human Resource Management, 6*, 1–35. DOI: 10.1080/09585192.2016.1192051

Andersson, U., Forsgren, M. and Holm, U. (2007). Balancing subsidiary influence in the federative MNC: A business network view. *Journal of International Business Studies, 38*(5), 802–818.

Andriopoulos, C. and Lewis, M. W. (2009). Exploitation-exploration tensions and organisational ambidexterity: Managing paradoxes of innovation. *Organisation Science, 20*(4), 696–717.

Antoncic, B. and Hisrich, R. D. (2001). Intrapreneurship: Construct refinement and cross-cultural validation. *Journal of Business Venturing, 16*(5), 495–527.

Audretsch, D., Lehmann, E. and Plummer, L. (2009). Agency and governance in strategic Entrepreneurship. *Entrepreneurship Theory and Practice, 33*(1), 149–166.

Barr, P. S., Stimpert, J. L. and Huff, A. S. (1992). Cognitive change, strategic action and organisational renewal. *Strategic Management Journal, 13*(1), 15–36.

Bartlett, C. A. and Ghoshal, S. (1989). *Managing across borders: The transnational solution*. Boston, MA: Harvard Business School Press.

Bartlett, C. A. and Ghoshal, S. (2002). *Managing across borders: The transnational solution. (second edition)*. Boston, MA: Harvard Business School Press.

Benner, M. J. and Tushman, M. L. (2003). Exploitation, exploration, and process management: The productivity dilemma revisited. *The Academy of Management Review, 28*(2), 238–256.

Birkinshaw, J. and Gibson, C. (2004). Building ambidexterity into an organisation. *MIT Sloan Management Review, 45*, 47–55.

Birkinshaw, J. and Gupta, K. (2013). Clarifying the distinctive contribution of ambidexterity to the field of organisation studies. *Academy of Management Perspectives, 27*(4), 287–298.

Birkinshaw, J. and Hood, N. (1998). Multinational subsidiary evolution: Capability and charter change in foreign-owned subsidiary companies. *The Academy of Management Review, 23*(4), 773–795.

Birkinshaw, J. and Hood, N. (2001). Unleash innovation in foreign subsidiaries. *Harvard Business Review, 79*, 131–137.

Birkinshaw, J., Hood, N. and Young, S. (2005). Subsidiary entrepreneurship, internal and external competitive forces, and subsidiary performance. *International Business Review, 14*, 227–248.

Birkinshaw, J. and Morrison, A. J. (1995). Configurations of strategy and structure in subsidiaries of multinational corporations. *Journal of International Business Studies, 26*, 729–753.

Boojihawon, D. K., Dimitratos, P. and Young, S. (2007). Characteristics and influences of multinational subsidiary entrepreneurial culture: The case of the advertising sector. *International Business Review, 16*, 549–572.

Bostjan, A. (2007). Intrapreneurship: A comparative structural equation modeling study. *Industrial Management + Data Systems, 107*(3), 309–325.

Brazeal, D. V. (1993). Organizing for internally developed corporate ventures. *Journal of Business Venturing, 8*, 75–90.

Brockhaus, R. H., Sr. (1980). Risk taking propensity of entrepreneurs. *Academy of Management Journal, 23*(3), 509–520.

Burgelman, R. A. (1983a). Corporate entrepreneurship and strategic management: Insights from a process study. *Management Science, 29*(12), 1349–1364.

Burgelman, R. A. (1983b). A process model of internal corporate venturing in the diversified major firm. *Administrative Science Quarterly, 28*(2), 223–244.

Burgelman, R. A. (1984). Designs for corporate entrepreneurship in established firms. *California Management Review, 26*, 154–166.

Burgelman, R. A. (1985a). Managing corporate entrepreneurship: New structures for implementing technological innovation. *Technology in Society, 7*, 91–103.

Burgelman, R. A. (1985b). Managing the new venture division: Research findings and implications for strategic management. *Strategic Management Journal, 6*(1), 39–54.

Burgers, J. H. and Jansen, J. (2008). Organisational Ambidexterity and Corporate Entrepreneurship: The Differential Effects on Venturing, Innovation and Renewal Processes. *Babson College Entrepreneurship Research Conference (BCERC)*, Wellesley, MA.

Cao, Q., Gedajlovic, E. and Zhang, H. (2009). Unpacking organisational ambidexterity: Dimensions, contingencies, and synergistic effects. *Organisation Science, 20*(4), 781–796.

Carrier, C. (1994). Intrapreneurship in large firms and SMEs: A comparative study. *International Small Business Journal, 12*(3), 54–61.

Casson, M. (1982). *The entrepreneur.* Totwa, NJ: Barnes and Noble Books.

Chadwick, C. and Dabu, A. (2009). Human resources, human resource management and the competitive advantage of firms: Toward a more comprehensive model of causal linkages. *Organisation Science, 20*(1), 253–272.

Corbett, A. C. and Hmieleski, K. M. (2007). The conflicting cognitions of corporate entrepreneurs. *Entrepreneurship Theory and Practice, 31*(1), 103–121.

Cornelius, B., Landström, H. and Persson, O. (2006). Entrepreneurial studies: The dynamic research front of a developing social science. *Entrepreneurship Theory and Practice, 30*(3), 375–398.

Coulson-Thomas, C. (2000). Developing a corporate learning strategy: Creating intrapreneurs. *Strategic Change, 9*(8), 469–479.

Covin, J. G. Green, K. M. and Slevin, D. P. (2006). Strategic process effects on the entrepreneurial orientation – sales growth rate relationship. *Entrepreneurship Theory and Practice, 30*, 57–81.

Covin, J. G. and Miles, M. P. (1999). Corporate entrepreneurship and the pursuit of competitive advantage. *Entrepreneurship Theory and Practice, 23*(3), 47–63.

Covin, J. G. and Miles, M. P. (2007). Strategic use of corporate venturing. *Entrepreneurship Theory and Practice, 31*(2), 183–207.

Covin, J. G. and Slevin, D. P. (1986). *The development and testing of an organisation-level entrepreneurship scale.* Wellesley, MA: Babson College.

Covin, J. G. and Slevin, D. P. (1989). Strategic management of small firms in hostile and benign environments. *Strategic Management Journal, 10*, 75–87.

Covin, J. G. and Slevin, D. P. (1991). A conceptual model of entrepreneurship as firm behavior. *Entrepreneurship Theory and Practice, 16*, 7–25.

Culpin, V. and Scott, H. (2012). The effectiveness of a live case study approach: Increasing knowledge and understanding of 'hard' versus 'soft' skills in executive education. *Management Learning, 43*(5), 565–577.

Czarniawska, B. (1999). *Writing management: Organisation theory as a literary genre.* Oxford: Oxford University Press.

Dess, G. G., Ireland, R. D., Zahra, S. A., Floyd, S. W., Janney, J. J. and Lane, P. J. (2003). Emerging issues in corporate entrepreneurship. *Journal of Management, 29*, 351–378.

Dimitratos, P., Liouka, I. and Young, S. (2009). Regional location of multinational corporation subsidiaries and economic development contribution: Evidence from the UK. *Journal of World Business, 44*, 180–191.

Dörrenbächer, C. and Geppert, M. (2008). A micro-political perspective on subsidiary initiative-taking: Evidence from German-owned subsidiaries in France. *European Management Journal, 27*(2), 100–112.

Doz, Y. and Prahalad, C. K. (1984). Patterns of strategic control within multinational corporations. *Journal of International Business Studies (pre-1986), 15*(2), 55–72.

Duncan, W. J., Ginter, P. M., Rucks, A. C. and Jacobs, T. D. (1988). Intrapreneurship and the reinvention of the corporation. *Business Horizons, 31*(3), 16–21.

Ebner, M., Korunka, C., Frank, H. and Lueger, M. (2008). Intrapreneurship in der beruflichen Erstausbildung: Versuch einer begrifflichen Klärung und Operationalisierung. *Zeitschrift für Personalforschung, 22*, 291–311.

Fish, S. (1990). How to recognise a poem when you see one. In Bartholomae, D. and Petrosky, A. (Eds.), *Ways of reading: An anthology for writers.* Boston, MA: Belford Books of St Martins Press, pp. 178–191.

Floyd, S. W. and Lane, P. J. (2000). Strategizing throughout the organisation: Management role conflict in strategic renewal. *Academy of Management Review, 25*(2), 154–177.

Frank, H. and Landström, H. (2016). What makes entrepreneurship research interesting? Reflections on strategies to overcome the rigour–relevance gap. *Entrepreneurship and Regional Development, 28*(1–2), 51–75.

Fry, A. (1987). The post-it note: An intrapreneurial success. *S.A.M. Advanced Management Journal, 52*(3), 4–9.

Garud, R., Jain, S. and Kumaraswamy, A. (2002). Institutional entrepreneurship in the sponsorship of common technological standards: The case of Sun Microsystems and Java. *Academy of Management Journal, 45*(1), 196–214.

Garvin, D. A. (2004). What every CEO should know about creating new businesses. *Harvard Business Review, 82*, 18.

Geneen, H. (1985). Harold Geneen: Why intrapreneurship doesn't work. *Venture, 7*, 46–52.

Ghoshal, S. and Bartlett, C. A. (1990). The Multinational corporation as an interorganisational network. *Academy of Management Review, 15*, 603–625.

Gilbert, C. G. (2006). Change in the presence of residual fit: Can competing frames coexist? *Organisation Science, 17*, 150–167.

Gill, T. G. (2014). The complexity and the case method, *Management Decision, 52*(9), 1564–1590.

Govindarajan, V. and Trimble, C. (2005). Building breakthrough businesses within established organisations. *Harvard Business Review, 83*, 58–68.

Grégoire, D. A., Noël, M. X., Déry, R. and Béchard, J.-P. (2006). Is there conceptual convergence in entrepreneurship research? A co-citation analysis of frontiers of entrepreneurship research, 1981–2004. *Entrepreneurship Theory and Practice, 30*(3), 333–373.

Gulati, R. (2007). Tent poles, tribalism, and boundary spanning: The rigor-relevance debate in management research. *Academy of Management Journal, 50*(4), 775–782.

Guth, W. D. and Ginsberg, A. (1990). Corporate entrepreneurship. *Strategic Management Journal, 11*, 297–308.

Hayton, J. C. (2005). Promoting corporate entrepreneurship through human resource management practices: A review of empirical research. *Human Resource Management Review, 15*, 21–41.

Hayton, J. C., Hornsby, J. S. and Bloodgood, J. (2013). Part II: The contribution of HRM to corporate entrepreneurship: A review and agenda for future research. *M@n@gement, 16*(4), 381–409.

Hayton, J. C. and Kelley, D. J. (2006). A competency-based framework for promoting corporate entrepreneurship. *Human Resource Management, 45*, 407–427.

Hedlund, G. (1986). The hypermodern MNC – A heterarchy? *Human Resource Management, 25*(1), 9–36.

Hills, G. E., Lumpkin, G. T. and Singh, R. P. (1997). *Opportunity recognition: Perceptions and behaviors of entrepreneurs*. Wellesley, MA: Babson College.

Hisrich, R. D. (1990). Entrepreneurship/intrapreneurship. *American Psychologist, 45*, 209–222.

Hitt, M. A., Ireland, R. D., Sirmon, D. G. and Trahms, C. A. (2011). Strategic entrepreneurship: Creating value for individuals, organisations and society. *Academy of Management Executive, 25*(2), 57–75.

Hoenen, A. K., Nell, P. C. and Ambos, B. (2014). MNE entrepreneurial capabilities at intermediate levels: The roles of external embeddedness and heterogeneous environments. *Long Range Planning, 47*, 76–86.

Hornsby, J. S., Kuratko, D. F., Shepherd, D. A. and Bott, J. P. (2009). Managers' corporate entrepreneurial actions: Examining perception and position. *Journal of Business Venturing, 24*(3), 236–247.

Hornsby, J. S., Naffziger, D. W., Kuratko, D. F. and Montagno, R. V. (1993). An interactive model of the corporate entrepreneurship process. *Entrepreneurship Theory and Practice, 17*, 29–38.

Hoy, F. (2006). The complicating factor of life cycles in corporate venturing. *Entrepreneurship Theory and Practice, 30*(6), 831–836.

Im, G. and Rai, A. (2008). Knowledge sharing ambidexterity in long-term interorganisational relationships. *Management Science, 54*, 1281–1296.

Ireland, R. D., Covin, J. and Kuratko, D. (2009). Conceptualizing corporate entrepreneurship strategy. *Entrepreneurship Theory and Practice, 33*(1), 19–46.

Ireland, R. D., Hitt, M. A. and Sirmon, D. G. (2003). A model of strategic entrepreneurship: The construct and its dimensions. *Journal of Management, 29*, 963–989.

Ireland, R. D. and Webb, J. W. (2007). A cross-disciplinary exploration of entrepreneurship research. *Journal of Management, 33*, 891–927.

Iser, W. (1978). *The act of reading*. Baltimore: Johns Hopkins University Press.

Iser, W. (1980). The reading process: A phenomenological approach. In Tompkins, J. P. (Ed.), *Reader response criticism*, pp. 50–69. Baltimore: Johns Hopkins University Press.

Jansen, J., Tempelaar, M., van den Bosch, F. and Volberda, H. (2009). Structural differentiation and ambidexterity: The mediating role of integration mechanisms. *Organisation Science, 20*, 797–811.

Jantunen, A., Puumalainen, K., Saarenketo, S. and Kyläheiko, K. (2005). Entrepreneurial orientation, dynamic capabilities and international performance. *Journal of International Entrepreneurship, 3*, 223–243.

Keupp, M. and Gassmann, O. (2009). The past and the future of international entrepreneurship: A review and suggestions for developing the field. *Journal of Management, 35*(3), 600–633.

Koen, P. A. (2000). Developing corporate intrapreneurs. *Engineering Management Journal, 12*(2), 3–8.

Kogut, B. and Zander, U. (1993). Knowledge of the firm and the evolutionary theory of the multinational corporation. *Journal of International Business Studies, 24*, 625–645.

Kuepp, M. M. and Gassmann, O. (2009). The past and the future of international entrepreneurship: A review and suggestions for developing the field. *Journal of Management, 35*(3), 600–633.

Kuratko, D. F. and Audretsch, D. (2009). Strategic entrepreneurship: Exploring different perspectives of an emerging concept. *Entrepreneurship Theory and Practice, 33*, 1–17.

Kuratko, D. F., Hornsby, J. S. and Goldsby, M. G. (2004). Sustaining corporate entrepreneurship: Modelling perceived implementation and outcome comparisons at organisational and individual levels. *International Journal of Entrepreneurship and Innovation Management, 5*(2), 77–90.

Kuratko, D. F., Hornsby, J. S. and Hayton, J. (2015). Corporate entrepreneurship: the innovative challenge for a new global economic reality. *Small Business Economics, 45*, 245–253.

Kuratko, D. F., Montagno, R. V. and Hornsby, J. S. (1990). Developing an intrapreneurial assessment instrument for an effective corporate entrepreneurial environment. *Strategic Management Journal (1986–1998), 11*(special issue), 49–58.

Le Breton-Miller, I. and Miller, D. (2006). Why do some family businesses outcompete? Governance, long-term orientations, and sustainable capability. *Entrepreneurship Theory and Practice, 30*(6), 731–746.

Lee, S. H. and Williams, C. (2007). Dispersed entrepreneurship within multinational corporations: A community perspective. *Journal of World Business, 42*, 505–519.

Ling, Y., Simsek, Z., Lubatkin, M. and Veiga, J. (2008). Transformational leadership's role in promoting corporate entrepreneurship: Examining the CEO-TMT interface. *Academy of Management Journal, 51*(3), 557–576.

Lu, T.-E., Chen, L.-J. and Lee, W.-R. (2007). Subsidiary initiatives in subsidiary role changing in the case of the Bartlett and Ghoshal typology. *Journal of American Academy of Business, Cambridge, 11*, 280–284

Lumpkin, G. T., Brigham, K. and Moss, T. (2010). Long-term orientation: Implications for the entrepreneurial orientation and performance of family businesses. *Entrepreneurship and Regional Development, 22*, 241–264.

Lumpkin, G. T., Cogliser, C. C. and Schneider, D. R. (2009). Understanding and measuring autonomy: An entrepreneurial orientation perspective. *Entrepreneurship Theory and Practice, 33*(1), 47–69.

Lumpkin, G. T. and Dess, G. G. (1996a). Clarifying the entrepreneurial orientation construct and linking it to performance. *Academy of Management Review, 21*, 135–172.

Lumpkin, G. T. and Dess, G. G. (1996b). Enriching the entrepreneurial orientation construct – a reply to 'Entrepreneurial Orientation or Pioneer Advantage'. *Academy of Management Review, 21*, 605–607.

Lumpkin, G. T. and Dess, G. G. (1997). Proactiveness versus competitive aggressiveness: Teasing apart key dimensions of an entrepreneurial orientation. In Reynolds, P., Bygrave, W., Carter, N., Davidsson, P., Gartner, W., Mason, C. and McDougall, P. (Eds.), *Frontiers of entrepreneurship research*. Wellesley, MA: Babson College, pp. 47–58.

McGaughey, S. L. (2004). 'Writing it up': The challenges of representation in qualitative research. In Piekarri, R. and Welch, C. (Eds.), *Handbook of qualitative research methods for international business*. Cheltenham, UK: Edward Elgar, pp. 529–550.

McGaughey, S. L. (2006). Reading as a method of inquiry in IB: Re-presentations of the 'born global'. *Management International Review*, Special Issue on Qualitative Methods in International Business, *46*(4), 461–480.

McGaughey, S. L. (2007a). Hidden ties in international new venturing: The case of portfolio entrepreneurship. *Journal of World Business, 42*, 307–321.

McGaughey, S. L. (2007b). *Narratives of internationalisation: Legitimacy, standards and portfolio entrepreneurs*. Cheltenham, UK: Edward Elgar.

McGaughey, S. L., Kumaraswarmy, A. and Liesch, P. W. (2016). Institutions, entrepreneurship and co-evolution in international business. *Journal of World Business. 51*, 871–881.

McGaughey, S. L. and Liesch, P. W. (2002). Management of the global sports-commerce nexus: The super league saga in Australia. *Journal of Management Studies, 39*(3), 383–416.

Menzel, H. C., Aaltio, I. and Ulijn, J. M. (2007). On the way to creativity: Engineers as intrapreneurs in organisations. *Technovation, 27*(12), 732–743.

Miller, D. (1983). The correlates of entrepreneurship in three types of firms. *Management Science, 29*, 770–791.

Miller, D. (1986). Configurations of strategy and structure: Towards a synthesis. *Strategic Management Journal, 7*, 233–249.

Miller, D. (1996). Configurations revisited. *Strategic Management Journal, 17*, 505–512.

Mom, T. J. M., van den Bosch, F. A. J. and Volberda, H. W. (2009). Understanding variation in managers' ambidexterity: Investigating direct and interaction effects of formal structural and personal coordination mechanisms. *Organisation Science, 20*(4), 812–828.

Monin, N., Barry, D. and Monin, D. C. (1996). Toggling with Taylor: A different approach to reading a management text. *Journal of Management Studies, 40*(2), 377–401.

Morris, M. H., Kuratko, D. F. and Covin, J. G. (2008). *Corporate entrepreneurship and innovation.* Mason, OH: South Western Cengage Learning.

Narayanan, V. K., Yang, Y. and Zahra, S. A. (2009). Corporate venturing and value creation: A review and proposed framework. *Research Policy, 38*, 58–76.

Nason, R. S., McKelvie, A. and Lumpkin, G. T. (2015). The role of organisational size in the heterogeneous nature of corporate entrepreneurship. *Small Business Economics, 45*, 279–304.

Nohria, N. and Ghoshal, S. (1994). Differentiated fit and shared values: Alternatives for managing headquarters-subsidiary relations. *Strategic Management Journal, 15*, 491–502.

O'Reilly, C. A. and Tushman, M. L. (2013). Organisational ambidexterity: Past, present and future. *Academy of Management Perspectives, 27*(4), 324–338.

OECD and Eurostat (2005). *Oslo manual – guidelines for collecting and interpreting innovation data.* Paris: OECD.

Paterson, S. L. and Brock, D. M. (2002). The development of subsidiary-management research: Review and theoretical analysis. *International Business Review, 11*, 139–163.

Petrakis, P. E. (2005). Risk perception, risk propensity and entrepreneurial behaviour: The Greek case. *Journal of American Academy of Business, Cambridge, 7*(1), 233–242.

Phan, P., Wright, M., Ucbasaran, D. and Tan, W. (2009). Corporate entrepreneurship: Current research and future directions. *Journal of Business Venturing, 24*(3), 197–205.

Pinchot, G., III. (1985). Introducing the 'Intrapreneur'. *IEEE Spectrum, 22*, 74–79.

Polkinghorne, D. E. (1988). *Narrative knowing and the human sciences.* Albany: State University of New York Press.

Porter, M. E. (1980). *Competitive strategy: Techniques for analyzing industries and competitors.* New York: The Free Press.

Porter, M. E. (1985). *Competitive advantage: Creating and sustaining superior performance.* New York: The Free Press.

Raisch, S. and Birkinshaw, J. (2008). Organisational ambidexterity: Antecedents, outcomes and moderators. *Journal of Management, 34*, 375–409.

Raisch, S., Birkinshaw, J., Probst, G. and Tushman, M. L. (2009). Organisational ambidexterity: Balancing exploitation and exploration for sustained performance. *Organisation Science, 20*, 685–695.

Reader, D. and Watkins, D. (2006). The social and collaborative nature of entrepreneurship scholarship: A co-citation and perceptual analysis. *Entrepreneurship Theory and Practice, 30*, 417–441.

Rosenblatt, L. M. (1978). *The reader, the text, the poem: The transactional theory of the literary work.* Carbondale, IL: Southern Illinois University Press.

Rugman, A., Verbeke, A. and Yuan, W. (2011). Re-conceptualizing Bartlett and Ghoshal's classification of national subsidiary roles in the multinational enterprise. *Journal of Management Studies, 48*, 253–277.

Rynes, S. L., Bartunek, J. M. and Daft, R. L. (2001). Across the great divide: Knowledge creation and transfer between practitioners and academics. *Academy of Management Journal, 44*(2), 340–355.

Schildt, H. A., Zahra, S. A. and Sillanpää, A. (2006). Scholarly communities in entrepreneurship research: A co-citation analysis. *Entrepreneurship Theory and Practice, 30*(3), 399–415.

Schuler, R. S. (1986). Fostering and facilitating entrepreneurship in organisations: Implications for organisation structure and human resource management practices. *Human Resource Management (1986–1998), 25*(4), 607–629.

Shane, S. (2003). *A general theory of entrepreneurship: The individual-opportunity nexus.* Cheltenham, UK: Edward Elgar.

Sharma, P. and Chrisman, J. J. (1999). Toward a reconciliation of the definitional issues in the field of corporate entrepreneurship. *Entrepreneurship Theory and Practice, 23,* 11–27.

Shepherd, D. A., Williams, T. A. and Patzelt, H. (2015). Thinking about entrepreneurial decision making: Review and research agenda. *Journal of Management, 41*(1), 11–46.

Simon, H. A. (1967). The business school a problem in organisational design. *Journal of Management Studies, 4*(1), 1–16.

Simon, H. A. (1982). *Models of bounded rationality.* Cambridge, MA: MIT Press.

Stake, R. E. (1978). The case study method in social inquiry. *Educational Researcher, 7*(2), 5–8.

Tang, G., Wei, L-Q., Snape, E. and Ng, Y. C. (2015). How effective human resource management promotes corporate entrepreneurship: Evidence from China. *The International Journal of Human Resource Management, 26*(12), 1586–1601.

Taylor, A. and Helfat, C. E. (2009). Organisational linkages for surviving technological change: Complementary assets, middle management and ambidexterity. *Organisation Science, 20,* 718–739.

Teece, D. J., Pisano, G. and Shuen, A. (1997). Dynamic capabilities and strategic management. *Strategic Management Journal, 18,* 509–533.

Thornhill, S. and White, R. E. (2007). Strategic purity: A multi-industry evaluation of pure vs. hybrid business strategies. *Strategic Management Journal, 28*(5), 553–561.

Venkataraman, S. (1997). The distinctive domain of entrepreneurship research: An editor's perspective. In Katz, J. and Brockhaus, R. (Eds.), *Advances in entrepreneurship, firm emergence and growth,* pp. 119–138. Greenwich, CT: JAI Press.

Verbeke, A., Chrisman, J. J. and Yuan, W. (2007). A note on strategic renewal and corporate venturing in the subsidiaries of multinational enterprises. *Entrepreneurship Theory and Practice, 31*(4), 585–600.

Verbeke, A. and Yuan, W. (2013). The drivers of multinational enterprise subsidiary entrepreneurship in China: A new resource-based view perspective. *Journal of Management Studies, 50*(2), 236–258.

Vernon, R. (1966). International investment and international trade in the product cycle. *Quarterly Journal of Economics, 80,* 190–207.

Weick, K. E. (2001). Gapping the relevance bridge: Fashions meet fundamentals in management research. *British Journal of Management, 12*(supplement 1), S71.

Weil, S., Oyelere, P. and Rainsburg, E. (2004). The usefulness of case studies in developing core competencies in a professional accounting programme: A New Zealand case study. *Accounting Education, 13*(2), 139–169.

Weil, S., Oyelere, P., Yeoh, J. and Firer, C. (2001). A study of students' perceptions of the usefulness of case studies for the development of finance and accounting-related skills and knowledge. *Accounting Education, 10*(2), 123–146.

Wolcott, H. F. (1999). *Ethnography: A way of seeing*. Walnut Creek, CA: AltaMira Press.

Wright, P. M. and McMahan, G. C. (2011). Exploring human capital: Putting human back into strategic human resource management. *Human Resource Management Journal, 21*(2), 93–104.

Zahra, S. A. (1991). Predictors and financial outcomes of corporate entrepreneurship: An exploratory study. *Journal of Business Venturing, 6*(4), 259–285.

2 Siemens Fire Safety

Introduction

In this chapter we provide the organisational and industry context for our study of apparent inertia in low levels of corporate entrepreneurship and business stagnation within the Fire Safety business unit of the Building Technologies division of Siemens AG. We begin with a short historical overview, highlighting the division's origins and its growth through the acquisition of the industry sector of Elektrowatt AG in 1997. This included Cerberus AG – a market leader in fire safety at the time of acquisition – which became the core of the Fire Safety business unit in Siemens AG. We then introduce the three case studies within the Fire Safety business unit used in our research to explore potentially different approaches and outcomes surrounding corporate entrepreneuring and to provide the rationales for their inclusion in our study. We conclude by offering a short note on method, where we describe the research process and key sources of data.

Historical overview of Fire Safety

Siemens AG offers many products, solutions, and services in the fields of general industry, healthcare, and energy generation and distribution. As of March 2011, these businesses were run by three sector organisations – Industry, Energy, and Healthcare – operating globally.[1] Within the industry sector, a building technology division integrates the Siemens offerings in fire safety, security, and building automation by four specific business units. The business unit Fire Safety (FS) represents the activities in the market of electronic products and solutions used to detect and suppress fires, as well as the product business in two adjacent fields of electronic security (i.e. access control and anti-intruder systems). The business unit Security Solutions (SES) provides its customer solutions based on the respective products of Fire Safety, and Building Automation (BAU) provides solutions for heating, ventilation, and air conditioning mainly based on the products obtained from the business unit Control Products and Systems (CPS). Headquarters of all Building Technology organisations are located in Zug, Switzerland. The business units focus on their specific area of market offerings as well as on combined solutions comprising all disciplines, called 'total building solutions'.

Historically the Building Technology division represents, primarily, the industry sector of Elektrowatt AG, taken over by Siemens at the end of 1997, with some similar but much smaller activities of Siemens added. As shown in Figure 2.1, within Elektrowatt Cerberus AG represented the business in fire safety and security products and solutions. Cerberus AG emerged as a spin-off from ETH[2] in 1941, industrialising the breakthrough invention of the ionisation detection principle by the Swiss Dr Walter Jaeger and Dr Ernst Meili in the same year – the first mechanism identified to detect fire aerosols electrically (Meili, 1990). Cerberus began its internationalisation in 1949 and 1951 with the granting of licences for the unique and patented design of the Cerberus smoke alarms to companies in Great Britain and USA (Meili, 1990).[3] In 1962 the first subsidiary outside Switzerland was founded in France by taking over Guinard SA (located in Buc near Paris and having its own local product assortment and R&D).

In 1972 the overall business strategy was reviewed fundamentally. Electronic fire detection had become a mature technology, and Cerberus was clearly dominant in the countries in which it was present. To further leverage from its superior

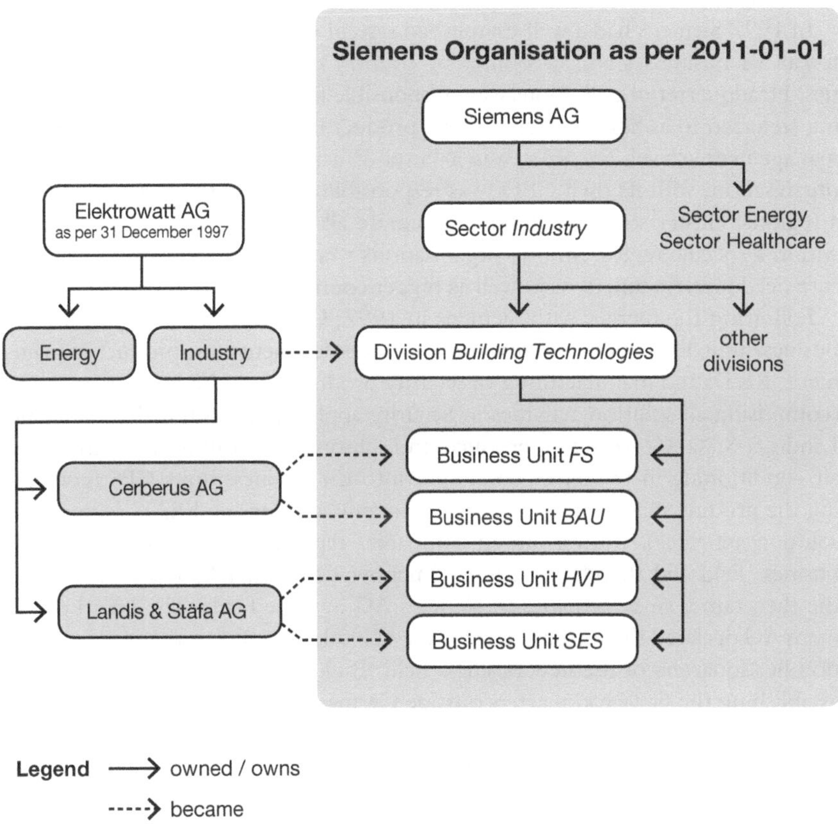

Figure 2.1 Origins and organisation of Fire Safety business unit

products, a strategy of worldwide geographic expansion by either taking over existing companies or setting up long-term partnerships was pursued. In subsequent years, several new subsidiaries were set up (Israel 1974, Spain 1975, Belgium 1977, Brazil 1978, United Kingdom 1982), and new partnerships were established with Siemens (Germany, Austria, and Nederland) and Ericsson (Sweden). Since the 1980s, Cerberus AG was also active in the adjacent business of various fields of electronic security products and applications. Key products and solutions were offered in the areas of access control systems, intruder detection, and CCTV equipment.[4]

Cerberus AG was considered the world market leader in the fire safety business from the mid 1990s, in what had become a multi-billion dollar business worldwide. United Technologies (UTC), Tyco International Ltd, and Honeywell International Inc. were its closest competitors on a global scale. Key for market growth was the establishment of strong national and international regulations, whereby such equipment was declared mandatory in most types of publicly accessible buildings. On the other hand, the abundance of country-specific regulations hindered the harmonisation of the products, inhibiting the business unit's ability to leverage from uniform global products.

In 1997 Siemens had a well-established system of German-based headquarters for all its businesses and a country-by-country organisation of all sales activities. Headquarter organisations were responsible for purchasing and manufacturing (referred to as 'level-1'), and R&D, product marketing, and overall business management ('level-2'). Sales was a 'level-3' activity, for which each country organisation, with its own CEO, was responsible. From 2008 there also existed a regional cluster setup intended to integrate all business planning and activity within a specific region. Matrix organisations were a preferred pattern to structure headquarters functions as well as bigger country offices.

Following the merger with Siemens in 1997, Cerberus AG was split into the business unit Fire Safety (representing all fire safety activities, product management, R&D, and manufacturing of security products) and the business unit SES (comprising all solution activities in Security applications). Similarly, the former Landis & Stäfa AG – offering products and solutions for heating, ventilation, and air conditioning in buildings – was split into the business units CPS (comprising the product management, R&D, and manufacturing) and BAU (comprising solution activities). Both acquired companies represented the core of the new business field and therefore created somehow a 'reverse-takeover' situation for the then rather small activities of Siemens AG in these fields. The board of Siemens AG declared the former Elektrowatt AG holding office as the new organisation headquarters of the new business field 'Building Automation BT', thereby establishing the first headquarters outside Germany.

Despite the strong position of the former Elektrowatt Group in the new Siemens organisation, a majority of employees disliked the integration. The Employees Survey 1999 recorded a very negative response to the statement *I am proud to be part of Siemens AG*. A first wave of key people left the company shortly after the merger. Turnover and EBIT declined year after year. In 2001 the board of

Siemens AG decided to replace the whole top management of Building Technologies and its six divisions and to integrate all independent Building Technologies sales offices into the unified Siemens country organisations. The majority of the former Cerberus Far East sales offices were closed down due to the negative cost effects of this integration (high expenses now had to be paid for sophisticated IT infrastructure, marketing, human resource management, and so on). A second wave of former key employees left Building Technologies. A consolidation of R&D sites took place in 2003 by closing down the redundant hardware development in the Munich office. Siemens Fire Safety decided in May 2004 to move its headquarters (including the main R&D facility) from Männedorf to Zug by October 2006. By June 2007, more than 60 per cent of the former R&D engineers in Switzerland had left the company. This drastic brain drain, combined with the resource-intensive development of a new global fire detection control panel, created the need for a significant increase in R&D headcount, rising from 120 in 1997 to 200 in 2008. In April 2008 Shinwha Electronics was bought. At the time it was the number two player in the fire safety market in South Korea, with its own product assortment developed by inhouse R&D.

In mid 2008 fire safety products were being developed at seven different locations: in headquarters in Zug (Switzerland, global product portfolio, fire research labs, 200 employees), in Munich (Germany, former Siemens headquarters, local portfolio, 80 employees), in Florham Park (United States, local portfolio, 50 employees), in Beijing (China, former joint venture company, global portfolio low end markets, 55 employees), in Buc (France, local portfolio, 40 employees), in Milan (Italy, focused on Management station software solutions, 35 employees), and in Seoul (South Korea, local portfolio, 21 employees). Technical standards still play an important role. The three major standards of EN54 (European community), UL (Underwriters Laboratories, United States), and GB (China) continued to be complemented with numerous country-specific standards, especially in Germany (VdS), France (CNPP), United Kingdom (BS), and South Korea. In particular, the local standards in France created huge additional efforts in product development. Purchasing and manufacturing were heavily optimised due to generally accepted and quite mature supply chain management processes and a full integration into Siemens-wide concepts and tool chains. Purchasing was done on a worldwide basis, and manufacturing sites were run in Switzerland, Germany, United States, and China.

Despite Cerberus AG being the world market leader in the fire safety business since the mid 1990s, the subsequent Siemens Fire Safety business unit lost this leading position. By the start of 2011 it had dropped to third position behind the new global leaders UTC and Tyco.[5] In fact, the fire safety industry is considered to have been in consolidation since the end of the 1990s, with bold acquisition moves by UTC, Tyco, and Honeywell. In the biggest acquisitions around the time of our study, Honeywell bought the main parts of Novar Plc. (UK) in December 2004 for US$2.3 billion, and the GE Security division was sold for US$1.8 billion in November 2009 to UTC. Despite having been part of the due diligence of almost all of the bigger acquisitions taking place in these years, Fire Safety did not manage to buy any of the competitors' activities (aside from the acquisition of Shinwha Electronics in South Korea, representing a local business). Key factors reported to explain this lack of success in securing desired acquisitions were slow internal decision-making in the bidding process and the difficulty of convincing the Siemens top management of the necessity of significant investments. This is especially attributed to the perceived low importance of the fire safety business when judged by created turnovers, profits, and strategic importance in the context of the overall Siemens operations.

A further key challenge for Fire Safety is an ongoing change in its industry towards significantly higher stakes of extinguishing products and solutions (i.e. automatic fire extinguishing by natural gases, chemical gases, water, and combined systems) in the overall fire safety business. These products and services represented around 60 per cent of the existing total market turnovers. With only 5 per cent of current turnover of Fire Safety created in this field, no profitable business performance in this segment could be achieved. Even worse, a major business shift from old-fashioned water sprinkler facilities towards high-tech water mist systems[6] – increasing the market attractiveness and profitability margins fundamentally – was missed by Fire Safety almost completely due to a lack of product innovation and market access. Additionally, IT companies like IBM and Cisco started to enter the business fields of software and networks on the side of fire detection. Fire extinguishing (as opposed to detection) technologies and products, however, are much harder to copy for IT firms. Therefore, comprehensive fire safety product portfolios and solutions still represent a high market-entry barrier.

Contrasting contexts of corporate entrepreneurship

Our interest in Siemens AG arose not only because it is a multinational enterprise (MNE) per se, but also because it is a special type of multi-establishment firm (Beugelsdijk and Mudambi, 2013). As discussed in Chapter 1, in the differentiated network of the MNE (Hedlund, 1994) subsidiaries often face diverse cultural, administrative, geographic, and economic contexts (Ghemawat, 2011) and perform different roles (Bartlett and Ghoshal, 2002; Alfoldi, Clegg and McGaughey, 2012). This enables us to explore corporate entrepreneuring across (internally and externally) heterogeneous units, but under common ownership and control.

To better understand impediments to corporate entrepreneuring – and, in particular, to explain the continuing business stagnation and perceived low levels of corporate entrepreneurship in Fire Safety – we selected three contrasting case studies within the business unit: (1) a SMART[7] project that takes place in the subsidiaries in China; (2) the acquisition of a South Korean competitor (Shinwha Electronics), involving the subsidiary and sales organisation in Korea; and (3) the Security Products (SP) new setup, which involves various European subsidiaries and sales organisations. Figure 2.2 shows the position of these case studies within the overall Siemens AG matrix organisation, with the Fire Safety business unit headquarters consistently being a part of them. In the following we provide short

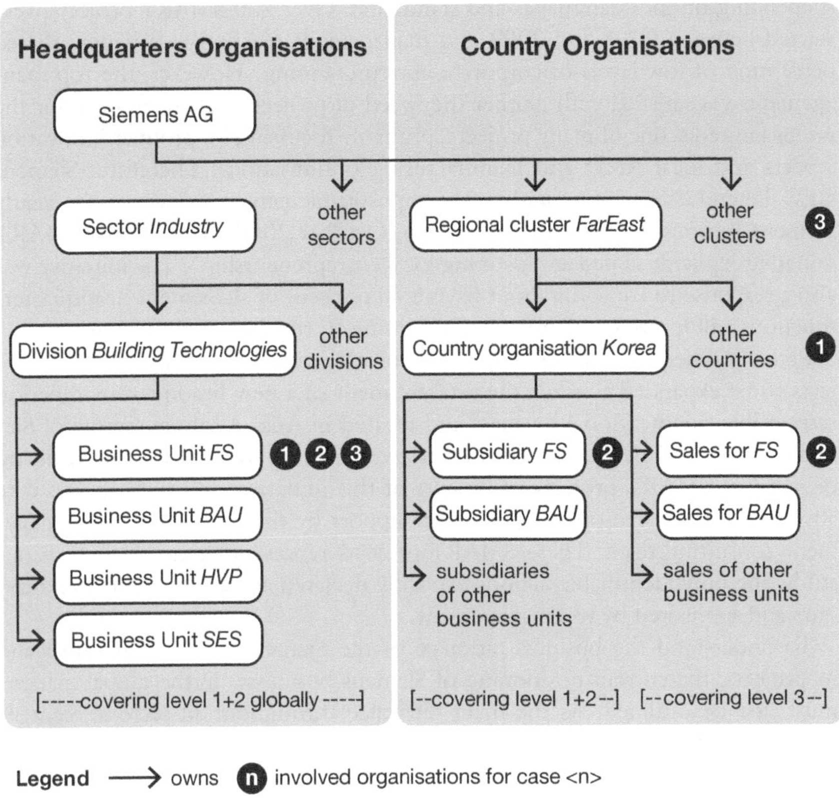

Figure 2.2 Case studies within Siemens Matrix Organisation (1 December 2009)

case study descriptions, including the nature of each entrepreneurial endeavour and their intended contributions to the study.

Entrepreneurial SMART initiatives

Siemens traditionally had a very centralised "Stammhaus"[8] model, consisting of global head offices for all divisions and sectors concentrated in Germany (with the exception of the Building Technologies division headquarters located in Switzerland). The SMART initiative sought to strengthen corporate venturing with significant levels of freedom from the established organisation. The process of breaking up this centralisation through the newly set-up SMART headquarters in the Far East had only just started at the time of our study, and was complemented by the twenty new regional cluster offices worldwide to provide more local business focus and increased efficiency in shared services.

SMART refers to Simple, Maintenance-friendly, Affordable, Reliable, and Timely. The SMART initiative was aimed at the launch of specific new businesses in lower-end markets as well as Asia-specific product adaptations and additions (depending on local languages and standards). Over 200 SMART projects were started between 2007 and 2009 as a management reaction to a widely shared perception of low levels of corporate entrepreneuring. However, the top management was satisfied with neither the speed of project implementation nor the rather limited scope of many projects, primarily focussing on product innovation aspects and local R&D and manufacturing optimisations. Therefore, Siemens CEO Peter Löscher presented to the top 300 Siemens managers at the yearly Siemens Business Conference in Berlin in October 2009 an additional SMART initiative explicitly aimed at "fostering local entrepreneurship". The initiative was also a response to concerns about having 70 per cent of all Siemens headquarters functions still located in Germany while trying to run a truly global business.

Peter Löscher asked the sector heads for a selection of twenty SMART projects to be expanded towards the establishment of a new headquarters function responsible for the global business and located in Asia. All three sectors of Siemens (Industry, Energy, and Healthcare) were invited to apply for their existing or planned SMART projects to be part of this initiative, and thus also to take advantage of the free-of-charge project support by the Siemens Top+ management consulting team. These SMART projects represented, at the time of our study, the only identifiable actions explicitly declared as entrepreneurial endeavours and sponsored by top management.

To understand the business rationale of the Siemens SMART initiative and its projects, the current positioning of Siemens businesses in the global markets must first be outlined. As the main reference throughout all sectors, Siemens was using a standardised model of market segmentation with four levels of complexity, size and pricing of product, and service offering, referenced to as 'M1' ('high-end') to 'M4' ('low-priced'). Traditionally, Siemens was only active in M1 and M2 markets, as compared to companies such as GE and ABB. M1 markets involve high value-added solutions, such as wind turbines and CT scanners at the premium end. M2 includes mass-produced solutions such as industrial sensor systems and smoke detectors for the middle market segments. In recent years, growing competition from companies in emerging markets (mainly in Brazil, Russia, India, China, and Middle East countries), such as Gulf, Chint, Nari, and Neusoft, emerged. These emerging market multinational enterprises also started to innovate towards higher end markets, as shown in Figure 2.3.[9] That is, they began to produce innovative solutions of good-enough quality that were affordable and dependable. In addition to expanding globally – thereby representing a serious threat for the existing business of Siemens – these emerging market multinationals were increasing business in the emerging markets, which were expected to experience the biggest growth rates in coming years. The SMART initiative thus represented a 'counterattack' by Siemens, involving the expansion of its product portfolios down towards the 'entry-level' market segment M3, particularly targeting emerging markets.[10] Here customers were highly price sensitive and yet remained quality conscious, requiring Siemens to create solutions that were simple, reliable, of good quality, and reasonably priced. Global

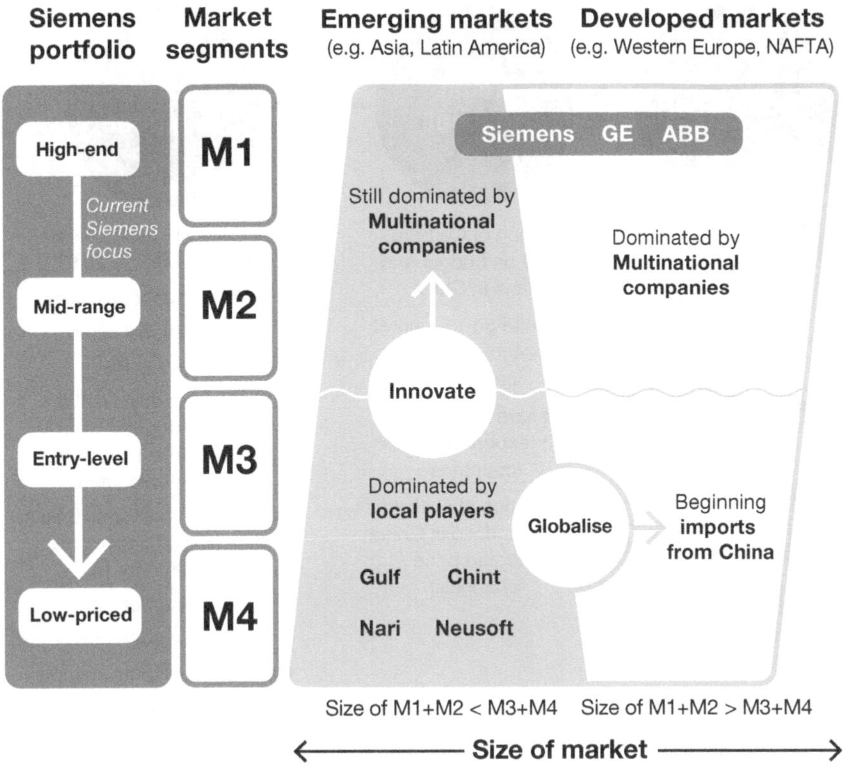

Figure 2.3 Rationale for the SMART initiative

M3 product responsibility was to be delegated to emerging markets, and local entrepreneurship strengthened to increase market penetration, customer loyalty, and local value added.

In 2007 Fire Safety had already started in its China subsidiary a new product development project aimed at addressing lower-end product distribution markets in China with moderately priced competitive fire detectors and fire panels (matching M3 in the Siemens model). Subsequently, when Siemens AG top management launched the overarching 'SMART initiative' to more successfully address such lower-end markets throughout all businesses with specific projects, the Fire Safety endeavour in China was selected as one of these projects (internally referenced as project "I-02"). Key to the concrete implementation of the Fire Safety SMART project, a three-step approach was defined, summarised in Figure 2.4.[11] A first step called "Start local"(2007–2008) was focussed on setting up a local organisation in Beijing, defining target markets within China, identifying required product features, and developing the products – mainly by simplifying and optimising the cost of existing products. The second step – "Local for local", 2009 – was the start of sales in China with respective

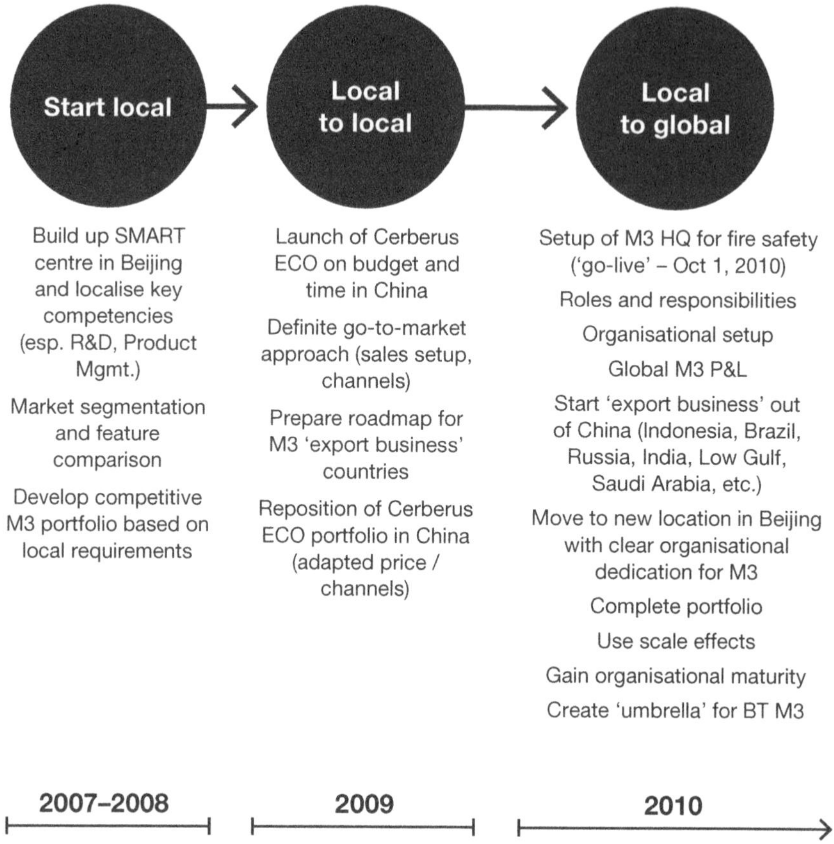

Figure 2.4 Implementation roadmap for the SMART initiative

go-to-market setups, product positioning in the market, and the preparation of roadmaps for exporting to further countries. Step three of the project was running from the start of 2010 and is called "Local for global". A global headquarters was set up with a global profit and loss responsibility for the M3 market in fire safety. By the start of 2011 product exportation to Russia and Brazil had commenced, and a new location in Beijing was used to centralise all M3 activities.

At the time of our study, the SMART project within the Industry sector and driven by the Fire Safety business unit was sufficiently mature to allow for insights regarding aspects of corporate entrepreneurship. This SMART project represents a significant new business venturing activity comprising the setup of a new organisational unit, a newly developed product portfolio, and entry to new markets worldwide. Furthermore, it involves explicit management sponsorship and was – at the time of our study – widely perceived within Siemens AG as a successful entrepreneurial endeavour, albeit not without challenges.

Acquisition of an entrepreneurial SME: Shinwha

In the climate of crisis and change at Siemens described in Chapter 1, the acquisition of Shinwha Electronics in South Korea by the Siemens business unit Fire Safety in 2008 was perceived by management and staff as one of the most visible elements of trying to develop new venturing and thus to overcome the firm stagnation. It was, and remains, the key business rationale of Fire Safety to try to reach dominant market positions in all major geographical markets worldwide. By the end of the 1990s the fire safety market in South Korea (subsequently referred to as 'Korea') was entered for the first time by selling existing European products directly (approved by local government authority KFI),[12] but only an insignificant market share of 0.6 per cent had been achieved by 2005. In contrast, Siemens Korea BAU and HVP organisations held number two market positions. Subsequently, driven by Daniel Bertok[13] – who had been appointed the new CEO of Building Technologies Korea from October 2005 – it was decided to investigate the options for a substantial local acquisition. Fire Safety market intelligence reported a market share of 27 per cent for the leading company Tyco Dongbang – a company that arose from the takeover of Korean Dongbang Ltd. by US conglomerate Tyco in 1999. The second biggest player was Shinwha Electronics Co. Ltd (hereafter Shinwha Ltd), with an estimated market share of thirteen per cent. Since Tyco Dongbang was not for sale and Shinwha Ltd was a well-known partner of Siemens, already selling the American product portfolio of Fire Safety in Korea, it was decided to explore the option of potentially acquiring Shinwha Ltd.

Shinwha Ltd was initially founded as a joint venture named Ewha Electronics in October 1970, and was held by Korean owners and Hochiki Corp, Japan.[14] Due to the unsatisfactory economic development of the company, Ewha Electronics was sold in February 1980 to Mr ST Park and renamed Shinwha Electronics Co. Ltd. In 1991 ST Park appointed his brother OK Park as the CEO and acted subsequently as the chairman only. By leveraging from its business with international Korean construction companies,[15] Shinwha Ltd managed to build up its own international project business. By the time of the acquisition, the Shinwha Ltd product portfolio consisted of a full range of conventional and addressable fire detection systems,[16] rounded off with stand-alone fire detectors for residential application ('Home Smokes'), a portfolio of Exit Lights, and a full assortment of automated Fire Extinguishing solutions. Only in the top end of the market, from 1996 Shinwha Ltd sold the Siemens FS Fire detection systems MXL and XLS[17] and some third party niche products. Overall, 80 per cent of all sold products were developed and manufactured by Shinwha Ltd itself, with an additional turnover of 10 per cent from Siemens Fire Safety products and another 10 per cent by other third party providers. The company turnover had grown by 86 per cent from 2003 to 2006. Further expansion planned by the owners required significant new financial resources.

In 2006 a 90 per cent stake of Shinwha Ltd's shares was held by the Park brothers. Both were approaching retirement age and had no obvious successor coming from their families to lead the firm in the future. In October 2006 Siemens started a first due diligence, and an indicative offer was accepted by Shinwha Ltd in July 2007. A detailed due diligence took place from August to November 2007. Deal negotiations finally led to the deal closing at the end of April 2008. Shinwha Electronics Co. Ltd consisted of Shinwha Electronics (fire detection) and SH Engineering (fire extinguishing) at the time of the takeover. Using European Union definitions, it was a small to medium enterprise (SME) employing around 250 employees, with a turnover of EUR 40 million in the business year of 2007.

According to the internal "Investment Proposal" document of Siemens BT, the main rationales given by Siemens for buying Shinwha Ltd were (1) the previous failure to establish their own sales channels in Korea; (2) the attractive Korean fire safety market (by total market size, sales margins, a strong high-end market segment, and estimated growth rates higher than in European markets); (3) the possibility to leverage on combined offerings, including products and services from the other Building Technologies business units; and (4) a reasonable price offered for becoming number two in the Korean fire safety market. From a Shinwha Ltd owner's perspective, the takeover (1) solved the successor problem; (2) provided a good selling price; and (3) opened access to substantial financial resources for future growth; as well as (4) access to the international sales channels of Siemens, the full product portfolio, and the global R&D and manufacturing network of Fire Safety. Unfortunately, this last aim from the seller's side collided with the primarily Korean-local market objectives from the buyer's side. Fire Safety was primarily interested in the market access to Korea and selling the global Fire Safety products there, with some minor adaptations in the future. Nevertheless, Fire Safety announced to all Shinwha employees that a main target of the acquisition would be to "[r]ealis[e] growth opportunities together with Shinwha [. . .] for the Korean and overseas market in fire safety".

It was decided at deal closing to keep OK Park as the CEO of the newly formed Siemens Shinwha subsidiary. Being the long-serving 'patron' with a high legitimacy among the employees, OK Park was guaranteeing continuity within the company and maintaining the strong personal relationships to key customers and local regulation authorities. OK Park was, for example, re-elected as a member of the governmental standards committee for Fire Safety in September 2008. TS Lim, the CFO of Building Technologies Korea, was additionally appointed CFO of Siemens Shinwha, thus replacing the former CFO KM Lim, who took over other responsibilities within the firm. The former chairman ST Park signed a one-year contract as a management consultant, whereas his position was replaced by a board of directors, comprising the CEO and CFO of Siemens Korea and TS Lim and OK Park. However, at the end of 2008 ST Park resigned as a consultant, and in May 2009 OK Park was replaced by Daniel Bertok. Furthermore, it was decided in May 2009 that Daniel Bertok would leave Korea at the end of September 2009 and that YK Lim (heading the sales of Siemens Shinwha at that time) would take over responsibility for Siemens Shinwha as a director (Siemens organisation did not contain a 'CEO' position within a regional company structure). SH Wong, the factory manager of Building Technology Korea, took over the same function for Siemens Shinwha by October 2008 to allow for a unified factory management.

The subsequent integration of Shinwha Ltd followed the comprehensive and standardised Siemens process defined as mandatory for all acquisitions company-wide. The integration process was officially closed by 1 December 2009 – exactly one and half years after the deal closing, as targeted by the Siemens integration process. However, turnover and profit of the new Fire Safety Korea entity did not develop as expected by the Siemens management at deal closing. A drastic drop in new order intake led to a dramatic decrease of turnover and a negative profitability by the end of business year 2010. In business year 2009, instead of the budgeted KRW 70 billion turnover and 4.5 billion profit, a turnover of only 52 billion (-26 per cent) and a profit of only 1.3 billion (-71 per cent) was achieved. In business year 2010 the initial budget of KRW 52 billion turnover with a profit of 2.1 billion was missed, with a realised turnover of 37.8 billion by 27 per cent, and a net loss of 3.7 billion resulted (equivalent to -9.7 per cent return of sales). During the business years 2009 and 2010, two waves of staff reductions throughout all functions (manufacturing, R&D, sales) took place to cut internal cost. The expected synergies on the sales side, by offering combined projects comprising all solution disciplines of Building Technologies, did not materialise; none of the offered 'total buildings solutions' were sold (as of the end of September 2010). It was a widely shared understanding within Siemens management that the drastic sales drops were primarily caused by the loss of key account managers.

The acquisition integration process revealed significant differences in the entrepreneurial orientation and behaviour of relevant Siemens headquarters, Siemens Korea, and Shinwha Ltd management representatives, with post-acquisition performance significantly below the economic performance of the Shinwha ventures in the years prior to the acquisition in 2008. Furthermore, the clash of the different company cultures of the involved Siemens entities and Shinwha Ltd – evident in the integration process – revealed exemplary differences in the 'way of corporate entrepreneurship'.

Initially, the selection of the Shinwha acquisition as a case to be studied afforded an opportunity to contrast the 'normal way of corporate entrepreneurship' at Siemens in a specific integration situation with the 'entrepreneurial way' within the formerly independent SME, Shinwha Ltd. Furthermore, the acquisition offered insights into entrepreneurial activities outside the official Siemens SMART initiative where management explicitly sponsored entrepreneurial behaviour. Subsequently, and unexpectedly, the Shinwha integration developed into rather a critical case (Yin, 2009), since the economic development of the new entity did not live up to the expectations. Indeed, by 2011 it was considered to be a failed acquisition by the Fire Safety management.

The SP 'new setup'

The Building Technologies business units Fire Safety and Security Solutions were active for many years in various fields of the adjacent business of electronic security products and solutions. Key areas of offering were access control systems, intruder detection, and CCTV[18] equipment. The product management, product development, and manufacturing of these security products were integrated into the Fire Safety business unit and referred to as Security Products (SP), whereas the sales of solutions and the subsequent entire life cycle business remained part of the operations of the business unit Security Solutions.

This security product business never reached significant levels of profitability within the Fire Safety business unit, and was consistently considered to be below a critical size in turnovers. An early initiative to significantly increase the business by substantial acquisitions was planned at the end of 2000. It aimed to quadruple the turnover within five years by adding new product portfolios and strengthened sales channels. But due to the crisis in paid share prices of companies focussed on IT technology starting in 2001 (i.e. the bursting of the '.COM bubble' in the financial markets) and the reduced profitability of Fire Safety and Security Solutions in parallel, neither the cash positions for direct company buys nor attractive share conditions for share-based deals existed six months after deciding upon the initiative. Therefore, the screening of potential acquisition targets again stopped, and new venturing activities refocussed towards activities for organic growth. Unfortunately, activities in product portfolio renewal and sales channel build-up were highly unsuccessful, leading to a further decrease in turnovers and profitability in the security business until 2005.

Due to better profitability of the Fire Safety business (and Building Technologies overall) and changing conditions in the financial markets, it was decided to restart the screening of potential acquisition targets in 2004. In November 2005 the Swedish company Bewator was acquired and integrated into Security Products of Fire Safety. It added significant new business in access control and anti-intrusion systems through its product portfolio and sales channels. Furthermore, in April 2007 the Chennai (India)–based iMetrex Ltd was acquired, adding substantially more security products and solutions with direct operations in India, Ireland, United Kingdom, Singapore, and Hong Kong. The iMetrex operation was subsequently split up into a solutions part (containing most of the India business) that was integrated into the business unit Security Solutions, whereas the development and manufacturing of the intrusions systems was added again to the Security Products portfolio within Fire Safety.

Unfortunately, the acquisition of Bewator and iMetrex was also unsuccessful. Key employees of Bewator left within the first six months after the deal closing, whereas many Siemens employees left in India after the merger with iMetrex. The consolidated Security Products business operation never reached operational profitability. Fire Safety top management declared the Security Products business (SP) within Fire Safety – built on the two previously acquired companies (Bewator Ltd in 2005, iMetrex Ltd in 2007) – as void of any prospect of ever becoming profitable within the Siemens organisation. Therefore, the management of Building Technologies searched for a potential buyer for the whole Security Products entity in mid 2008, but failed.

A new project was therefore started in 2009 for the planned carve-out of the business into an independently run company, hopefully to be sold to a new shareholder in the best-case scenario. As part of this project, it was decided to close down the CCTV product line, to reduce the intrusion product portfolio and the number of related staff in product management, R&D, and manufacturing, and to set up the new and quite small company for the remaining business parts. This entity – referred to as 'SP new setup' – was kept highly independent from the Siemens organisation and its processes, led by a new management team, and intended to be ready for a carve-out (divesture from Fire Safety) by the end of 2011. In October 2014 Vanderbilt Industries announced it had signed a Purchase Agreement to acquire Siemens' Security Products, with the deal concluded in June 2015.[19]

Similar to the acquisition circumstances of Shinwha Ltd described previously, this case has the potential to highlight the shortcomings of entrepreneurial endeavours in Fire Safety when attempting business expansion and renewal by acquisitions. It delineates business circumstances considered by the Siemens management as impossible to deal with successfully within the given boundaries of the Siemens organisation, thus revealing the limitations to entrepreneurial activity within Siemens. It also represents an alternative model of organisation and operations, shedding many of the constraints imposed by being embedded in the Siemens context and leveraging from the advantages of being a small and independent SME organisation.

Summarising case study contributions

The contrasts between the three case studies and their respective contributions, discussed previously in detail, are summarised in Table 2.1. Looking at the cases from a Fire Safety business unit perspective (see Figure 2.5), the SMART project represents an entrepreneurial activity within the existing Fire Safety entity and with explicit Siemens AG top management support; the Shinwha acquisition represents the entrance of a formerly independent and highly entrepreneurial entity; and the SP new setup involves the separation of a then integrated business into a new and independent entity in preparation for its sale. Within this case selection, the Shinwha acquisition was especially anticipated to reveal entrepreneurial behaviour in a small to medium enterprise (SME) and effects of change when being merged into a MNE such as Siemens. The SMART project was hoped to reveal mechanisms of entrepreneurial activity when launching an explicitly entrepreneurial endeavour entirely embedded in the MNE. Finally, the SP new setup illustrated the limitations of business opportunity recognition and exploitation

Table 2.1 Intended contribution of each Fire Safety case study

Case name		
SMART project	*Shinwha acquisition and integration*	*SP new setup*
Case description		
Entrance of low-end fire safety markets by setting up a newly developed product portfolio, a global headquarters organisation in China, and a product roll-out globally.	Acquisition of Shinwha Ltd. (Korea) and its integration into the global Siemens Fire Safety organisation, as well as the Siemens organisation in Korea.	Acquisitions of Bewator (2005) and iMetrex (2007) by Fire Safety, a failed merger with similar operations, and the subsequent restructuring and carve-out into a new and highly independent legal entity.
Main contribution		
New business venturing activity entirely embedded within Fire Safety, with explicit top management sponsorship. Widely perceived as a successful entrepreneurial endeavour, comprising product innovation, the setup of a new global headquarters, and the entering of new markets worldwide.	Revelation of the 'normal way of corporate entrepreneurship' at Siemens by especially contrasting its specific integration situation to the 'entrepreneurial way' within the formerly independent SME Shinwha Ltd.	Revelation of the limitations to corporate entrepreneurship within the Siemens context of complex MNE organisations, processes and rules, and pointing to an alternative model.

within an MNE, and the subsequent (hoped for) successful breakup of the business into a new SME setup.

A note on method

Our approach to case selection is best described as an embedded case study design in which we explore the entrepreneurial behaviour of the previously described three local entities within the Siemens AG business unit Fire Safety. In selecting cases we used a maximum variation approach (Patton, 2005) with 'polar' cases (Eisenhardt and Graebner, 2007). Data collection was undertaken from September 2007 to October 2010 in Shinwha Siemens (including a pilot study), and from January 2008 to October 2010 in the other two entities, as illustrated in Figure 2.6. The first author, Joe Amberg, was engaged with the Shinwha merger since the Siemens due diligence phase II commenced in July 2007, and subsequently continued working as an integration manager in the new Shinwha subsidiary. This enabled a real-time longitudinal approach to data collection, drawing

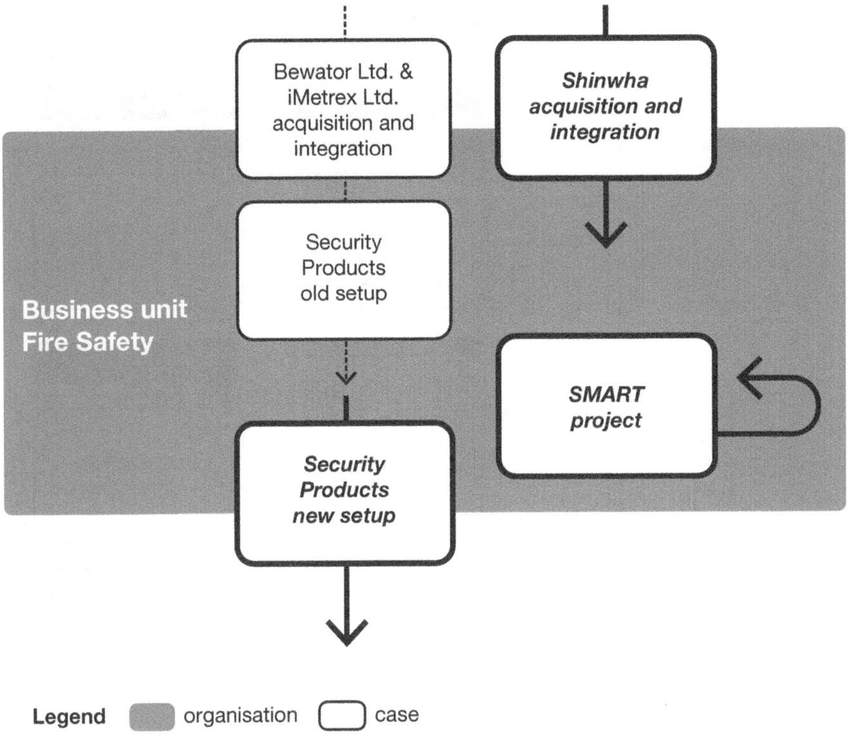

Figure 2.5 Selected cases in the context of the Fire Safety business unit

extensively on naturally occurring data through participant observation that afforded close contact with key decision makers, semi-structured interviews, and corporate documents used in Amberg's daily activities. For the remaining two cases we primarily focussed on semi-structured interviews with executive and middle managers who were responsible for comparable value chain elements within all three cases. Also included were two representatives of the Siemens corporate management as the initiators of the SMART initiative and those responsible for the definitions of the Siemens human resource models. To identify appropriate interviewees, the Siemens Reference Process House[20] was used as a guiding structure. This sampling approach used in relation to the selection of interview participants was intended to uncover different (and not just dominant) views within the organisation and specific case studies (Guba and Lincoln, 1989). Overall, formal interviews were conducted with nineteen top and middle managers from Europe and Asia, drawn from both relevant headquarters and local entities.

Data sources are detailed in Table 2.2. All names of interviewees are changed to afford some degree of anonymity, although position titles are disclosed. All interviews were conducted in English, audio recorded, and transcribed in full. The

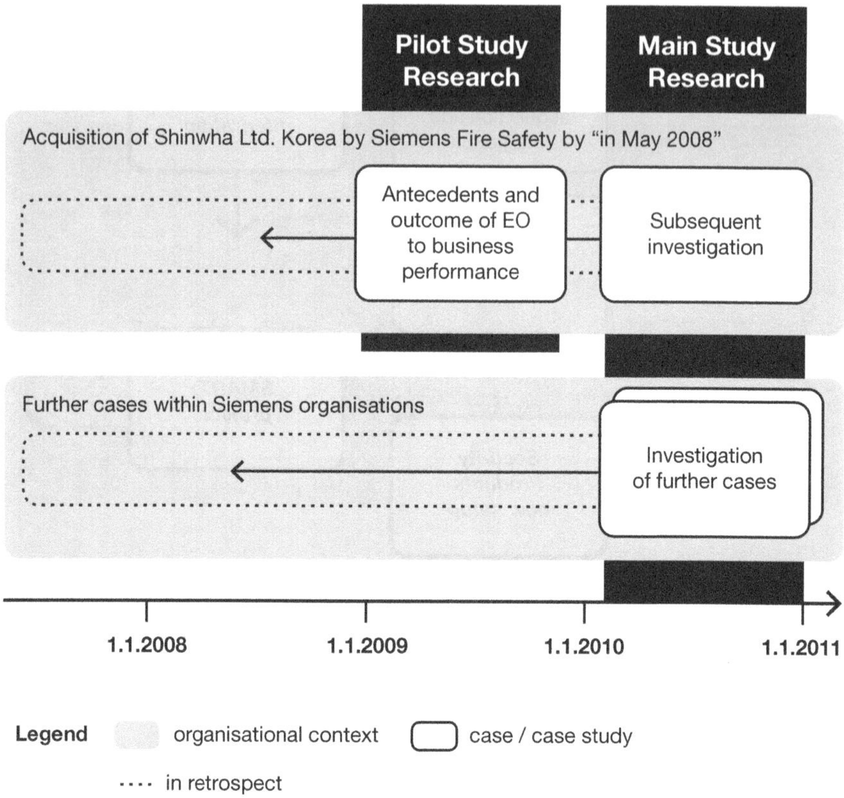

Figure 2.6 The research process

chosen monolingual approach using English as the sole language of interviews may have limited the possibilities of non-native speakers for delineating details and providing authentic and "rich" responses exhibiting "subtle nuances", thus potentially just "repeating company policy and falling back on jargon" (Welch and Piekkari, 2006, p. 428). However, all interviewees were fluent English speakers (with English being the corporate language). For the interview questions, an "international" English devoid of dialect, idioms, and colloquialisms was used "to reduce the impact of interviews that are 'linguistically dysfunctional'" (Welch and Piekkari, 2006, p. 429). Furthermore, distortion and inaccuracies of answers caused by language translations could be avoided. The project was approved by the management of Siemens I BT FS headquarters in Switzerland, who then remained at arms-length. All participants were advised of the researchers' activities, the purpose of the research, and their own potential role in it should they agree to be involved.

In addition to interviews, notes from opportunistic observations in the context of the cases were taken over the full period of data collection, and extensive

Table 2.2 Case-specific data sources

<table>
<tr><th colspan="2" rowspan="2">Organisations and roles</th><th colspan="3">Interviewees by cases</th><th rowspan="2">Siemens AG corporate perspective</th></tr>
<tr><th>Shinwha acquisition</th><th>SMART project</th><th>SP new setup</th></tr>
<tr><td rowspan="3">Headquarters management</td><td>CEO/PL</td><td colspan="3">• CEO BT FS</td><td>• Global Project Lead SMART Initiative</td></tr>
<tr><td>R&D, PM, Sales</td><td>• Regional Manager for Korea in FS HQ</td><td>• Global Head of FS SES</td><td>• Integration Manager iMetrex;
• Global Head of Product Line Intrusion (before SP new setup)</td><td></td></tr>
<tr><td>HRM</td><td colspan="3">• Global Head of FS Human Resources</td><td>• Management Development HQ</td></tr>
<tr><td rowspan="3">Local entity management</td><td>CEO/CFO/PL</td><td>• CFO BT Korea</td><td>• Global Head FS SYS</td><td>• CEO SP new setup</td><td rowspan="3"></td></tr>
<tr><td>former CEO/ CFO</td><td>• CEO BT Korea.
• CEO of Shinwha and CEO, Shinwha Siemens</td><td></td><td>• Chief Marketing Officer BT</td></tr>
<tr><td>R&D, PM, Sales</td><td>• Head of R&D and Manufacturing at FS Korea;
• Head of BT FS Korea and former CEO of Shinwha Fire Protection</td><td>• Head of Product Management FS China;
• Regional Coordinator for Korea and China</td><td>• Head of Product Line within SP new setup</td></tr>
<tr><td rowspan="5">Other data sources</td><td rowspan="5"></td><td>participant observation</td><td colspan="3"></td></tr>
<tr><td colspan="4">financial reports (monthly, quarterly, yearly)</td></tr>
<tr><td colspan="2">project planning and reports</td><td colspan="2"></td></tr>
<tr><td colspan="3">employee surveys</td><td></td></tr>
<tr><td colspan="4">management reports</td></tr>
</table>

Legend: PL = project lead, PM = product management, HRM = human resource management, R&D = research and development, CEO = chief executive officer, CFO = chief financial officer, BT = Building Technologies, FS = Fire Safety, SMART = simple, maintenance-friendly, affordable, reliable, and timely, SP = security products, HQ = Siemens AG Corporate Headquarters, SES = Security Solutions corporate documents were available due to the first author's immersion into the Siemens organisation as an acting senior manager. Additional data sources included the financial reports (monthly, quarterly, yearly) of the researched projects and business units, as well as those of Siemens AG, due diligence reports, investment proposals and takeover reports, project planning and reports, employee surveys (regular and project specific) conducted by the organisation, specifically created management reports (especially reporting the SMART project advancement) and corporate presentations, and an array of policy documents at various levels of the organisation.

By investigating three cases of different nature and multiple sources within, we sought 'data triangulation', thereby improving the completeness and reliability of the data used in analysis (Eisenhardt, 1989; Yin, 2009). 'Investigator triangulation' (Denzin, 1978) – with the authors representing an industry practitioner and university-employed academic, respectively – enhances the likelihood of insights being generated that blend contributions to theory with practical relevance. All three cases take place within the organisation of Building Technologies division. However, the majority of interviewees are not only engaged in one specific case but are also active in many further proceedings of the business unit, the division, or even the top corporate level. Therefore, the views and information provided by respondents may also include knowledge and experiences beyond one specific case. To reveal case specifics, interview questions were explicitly designed to focus on the case of interest. Nonetheless, many of the participant responses cannot be assigned to one specific case only, but instead reflect patterns existing throughout the entire Fire Safety business unit, the Building Technologies division, or even Siemens AG. The ability of respondents to look beyond a specific case was an advantage to the study, since a core aim of this research was to better understand impediments to corporate entrepreneuring, which was most likely also affected by higher organisational levels, and to identify activities and factors that could foster entrepreneurial behaviour within Siemens or similar organisations.

NVivo software was used to support data analysis. A first cycle of data reduction using thematic coding not only drew on the extant literature and an extensive interview protocol, but also allowed unanticipated meanings to emerge. Following the thematic coding, data displays and detailed descriptions of the cases and findings were generated (see Miles and Huberman, 1994). These aimed at capturing and describing the central themes and relationships that cut across the heterogeneous case study entities and levels (see Table 2.2), as well as explaining differences. For example, in relation to factors affecting the dual needs for exploration and exploitation, we generated a table that recorded perspectives of each interviewee in relation to these dual needs, for each of the three embedded cases, and in relation to Siemens AG as a whole. Within each of these four locales we distinguished between perceptions at different levels of the organisation (i.e. senior executives and middle management in headquarters or in a subsidiary), linking perceptions to specific (anonymised) individuals. In a subsequent table, we provided a count of occurrence for each of the themes identified and clustered individuals within each theme, while retaining the distinctions between respondents in terms of locale and position in the organisational hierarchy. Hence, our data displays generated from the analysis sought to retain both the richness of the respondents' words as well as summary patterns, thereby allowing comparisons across organisational units and levels.

These interim findings led to further cycles of (mainly secondary) data gathering and subsequent analysis and, in particular, efforts to derive causal networks (Miles and Huberman, 1994) that showed the relationships between organisational antecedents and individual behaviours related to CE. The resulting data displays (e.g. concept and thematic tables, causal networks) helped to reduce the 'extended text' of the collected data and garner insights by building clusters, identifying relationships, and making contrasts and comparisons within each case study and, subsequently, between case studies. Our methodological approach is best described as ***abductive*** (Dew, 2007; Alfoldi et al., 2012; Amberg and McGaughey, 2016) in that we started with theory but engaged in a constant iteration between theory and data over the life of the research project.

Our procedures were consistent with those recommended for establishing data 'trustworthiness' (Guba and Lincoln, 1994): the first author had 'prolonged engagement' with the research site during the real-time data collection and afterwards; data collection and analysis were concurrent; sources of data were 'triangulated' (Yin, 2009); raw data is cross-referenced to provide an 'audit trail' (Morse, 1994); and 'member checks' whereby the emerging framework and interpretations were presented to senior executives and broader networks provided useful verification or challenges to interpretations, and sometimes led to additional data that further elaborated the findings. We start exploring findings from our study in the next chapter, where we present the perspectives of our research participants concerning the extent and nature of corporate entrepreneurship within Siemens Fire Safety and the Building Technologies division more broadly.

Notes

1 Organisation valid until March 2011 (from 1 April 2011, a further sector was founded)
2 Eidgenössische Technische Hochschule, Zürich, Switzerland
3 Ernst Meili was the founder and charismatic CEO of Cerberus AG for 38 years. His book about his life with Cerberus provides a rich historical account.
4 Closed-Circuit Tele Vision: video cameras and related monitors within a closed system, typically used in higher security areas, shopping malls, etc.
5 As reported by external market intelligence firms like Memoori Business Intelligence Ltd. (http://memoori.com)
6 Water mist systems use highly elaborated valve technologies blending air and water into a fog, thus requiring much less water for the same extinguishing impact as pure water-based sprinklers.
7 Simple, Maintenance-friendly, Affordable, Reliable, and Timely – Siemens' definition for products aimed at lower-end world markets.
8 German; i.e. head office
9 Based on interviews and Siemens internal presentations and media releases.

10 There were some inconsistencies about the geographic responsibilities and target: several internal presentations and documents refer to BRIC and ME only, while others refer to "global competence".

11 Source: Based on interviews, presentation by Fire Safety Product Management Head, June 2010, and media releases.

12 Selling of the fire detection system AlgoRex; only four systems could be sold between 2001 and 2005.

13 Virtually all names within this monograph have been altered to preserve a degree of anonymity for those interviewed.

14 A key player in the Japanese Fire Safety market as well as on the world markets. Compare http://www.hochiki.co.jp/overseas/ (accessed in May 2009)

15 Korean construction companies realised international business of approximately US $40 billion in 2008, with Hyundai considered the biggest firm in this market worldwide.

16 Fire detection systems are primarily distinguished by the technology used on the field buses. *Conventional* systems are only capable of receiving summary signals from fire detectors, whereas in *addressable* systems each sensor or actor is distinguishable. Shinwha's conventional products are named 'SPH', whereas the addressable systems are labelled 'SRF'.

17 This collaboration started in 1996 and was also based on the market requirement of having 'international' products offered in the highest market segment (highest reliability and complexity).

18 Closed-Circuit Tele Vision: the use of video cameras and respective monitors within a closed system, typically used in higher security areas, shopping malls, etc.

19 See <http://vanderbiltindustries.com/news/vanderbilt-completes-acquisition-of-security-products-from-siemens-press-release/> and <http://vanderbiltindustries.com/news/vanderbilt-establishes-international-headquarters-in-germany/>, last accessed 2016-05-11.

20 The Siemens Reference Process House is the overall process framework to be used throughout the whole organisation. It defines the three key business process areas: Customer Relationship Management CRM (sales), Product Lifecycle Management PLM (R&D and product management), and Supply Chain Management SCM (manufacturing). This is accomplished by the overall Management Process (general management) and Support Processes (human resource functions, IT, controlling, etc.).

References

Acs, Z. J. and Audretsch, D. B. (Eds.). (2005). *Handbook of entrepreneurship research: An interdisciplinary survey and introduction.* New York: Springer.

Alfoldi, E. A., Clegg, L. J. and McGaughey, S. L. (2012). Coordination at the edge of the empire: The delegation of headquarters functions through regional management mandates. *Journal of International Management, 18*, 276–292.

Amberg, J. J. and McGaughey, S. L. (2016). Human resource activities and corporate entrepreneurship in a multinational enterprise. *The International Journal of Human Resource Management, 6*, 1–35. DOI: 10.1080/09585192.2016.1192051

Bartlett, C. and Ghoshal, S. (2002). *Managing across borders: The transnational solution (2nd edition).* Boston, MA: Harvard Business School Press.

Beugelsdijk, S. and Mudambi, R. (2013). MNEs as border-crossing multi-location enterprises: The role of discontinuities in geographic space. *Journal of International Business Studies, 44*(5), 413–426.

Denzin, N. K. (1978). *Sociological methods: A sourcebook.* New York: McGraw-Hill.
Dew, N. (2007). Abduction: A pre-condition for the intelligent design of strategy. *The Journal of Business Strategy, 28*, 38–45.
Eisenhardt, K. M. (1989). Building theories from case study research. *The Academy of Management Review, 14*, 532–550.
Eisenhardt, K. M. and Graebner, M. E. (2007). Theory building from cases: Opportunities and challenges. *Academy of Management Journal, 50*(1), 25–32.
Ghemawat, P. (2011). The cosmopolitan corporation. *Harvard Business Review, 89*, 92–99.
Guba, E. G. and Lincoln, Y. S. (1989). *Fourth generation evaluation.* Newbury Park, CA: Sage.
Guba, E. G. and Lincoln, Y. S. (1994). Competing paradigms in qualitative research. In Denzin, N. K. and Lincoln, Y. S. (Eds.), *Handbook of qualitative research.* New York: Sage, pp. 105–117.
Hedlund, G. (1994). A model of knowledge management and the N-form corporation. *Strategic Management Journal, 15*(S2), 73–90.
Heinonen, J. and Toivonen, J. (2008). Corporate entrepreneurs or silent followers? *Leadership & Organization Development Journal, 29*, 583–599.
Meili, E. (1990). *My life with Cerberus.* Männedorf, Switzerland: Cerberus AG.
Miles, M. B. and Huberman, A. M. (1994). *Qualitative data analysis (2nd edition).* Thousand Oaks, CA: Sage.
Morse, J. M. (1994). Designing funded qualitative research. In Denzin, N. K. and Lincoln, Y. S. (Eds.), *Handbook of qualitative research.* New York: Sage, pp. 220–235.
Patton, M. Q. (2005). *Qualitative research.* Hoboken, NJ: John Wiley & Sons.
Welch, C. and Piekkari, R. (2006). Crossing language boundaries: Qualitative interviewing in international business. *Management International Review, 46*(4), 417–437.
Yin, R. K. (2009). *Case study research: Design and methods.* New York: Sage.

3 Perceptions of corporate entrepreneurship

Introduction

The previous chapter described the historical development of Fire Safety within Siemens AG and the key characteristics and contrasts between the case studies, and gave a brief overview of the research methods used in this study. In this chapter we begin presenting our findings from the field research, asking two broad questions: *what does it mean to those working within Siemens Fire Safety to be an entrepreneur or to act entrepreneurially?*, and *to what extent was entrepreneurial behaviour evident in Fire Safety at the time of our study?* We first describe respondents' understandings and perceptions of what an entrepreneur and entrepreneurial behaviour are, and the extent to which they perceive it as important to the business performance and sustainability of Fire Safety. This sets the stage for exploring to what extent and where entrepreneurial behaviours are manifest in Siemens Fire Safety, using the perceptions of those interviewed, observations of the first author as he engaged in his daily work as an executive within Fire Safety and as a researcher, and analyses of strategic moves and the market position development of Fire Safety based on corporate documents and secondary data.

Perceptions of entrepreneurship in Siemens Fire Safety

What is an entrepreneur and entrepreneurship?

The terms 'entrepreneur' and 'entrepreneurship' were sparsely used in daily life at Siemens Fire Safety at the time of our study. Nonetheless, when those interviewed were asked for their definition of key features of an entrepreneur in a corporate environment, a high degree of consistency in responses emerged among respondents across all levels, as shown in Table 3.1. To a large extent the attributes of a successful entrepreneur in a corporate environment described by the participants were in accord with the dimensions defined in an 'entrepreneurial orientation' (EO) (Lumpkin and Dess, 1996a, 1996b) discussed in Chapter 1 – that is, being innovative, taking risks, being proactive in anticipating and acting on future opportunities, having the propensity to act autonomously, and tending to directly and intensely challenge competitors to achieve entry or to improve market positions.

Table 3.1 Understandings of entrepreneurship within Siemens

		Shinwha – FS Korea	*SMART*	*SP*	*Siemens in general*
CEO / CFO / PL	**in HQ**		RD 1 an entrepreneur is the same for the business as is an inventor for the R&D 2 takes the risk, the responsibility, explores the path 3 thinks outside the box and beyond the obvious 4 CE have two functions, (1) integrating business in the whole corporation, and (2) acting as entrepreneurs at headquarters	KS 1 "bias for decision": decide, don't ask too many people, don't worry too much about decisions 2 it is *essential* to take more decisions then we see today, or you will miss many opportunities 3 to be open for contrarian views 4 CE: you need to have the buy-in of the organisation 5 CE has per definition a different baseline (complexity of processes and organisations) than does independent entrepreneurship	PM 1 entrepreneurship is being successful with the 80% approach, meaning a fast decision is better than no decision 2 Corporate entrepreneurship is to be successful in finding the balance of doing entrepreneurship within a corporate matrix HM 1 "Entrepreneurship is an attitude of a person: how he handles his activities inside the company" 2 entrepreneurship is *not* a process 3 entrepreneurship is essential to survive as a company
	in entities	HWK 1 "It means I am having all power to implement our business to achieve a target, to expand the market share, to increase the business sales volume." 2 it is like the landlord – I have the ownership	KH 1 entrepreneurship is primarily ownership 2 an entrepreneur has a clear vision 3 an entrepreneur is decisive 4 an entrepreneur is a good communicator (→ buy-in)	JD 1 "you are looking at opportunities, and responding to them in an innovative, creative way, where you are finding a quick and different solutions in a profitable manner to opportunities that you are able to identify in the market place"	

(*Continued*)

Table 3.1 (Continued)

		Shinwha – FS Korea	*SMART*	*SP*	*Siemens in general*
		3 corporate entrepreneurship is stewardship for the shareholder, also to administer the risk → the long-term risk of the company – to lose the market – is in having *no* entrepreneurship	5 also for a CE the key question is: would I do that if it would be my money?	2 corporate entrepreneurship is tremendously influenced by the existing organisation, culture, requested KPIs 3 Apple is a good example of successful CE, the right culture, quick responses to customer needs	
Middle management	**in HQ**	MB 1 entrepreneurship is the ability to spot a gap in the market and to develop a solution that can make money 2 market focussed, and quick in reaction 3 a CE can successfully work in a corporate framework, understands the boundaries, and can localise the global framework	PA 1 "Clear business responsibility, to have the freedom to take risks – allowed to take risks, and forced to take risks – and to make decisions" 2 profit and loss responsibility on the commercial side	CC 1 "Taking ownership of a topic, driving it actively, and being accountable". All together are required – AND! 2 CE means that a "company[. . .] creating the environment and culture, supporting that individuals can be entrepreneurs". 3 a corporate entrepreneur is "somebody who is involving himself, but just for the full benefit of Siemens". (not primarily for his own sake – his own career)	SA 1 strategic innovative orientation 2 thinks into the future, takes an idea to the next level 3 creativity 4 business result orientation

				JT 1 an entrepreneur believes in his idea and is willing to give his last shirt to make it happen 2 successful entrepreneurs are strong characters 3 a successful entrepreneur does not just need a brilliant (technical) idea – he needs to understand and interpret the market 4 a good intrapreneur does not ask for permission, he asks for excuse – afterwards if it did not work 5 a good intrapreneur is prepared to be fired every day	
	in entities	SHW 1 should know about the market, the trends, the technology; customer oriented 2 should have a very good networking 3 should be creative 4 should challenge the business, ideas,[. . .] 5 strong leadership	YW 1 entrepreneurship means: ownership, accountability, decision power, your own resources supporting the business 2 corporate entrepreneurship is very difficult because of missing competences / responsibilities 3 entrepreneurship is of key importance, we could be severely hit by the bold moves of our competitors	RS 1 an entrepreneur takes all the responsibility and decisions from A–Z 2 a corporate entrepreneur has "50 per cent non-egoism to something which is besides or even against his own part" → go for all the surrounding stuff as well 3 a corporate entrepreneur has to integrate all aspects, has to be a good communicator	

Within the EO concept, the aspect of risks (e.g. taking risks or being risk averse) goes beyond the classical business focus on a risk-return trade-off, where 'risk' refers specifically to the probability of a negative outcome or related loss (Yates and Stone, 1992; Forlani and Mullins, 2000). Rather, it is characterised in a more comprehensive way as the attitude toward risk and uncertainty of a potential entrepreneur (Shane, 2003, p. 61; Acs and Audretsch, 2005, p. 37). Frank H. Knight (1885–1972) long ago proposed in his dissertation titled "Risk, Uncertainty, and Profit" (1921) a still widely accepted definition of risk as randomness with knowable probabilities, whereas uncertainty is captured by randomness with unknowable probabilities. He postulated that the risk could be easily insured, whereas the entrepreneur primarily would bear the uncertainty of his economic endeavours. Schumpeter (1934) proposed an expansion of the original focus on individuals behaving entrepreneurially towards firm-level entrepreneurship. The attitude towards taking risks has also been characterised by the term 'risk propensity' (Brockhaus, 1980; Petrakis, 2005; Ling, Simsek, Lubatkin, and Veiga, 2008), which is seen as a personal trait as well as an attribute of teams and organisations. In accord with this dimension of EO, when asked *what comes to mind if you hear the term 'entrepreneurship'?*, the regional coordinator for Korea and China in Fire Safety R&D (HQ) responded:

> Clear business responsibility, to have the freedom to take risks – allowed to take risks, and forced to take risks, and to make decisions. In the end, it is also – from the commercial [aspect] – P&L [profit and loss] responsibility.

Miller described the non-entrepreneurial firm as "one that innovates very little, is highly risk averse, and imitates the moves of competitors instead of leading the way" (1983, p. 771). He proposed a distinction between simple firms, planning firms, and organic firms. The definition of the planning firm as being a bigger firm, focussed on the "smooth and efficient operation through the use of formal controls and plans" (1983, p. 770) is, as subsequent chapters show, perhaps the most appropriate depiction for the researched Siemens entities. Not surprisingly, the maturity of a business or firm is often linked to the level of risk propensity towards new entrepreneurial endeavours: "Risk aversion is the sine qua non of mature businesses" (Sykes and Block, 1989, p. 164). As discussed in Chapter 1, the entrepreneurial process raises an important issue in established firms, known as "the productivity dilemma" (Abernathy, 1978; Benner and Tushman, 2003): the requirement to protect the operation of the established business by rules and controls that minimise risks while also seeking new endeavours that are unavoidably linked to risks and uncertainty.

The effect of the size of the organisation on elements of entrepreneurial orientation can be one of the key challenges for fostering entrepreneurship in large, established organisations. Current research results indicate high levels of desired and required individual autonomy and innovative, proactive, and risk-seeking behaviour of successful entrepreneurs. But how can such attitudes manifest in large MNEs, where many potential intrapreneurs are not in top management positions linked to high levels of decision autonomy? As Heinonen and Toivonen (2008, p. 594) observe, "A true corporate entrepreneur is not a follower, [. . . but . . .] managers are likely to restrict the activities of corporate entrepreneurs even though strong empowerment would be needed". Autonomy refers to the independent action of an individual or team in bringing forth an idea or a vision and carrying it through to completion (Lumpkin and Dess, 1996a). While autonomy was a powerful theme in the responses surrounding the nature of entrepreneurship, it was strongly linked in our study to ownership and accountability, as shown in Table 3.1 and the following quotes.[1]

> Taking ownership of a topic, driving it actively, and being accountable. And it is always an AND between those three [. . .]
>
> [Connie Clark, Global Head of Product Line Intrusion]

> My understanding of the entrepreneurship is: number one is the ownership. Means that you are finally accountable for the thing you are doing, for the business you are running. And number two, which means you have a certain kind of decision power, you need to have a certain kind of decision power [. . .] And [. . .] number three is that you need to have a certain kind of resources, supporting you to make the decisions.
>
> [Jan Traber, Head of Product Management, FS China]

> It means I am having all power to implement our business to achieve a target, to expand the market share, to increase the business sales volume. It's like the land lord, it's a landlordship, it's like the [. . .] I am the owner of the building [. . .] this is the entrepreneurship.
>
> [HW Kim, CFO, BT FS Korea]

The importance of ownership and accountability is largely overlooked in typical depictions of the EO concept. Indeed, it is not once mentioned by Lumpkin and Dess (1996a) in their elaboration of the dimensions of EO. While it may be taken for granted in individual entrepreneurship or in small firms with a strong founder, this is not typically the case with corporate entrepreneurship.

In accord with EO dimensions, being innovative (e.g. thinking 'out of the box') and proactive (e.g. driving it forward) were important elements in the perceptions of what constitutes entrepreneurship and entrepreneurial behaviour, as captured in the below quotes:

> For me, the entrepreneur is a similar thing for the business like the innovator, or inventor is for R&D. [. . .] It's a business leader [who] is to explore a path, and also to take risk and responsibility. And I think what distinguishes just a normal manager from an entrepreneur is: the normal manager for me is more something [. . .] who is dealing well with day to day business, but somehow is not looking outside of the box, beyond the obvious; and an

> entrepreneur is also willing to take bold moves from time to time, and then of course, with enthusiasm, drive it forward and implement it.
>
> [Ralf Dunkel, Global Project Lead SMART Initiative]

> [Y]ou have an idea, which – right or wrong – you think it's the greatest thing on earth, and you believe in it, and you are willing to give your last shirt to make it happen.
>
> [Jan Traber, BT Integration Manager iMetrex]

Notably, however, the importance of competitive aggressiveness featured little in the descriptions of the respondents of entrepreneurs and entrepreneurial behaviour in Siemens Fire Safety. Where competitors were mentioned, they were typically seen as a threat. For example:

> I think if we don't have [entrepreneurship], with the attack of the competitors, and the change of the environment, we will have [. . .] somehow not a disaster, but we will have a big impact to the company [. . .]
>
> [Yao Wang, Head of Product Management, FS China]

The EO dimensions of proactiveness and competitive aggressiveness have been linked in prior studies to the nature of the relevant industry environment and achievable competitive advantage therein, since proactiveness represents firm initiatives towards opportunities in the specific market, and competitive aggressiveness summarises firm reactions to competitive trends and demands that already exist (Lumpkin and Dess, 2001). Lumpkin and Dess found evidence for the relevance of emphasising proactiveness primarily in emerging new industries to anticipate all the new opportunities, whereas competitive aggressiveness becomes most important in mature industries – such as those in which Fire Safety operates – by successfully responding to threats (2001, p. 446).

How important is it to behave entrepreneurially?

Against this backdrop of what is an entrepreneur, participants were asked how important it would be to behave entrepreneurially for Siemens Fire Safety. In similar ways, all interviewed CEOs, CFOs, and senior managers confirmed the relevance of being entrepreneurial for resulting firm performance and firm survival, in accord with numerous prior studies (Zahra, 1991; Zahra and Garvis, 2000; Lumpkin and Dess, 2001; Birkinshaw, Hood, and Young, 2005; Rauch, Wiklund, Lumpkin, and Frese, 2009):

> [Being entrepreneurial] is very important, because it's similar like innovation, I think it's the thing which will drive us forward, and [. . .] it is our vision in terms of: we are pioneers, and of course innovation is a very, very core element

> of what we are [. . .] I think we have the entrepreneurial power within Siemens, but of course we do better, to more explore it, and to more make it happen.
> [Ralf Dunkel, Global Project Lead SMART Initiative]

> Entrepreneurship is so important for our business! Also for the FS [Fire Safety]. If I have the entrepreneurship, then I really mean to lead the business!
> [HW Kim, CFO Building Technologies (BT) Korea]

> [. . .] entrepreneurship ensures the survival of the company!
> [Hans Meier, Global Head of FS Human Resources]

This positive perception of the relevance of entrepreneurship in the researched Siemens entities can be seen as essential for the implementations of initiatives to foster entrepreneurship or to harness entrepreneurial behaviour. While entrepreneurship and entrepreneurial behaviour is clearly considered relevant to Siemens' corporate success, how *prevalent* is it?

Extent of entrepreneurship within Siemens Fire Safety

It is not easy to assess the extent of corporate entrepreneurship or entrepreneurial behaviours. To operationalise the EO concept – especially in the context of corporate entrepreneurship – specific measurement scales have been developed in recent decades, one example of which is the "Enterscale"[2] (Khandwalla, 1977; Miller and Friesen, 1978, 1984; Covin and Slevin, 1986, 1989; Knight, 1997). The original Enterscale involves the aspects of innovation (setting up new lines of products or services, emphasis on R&D, technological leadership, and disruptive moves), proactivity, competitive aggressiveness, and taking risks.[3] The utility of the Enterscale questionnaire (as the most used instrument) was tested during a pilot study and in the early phase of our main study, but was found to be inappropriate for three reasons. First, participants were obviously not familiar with the elaborated concepts and terms used, and the research participants were executives with significant time pressures. The limited interview time available did not allow for a sound explanation necessary for the participants to make informed judgments, thereby undermining the validity of any results. Second, many participants openly stated they simply did not have enough market and competitive information to make judgments relative to competitors, as required by the survey instrument. Third, the questions do not hone in on actual entrepreneurial activities taking place, but rather the perceived individual notion of pursuing such endeavours. Therefore, it was decided to ask interview participants for concrete, candid examples of entrepreneurship, comprising people and functions perceived as behaving entrepreneurially and examples of entrepreneurial activities actually taking place. Subsequently, each of the individual dimensions of entrepreneurial orientation was explored in interviews more deeply.

Perceptions of entrepreneurial behaviour

A majority of interviewees had some difficulty naming persons or functions they perceived as behaving entrepreneurially in 2010 within the existing Building Technologies organisation. The only person seen as an entrepreneur by the interviewees – when considering the whole existing Building Technologies organisation – was Dr Milde (CEO Building Technologies). Additionally, Keiko Safaia (BT HQ Chief Marketing Officer, and previous founder and CEO of iMetrix) and John Davis (CEO of SP new setup) were seen as highly entrepreneurial. This is perhaps not surprising, since both had led independent and quite entrepreneurial companies just before joining Building Technologies in 2009. On the level of business renewal activities, a majority of respondents perceived only incremental technical innovations taking place, with little activity towards entering new business fields or new business approaches. The challenges were explained by the Regional Manager of Korea in 2010 as follows:

> Entrepreneurship for me is the ability to spot a gap in the market and develop a solution that can make money, and is attractive to close it [. . .] In principle, entrepreneurship is [. . .] whether it is a corporate or in a small standard line, it is essentially the same topic. But I would say inside a corporation, there are some boundaries around what a corporate entrepreneur can do [. . .] and therefore it attracts a different kind of person. But I think the entrepreneurship within a corporate organisation like our own is about understanding about those boundaries, and understanding where is there flexibility, and understanding how to harness that to meet local market needs. So it's about localising global frameworks in a way to breach the gaps that you have inside the market [. . .] The opportunities that you see, trying to find ways to close them within the corporate framework. And that is a very challenging task! It is harder I think to be an entrepreneur in a corporate than an SME. Because many entrepreneurs feel their hands are tied inside our organisations [. . .]
>
> [Mark Bossard, Regional Manager for Korea in FS HQ]

Evidence of entrepreneurial behaviour

Two specific programmes especially relevant for the entrepreneurial behaviour and activity within Siemens AG are the 3i programme and Top+ program. Top+ is the corporate business excellence programme of Siemens launched in 1998. It aims at the improvement of Siemens' products, solutions, services, and processes by establishing: (1) a high-performance culture based on business benchmarking and subsequent internal improvement activities; (2) the introduction of toolboxes containing respective methodologies and best practice; and (3) specific initiatives in the fields of asset management, quality, and innovation.[4] The SMART initiative and its projects, as described in the previous chapter, are part of this last facet of innovation initiatives.

Intended to contribute to the sharing of best practices, Top+ awards are granted on a yearly basis. The Building Technologies division rewards employee initiatives in the disciplines of 'innovation', 'customer focus', 'global competitiveness', and 'quality or continuous improvement projects to reduce non-compliance costs' by granting specific 'Top+ awards'. On the level of Siemens AG, endeavours in 'innovation', '3i' (ideas, impulses and initiative), 'SMART growth', 'sustainability', and 'cost optimisation and financial excellence' are rewarded, with additional prizes for the 'best cluster' and the 'best business unit'. Notably, the categories of rewards granted were not aligned between the Building Technologies division and Siemens AG.

Top+ award applications must come from entire teams and require management sponsorship. Direct applications of individuals and teams are not possible, and endeavours in the field of corporate entrepreneurship – in the sense of disruptive innovations, entering new business fields, and substantial company renewal activities – are not specifically addressed. On the level of Siemens AG awards, detailed pre-checks are required for potential applications to be admitted for competition. At the time of our study no project could be identified in the Building Technologies division that had been set up in the context of going specifically for a Top+ award; all of the endeavour reports submitted were based on activities that were planned as a part of the normal business processes and respective yearly budgets. Building Technologies division was granted two Top+ awards between 2007 and 2010: its US operation was honoured for cost savings in 2009, and the German sales organisation for pushing the profit level to eleven per cent in 2007 (in the category 'global competitiveness'). Despite its wide acclaim and recognised success, the Top+ programme is more about operational excellence and innovation than it is about corporate venturing or strategic renewal.

The 3i programme – 'Ideen, Impulse, Initiativen' ('ideas, impulses, and initiative')[5] – is an idea collection programme open to all employees, first established in 1997 and aimed at encouraging, implementing, and rewarding employee ideas that add value through cost savings, revenue generation, process improvement, or customer satisfaction. Siemens has a long history of engaging employees in business improvements, with premiums for 'improvement suggestions' being offered for the first time in October 1910 at Siemens' Kleinbauwerk in Berlin. The earliest recorded list of suggestions dates from 1913 and contains 21 ideas that were implemented. As of 2010 Siemens estimates it has received more than 1.5 million ideas from employees that have been put into practice, by which the company has saved over €3 billion, with employees rewarded by premiums totalling €300 million.[6] According to internal documentation at the time of our research, "[T]o compete in the 3i category, applicant teams must have created a business value of at least €20,000 as defined within the context of 3i and must have demonstrated an exceptional commitment to the 3i program".[7] This revised initiative was introduced in Switzerland and Germany in 2008, and allows direct entering of respective ideas into an IT tool via the intranet. Unfortunately, the initial effort in 2008 to motivate Building Technologies employees to participate, and to publish and celebrate respective achievements, had significantly ceased in 2009 and 2010 during our fieldwork.

The perceptions among our research participants of low levels of corporate entrepreneuring were also supported by the results of the analysis of strategic moves and developments in the market position of Fire Safety, based on corporate documents and secondary data. At the time of our study no new business fields had been entered in the previous ten years in Fire Safety and, as described in the preceding chapter, it was even decided to carve out and sell the business segment of Security Products (SP) due to continual operational losses. Furthermore, the Fire Safety business unit – world market leader since the mid 1990s – had lost its leading role to UTC and Tyco, primarily because of missed acquisitions. Further evidence from secondary data for low levels of entrepreneurial activity was the continuing lack of initiative in the fire extinguishing business for Fire Safety – a market segment representing 60 per cent of global turnovers and experiencing a major business shift from old-fashioned sprinkler facilities towards high-tech water mist systems. The increasing threat of IT companies such as IBM and Cisco entering the field of fire detection did not exist on the fire extinguishing side of the business; as noted previously, fire extinguishing technologies and products for such firms are much harder to copy and represent a significant market-entry barrier. Despite these known circumstances, as of the end of 2009 no significant new business planning took place in Fire Safety to significantly grow the extinguishing business, either by internal growth based on new products and additional sales activities or by considering relevant acquisitions.

In the field of product and service innovation, Fire Safety had been investing an almost constant amount of five per cent of its turnover in R&D activities for the ten years up to 2009. Over 95 per cent of the money was spent on incremental innovation, whereby old products were replaced with implementations that had comparable characteristics, but that were based on the newest technologies in hardware and software. The last 'breakthrough' product innovation was a new optical flame detector launched in the mid 1990s, based on highly innovative mathematical approaches and protected by several specific patents. In the ten years prior to our study, research towards disruptive innovations was done in relation to new approaches for fire detection principles based on created carbon monoxide (CO) gas, but this had not yet led to any saleable product at the time of our study. Overall, a picture of low levels of corporate entrepreneuring, of any form, emerges.

Of course, the nature of multinational enterprises makes entrepreneurial behaviour at the local level perhaps less visible than it does in more simple organisational structures. Alfoldi, Clegg, and McGaughey (2012) observe, for example, that due to the vast geographic reach of MNEs such as Siemens, the processing of large volumes of diverse local information requires increasingly tailored information processing capabilities and can be overwhelming for corporate headquarters. Similarly, administratively oriented regional headquarters tend to suffer from weak links to subsidiaries' operating activities. Distant subsidiaries may also offer a 'safe haven' in which experimentation is protected and the emergence of novel ventures is nurtured (McGaughey, 2007a, 2007b), away from the 'corporate immune system' or possible constraints imposed from above. Hence, the level of CE within Siemens may well be underestimated:

> [. . .] headquarters are not made aware of all the creativity that goes on in the regions. For fear of analysis, too many questions, hindering [. . .] or even stopping them from doing it again. So, some of the [. . .] entrepreneurial behaviour is not visible to us here, because the regions don't want it to be. And that's a cultural thing we need to break [. . .]
>
> [Regional Manager for Korea in FS HQ]

Concluding remarks

Overall, participants in the three case studies presented a somewhat coherent picture of what they perceived to be the key characteristics of entrepreneurs and entrepreneurial behaviour, and the strong importance placed on such activities for sustainable business performance. While these characteristics of entrepreneurship and entrepreneurial behaviour closely aligned with the concept of an entrepreneurial orientation, a marked addition was the importance of ownership and accountability, neither of which are overtly recognised in literature concerning the dimensions of EO. In contrast, 'competitive aggressiveness' was omitted in responses as an important ingredient in entrepreneurship and entrepreneurial behaviour. This omission is consistent with findings discussed in subsequent chapters concerning a strong 'inward orientation' within Siemens Fire Safety, evidenced by a focus primarily on exploiting existing technologies, incremental innovations within existing product and market approaches, and applying well-defined internal processes.

Among those interviewed, there was a clear sense that corporate entrepreneurs face challenges not as evident in entrepreneurial activities of individuals or owners of small firms, captured succinctly in the musings of the Integration Manager of iMetrix:

> There is a fundamental contradiction in 'corporate' and 'entrepreneurship'. So, yes, there are corporate entrepreneurs, no doubt about that, but it needs a certain willingness to bear the pain and the suffering to be in a corporate environment, [. . .] but by heart being an entrepreneur!

Consistent with this observation, there was a shared view among participants that the level of entrepreneurial behaviour in Fire Safety business unit is low, which was supported by performance in the Siemens-wide Top+ and 3i awards, and by the results of the analysis of strategic moves and the market position development of Fire Safety based on analyses of secondary data. Of course, some entrepreneurial behaviour may be hidden in such large MNEs either intentionally or due to the effect of distance. The suggestion that entrepreneurship in established companies is not restricted to the top management team as the seemingly sole entrepreneurs – as often depicted in the case of Apple Inc. with CEO Steve Jobs as the visible corporate entrepreneur – opens up an important but little researched field of top-down and bottom-up effects mutually influencing individual-level and organisational-level factors that foster entrepreneurial behaviour (Heinonen and Toivonen, 2008, p. 595). In the next three chapters we explore key organisational characteristics of Siemens AG, the Building Technologies division, and the Fire Safety business unit that were found in our study to play a significant role in shaping entrepreneurial behaviour of individuals, with implications for business performance. We begin in the next chapter with findings on the effect of Siemens' 'process orientation' on corporate entrepreneuring.

Notes

1 Please see Chapter 2 for the overview of all interviewees and their corporate functions.
2 The original Enterscale questionnaire using eight dimensions can be found in Appendix A of Knight (1997).
3 Based on this, a further expanded "CE scale" comprising 25 indicators was derived (Zahra, 1991, 1993b), followed by a further expansion towards a "Corporate Entrepreneurship Assessment Instrument (CEAI)" involving 84 Likert-style questions (Hornsby, Kuratko, and Zahra, 2002).
4 Sources: Internal corporate documents, as of 2011-02-02, including 'Top+ Overview Presentation 6-2010'
5 German, i.e., ideas, impulses, initiatives. Interestingly, there was no official English wording provided for 3i in 2011.
6 Siemens Press Release 2010 "Every employee is a pioneer: 100 years of idea management at Siemens. www.siemens.com/press/pi/AXX20101003e, (last accessed 2016-05-12).
7 Source: Internal corporate documents as of 2011-02-02.

References

Abernathy, W. J. (1978). *The productivity dilemma.* Baltimore: Johns Hopkins University Press.

Alfoldi, E., Clegg, J. and McGaughey, S. L. (2012). Coordination at the edge of the empire: Subsidiary regional management mandates in the multinational enterprise. *Journal of International Management, 18*, 276–292.

Benner, M. J. and Tushman, M. L. (2003). Exploitation, exploration, and process management: The productivity dilemma revisited. *The Academy of Management Review, 28*(2), 238–256.

Birkinshaw, J., Hood, N. and Young, S. (2005). Subsidiary entrepreneurship, internal and external competitive forces, and subsidiary performance. *International Business Review, 14*, 227–248.

Brockhaus, R. H., Sr. (1980). Risk taking propensity of entrepreneurs. *Academy of Management Journal, 23*(3), 509–520.

Covin, J. G. and Slevin, D. P. (1986). *The development and testing of an organization-level entrepreneurship scale.* Wellesley, MA: Babson College.

Covin, J. G. and Slevin, D. P. (1989). Strategic management of small firms in hostile and benign environments. *Strategic Management Journal, 10*, 75–87.

Forlani, D. and Mullins, J. W. (2000). Perceived risks and choices in entrepreneurs' new venture decisions. *Journal of Business Venturing, 15*, 305–322.

Hornsby, J. S., Kuratko, D. F. and Zahra, S. A. (2002). Middle managers' perception of the internal environment for corporate entrepreneurship: Assessing a measurement scale. *Journal of Business Venturing, 17*, 253–273.

Khandwalla, P. (1977). *The design of organizations.* New York: Harcourt Brace Jovanovich.

Knight, F. H. (1921). *Risk, uncertainty and profit.* Boston, MA: Hart, Schaffner & Marx; Houghton Mifflin.

Knight, G. A. (1997). Cross-cultural reliability and validity of a scale to measure firm entrepreneurial orientation. *Journal of Business Venturing, 12*, 213–225.

Ling, Y., Simsek, Z., Lubatkin, M. and Veiga, J. (2008). Transformational leadership's role in promoting corporate entrepreneurship: Examining the CEO-TMT interface. *Academy of Management Journal, 51*(3), 557–576.

Lumpkin, G. T. and Dess, G. G. (1996a). Clarifying the entrepreneurial orientation construct and linking it to performance. *Academy of Management Review, 21*, 135–172.

Lumpkin, G. T. and Dess, G. G. (1996b). Enriching the entrepreneurial orientation construct – a reply to 'Entrepreneurial Orientation or Pioneer Advantage'. *Academy of Management Review, 21*, 605–607.

Lumpkin, G. T. and Dess, G. G. (2001). Linking two dimensions of entrepreneurial orientation to firm performance: The moderating role of environment and industry life cycle. *Journal of Business Venturing, 16*, 429–451.

McGaughey, S. L. (2007a). Hidden ties in international new venturing: The case of portfolio entrepreneurship. *Journal of World Business, 42*, 307–321.

McGaughey, S. L. (2007b). *Narratives of internationalisation: Legitimacy, standards and portfolio entrepreneurs.* Cheltenham, UK: Edward Elgar.

Miller, D. (1983). The correlates of entrepreneurship in three types of firms. *Management Science, 29*, 770–791.

Miller, D. and Friesen, P. H. (1978). Archetypes of strategy formulation. *Management Science, 24*, 921–933.

Miller, D. and Friesen, P. H. (1984). *Organizations: A quantum view.* Englewood Cliffs, NJ: Prentice-Hall.

Petrakis, P. E. (2005). Risk perception, risk propensity and entrepreneurial behaviour: The Greek case. *Journal of American Academy of Business, Cambridge, 7*(1), 233–242.

Rauch, A., Wiklund, J., Lumpkin, G. and Frese, M. (2009). Entrepreneurial orientation and business performance: An assessment of past research and suggestions for the future. *Entrepreneurship Theory and Practice, 33*, 761–787.

Schumpeter, J. (1934). *The theory of economic development.* Cambridge, MA: Harvard Business Press.

Shane, S. (2003). *A general theory of entrepreneurship: The individual-opportunity nexus.* Cheltenham, UK: Edward Elgar Publishing.

Sykes, H. B. and Block, Z. (1989). Corporate venturing obstacles: Sources and solutions. *Journal of Business Venturing, 4*, 159–167.

Yates, F. and Stone, E. R. (1992). The risk construct. In Yates, J. F. (Ed.), *Risk-taking behaviour.* New York: Wiley, pp. 1–26.

Zahra, S. A. (1991). Predictors and financial outcomes of corporate entrepreneurship: An exploratory study. *Journal of Business Venturing*, *6*(4), 259–285.

Zahra, S. A. (1993). Environment, corporate entrepreneurship, and financial performance: A taxonomic approach. *Journal of Business Venturing*, *8*, 319–340.

Zahra, S. A. and Garvis, D. M. (2000). International corporate entrepreneurship and firm performance: The moderating effect of international environmental hostility. *Journal of Business Venturing*, *15*, 469–492.

4 A process-oriented organisation

Introduction

Organisational design (of which formal structure is only one part) has been shown in prior studies to have a significant impact on the nature of corporate entrepreneurship. Siemens is widely perceived – by both internal and external stakeholders – to be a process-driven organisation. This entails a view of the organisation as a system of interlinked processes and concerted efforts to map, adhere to, and improve organisational processes (Benner and Tushman, 2003). Siemens' process definitions are significantly more stable over time than its formal organisational structures, with a key objective being to make the way tasks are carried out independent of which actual employees are involved. In this chapter we describe the pervasive 'process orientation' within Siemens AG, the Building Technologies division, and Fire Safety business unit and ask *what are the consequences – good and bad – of this pervasive process orientation within Siemens AG, including the strengthened compliance following the historic bribery scandal?* In particular, we explore the implications for corporate entrepreneuring of 'people independence' arising from 'process maturity', the dominance of an inward orientation, the growth in compliance processes and their implications for organisational trust, and the effect of, at times, overwhelming organisational complexity. Throughout, we acknowledge different perspectives of respondents from across the case studies and corporate headquarters, avoiding the 'narrative smoothing' (Clandinin and Connelly, 2000) that homogenises diverse contexts and perspectives and that can lead to overestimation of the causal fabric of experience.

A process-driven organisation

Business process management encompasses all activities of identification, definition, analysis, design, execution, monitoring, measurement, and continuous improvement of business processes. Within Siemens AG, it involves defining performance goals for processes 'top down'. Process standards and a common process framework are seen as a fundamental basis for a systematic design and optimisation of results, processes, and resources (Rohloff, 2011). The Siemens Process Framework consists of a 'Reference Process House' and common methods for process management across Siemens AG, known as 'reference process definitions'. These process definitions are fundamental for process standardisation and are intended to provide a stable basis for process management. There are five key process areas within the Siemens Reference Process House: Customer Relationship Management, Supply Chain Management, Product Lifecycle Management, overarching Management Processes, and additional Support Processes. The framework, shown in Figure 4.1,[1] also defines four levels of further refinement, thus allowing the adaption to specific business types and business needs. The implementation of the process definitions down to concrete and detailed activities and document templates is division specific.

Using this Reference Process House definition as the basis, the Building Technologies division defined a three-level concept as the core approach to defining its organisational architecture, with the Supply Chain Management referred to as 'level-1', the Product Lifecycle Management as 'level-2', and Customer Relationship Management – or 'sales' – as 'level-3'. Headquarters and subsidiaries are directly responsible for level-1 and level-2 functions, whereas customer relationship management (level-3) is done within country organisations, with an

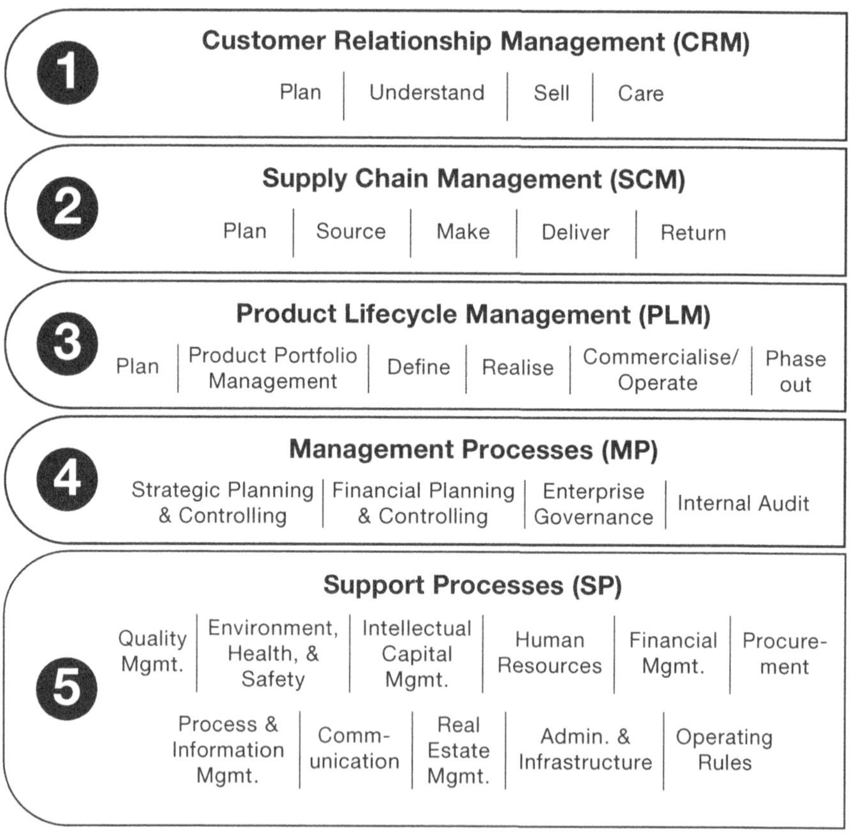

Figure 4.1 Siemens Reference Process House

overarching organisation coordinating the sales activities of all business segments within a specific country. A subsidiary in a specific country can be combined with the sales function (e.g. Fire Safety Korea), or the organisations can exist separately (with separated heads of organisation, e.g. Fire Safety China). Additionally, country organisations interact with regional cluster organisations. These regional cluster organisations were established by the then relatively new CEO Peter Löscher in 2008. They were intended to integrate and coordinate business planning and activities in twenty distinct geographic regions worldwide and to offer centralised business services.

As of 2011, only comprehensive processes for Product Lifecycle Management and Supply Chain Management had been defined and rolled out at the Building Technologies division, with a somewhat weak definition for Customer Relationship Management and no defined activities for Management Process. The Building Technologies implementation of Product Lifecycle Management was called Product Evolution Process (PEP) and covers all steps (plan, define, realise, commercialise/operate, phase out, and the overarching portfolio management), with detailed descriptions of process steps, roles, responsibility, and so on. To allow for optimised processes in small and simple – as well as large and complex – projects, three different types of PEP are provided: 'PEP real tiny, 'PEP tiny', and 'PEP standard'.

Siemens' process definitions are significantly more stable over time than is the formal organisational structure. At the time of our study, Siemens Process House definitions had been in place for more than fifteen years already, whereas the last fundamental organisational changes – the establishment of cluster offices or the founding of SMART headquarters – just took place in 2008. Within Building Technologies, the PEP process definitions were the most comprehensive definitions and had been set up in 2004; the organisational structure within Building Technologies had changed twice since then up to 2011.

The process orientation of Siemens AG is in part forced by the compliance to various industrial standards required by law or customer demand (e.g. ISO 9000:2000, ISO 14001) and an industry code of practice that expects proof of minimal levels of process maturity. The first stages of process maturity aim typically at people independence – that is, the way tasks are carried out must not depend on which actual employees are involved:

> [. . .] once the processes are clear, and you are independent from people, you can replace people and top managers, or top project leads more easily, because you are backed up by processes.
>
> [CEO BT FS]

Having activity primarily based on defined processes is also seen as an explicit goal of the management:

> That is clearly the ambition: with the processes you become person independent [. . .]
>
> [Integration Manager iMetrex]

By way of example, Building Technologies product development procedures must reach a level-3 of maturity when assessing them based on the Capability Maturity Model Integration (CMMI). CMMI maturity level-2 primarily focuses on people independence of activities carried out regarding content and quality of results. The ability to achieve the 'person independence' sought at Siemens may be assessed positively as evidence of 'process maturity' (Rohlof, 2011) and, related, as an indicator of the value of the prescribed business process as a potential source of competitive advantage (Kohlbacher, 2010; Kohlbacher and Reijers, 2013). This was not, however, a view all respondents shared, and the comprehensiveness and maturity of defined processes implemented across the three case studies – SMART Project, Shinwha, and SP new setup – varied markedly.

Consequences for corporate entrepreneurship

Person independence through process maturity

When suggesting to the interviewees that key elements of entrepreneurial activity – especially the aspects of opportunity recognition and evaluation – be added to the existing processes within Siemens' Building Technologies, surprisingly negative feedback emerged:

> [. . .] hopefully I never will see something like this! Because when we would start to describe how to be an entrepreneur and put it into a process, then [. . .] this would be for me the old Siemens [. . .] where you have 'Rundschreiben' [management circulars], and everybody [. . .] everything is explained [. . .] I mean, if we do not recruit these kinds of people with this [entrepreneurial] mindset, then we have a problem. So please: never ever describe a process: what is an entrepreneur!
>
> [Karl Huber, Global Head of FS SYS]

> I don't think that you can define a process to guide entrepreneurial activity [. . .]
>
> [Keiko Safaia, Chief Marketing Officer BT]

> [T]he more important human interaction is, the less it is people independent! Either in the sense of sales, for instance, or is it for instance a managerial task, which is a main people task, OK?
>
> [Jan Traber, Integration Manager iMetrex]

A majority of interviewees shared this same perception: entrepreneurship is something "personal" – a kind of "personal art". Hence, translating key activities into the company process definitions is "impossible". But was there any evidence in support of this perception regarding the impossibility of integrating entrepreneurial behaviours with process definitions? Subsequent investigations at Building Technologies division and Fire Safety business unit could not confirm *any attempt* at trying to include entrepreneurial activities in the established processes in recent years. Furthermore, a comprehensive idea process developed at Building Technologies Innovation Department in 2006 and 2007[2] explicitly involved activities in the Management Process and the Product Lifecycle Management processes to address all kinds of new business ideas (technical, market, incremental, or disruptive innovation, and entry into new business fields). However, no implementation of this idea process into the Siemens Reference Process House – and thus the roll-out into the wider organisation – ever took place, arguably due to the parallel introduction of the "3i" initiative described in Chapter 3. While evidence for the explicit integration of entrepreneurial activities into successfully implemented process definitions could not be found – supporting the perceptions of respondents – this alone does not preclude the *possibility* of success in such endeavours.

Important consequences – good and bad – arise for CE when organisational processes are designed and intended to create 'person independence' in the knowledge coordination and deployment underpinning entrepreneurial activity. On the positive side, process maturity may be seen not only as an indicator of the value of the prescribed business process in achieving competitive advantage around established markets and products (Kohlbacher, 2010; Rohlof, 2011), but even an enabler of entrepreneurial endeavours:

> Entrepreneurship requires very good processes, because having very good processes means that you can be confident that you are doing the basics well. [. . .] I think the overall thing about Siemens processes is excellent. [. . .] Having strong processes means that you can think more about the ideas how to solve customer needs. If you don't have strong processes, you'll end up failing as a business anyway. So it is not about processes, it is about [. . .] it is about processes, but doing them in a very light and responsive manner.
>
> [CEO of SP new Setup]

At the same time, however, person independence through process maturity negates what Wright and colleagues (2011) identify as a distinguishing characteristic of human resources – as opposed, for example, to financial or physical resources – namely 'free will'. Free will refers to the ability of employees, and people more generally, to choose how to act. While employees may acquire human capital – the knowledge, information, ideas, skills, and abilities of individuals (Wright, Dunford, and Snell, 2001) – through an employment contract, the employee can choose to withhold effort or behaviour that the firm may seek, to engage in unfavourable behaviours, or even to leave the firm. This 'free will' possessed by employees makes the use of human capital as a source of competitive advantage problematic: employees engage in discretionary behaviour and can choose *how*, to *what extent* and *when* to contribute to, or potentially to counter, organisational goals (Wright et al., 2001). Yet free will also underpins the spontaneous informal managerial entrepreneurship essential for CE. As noted in

Chapter 1, both Ricardian and entrepreneurial rents flow from organisations leveraging the *unique* abilities of individuals, the evolution of these abilities, and the related discretionary behaviours of employees (Chadwick and Dabu, 2009). Even unintentional supplanting of, or excessive constraints on, free will and discretion by inappropriate use of process definitions designed to engender operational efficiency, quality, or risk minimisation may place entrepreneurial outcomes at risk (Amberg and McGaughey, 2016).

A complexity in the use of formal business processes thus includes knowing when, or when *not*, to devise and deploy them. On the one hand, the research participants in Siemens saw significant merit in the development of processes for the exploitation of entrepreneurial opportunities. On the other hand, there was strong and largely intuitive resistance to the suggestion of developing processes for exploration activities. This is not inconsistent with extant theory. Both exploration and exploitation in entrepreneurial activities involve some degree of learning, although the nature and extent of the learning differs across the two. As March (1991) states, "The essence of exploitation is the refinement and extension of existing competencies, technologies, and paradigms [. . . .] The essence of exploration is experimentation with new alternatives" (p. 85). That is, exploration and exploitation differ in the type and amount of learning that is needed (Gupta, Smith, and Shalley, 2006).

Explorative learning is characterised by higher levels of uncertainty, in the sense that what is found is new, unknown, and unpredictable. In requiring experimentation, explorative learning draws on the 'free will' and individual discretion that Wright and colleagues (2001, 2011) observe distinguishes human resources from other types of resource. This makes devising business processes for exploration more problematic; by definition, they shape, and thus have the potential to constrain, behaviours and thus the emergence of the 'new' (Benner and Tushman, 2003), experimentation, and individual discretion. In contrast, exploitation of entrepreneurial opportunities often succeeds over the long run by reducing variability and maximising efficiency through tight coordination. In shaping human resource activity, formal business processes restrict discretionary behaviour, thereby reducing variability and enhancing efficiency.

That said, our data also suggests that while process definitions intended to support the exploitation of opportunities may not *directly* guide explorative behaviour through the assignment of opportunity search roles and tasks, they may also function as mechanisms for knowledge exchange and thereby help create a context conducive to the exploration of entrepreneurial opportunities. For example, the absence of process definitions in Customer Relationship Management (CRM) was perceived as a missing ingredient in the exploitation of previously identified opportunities and credited with being a major cause of declining sales in Siemens Fire Safety. However, the implementation of formal CRM processes could also create a context and mechanisms for greater social interactions between employees and customers – existing or new. Through these interactions, novel, external knowledge (e.g. of emerging customer needs) can be more readily identified and brought into the firm for entrepreneurial endeavours. Employees can further engage in spontaneous, discretionary behaviour within the framework of defined processes and in the context of developing broader relationships and knowledge. Hence, formal CRM processes form part of the infrastructure by which entrepreneurial knowledge can be generated and leveraged (i.e. an example of formal managerial entrepreneurship), and can further foster informal managerial entrepreneurship for the *exploration* of entrepreneurial opportunities, and not only exploitation. To the extent that CRM process definitions focus on only existing customers, this may result in predominantly incremental innovations (Benner and Tushman, 2003), while the additional orientation towards possible future customers may foster identification or exploration of more radical opportunities. Hence, the absence of well-defined formal CRM processes in Fire Safety conceivably hampered both formal and informal managerial entrepreneurship.

A dominant inward orientation

As alluded to previously, imbalance in process maturity across process categories deployed in Siemens Fire Safety posed a challenge for corporate entrepreneuring. That is, there were only well-developed process definitions for Product Lifecycle Management and Supply Chain Management, weak Customer Relationship Management process definitions, and no Management Process definitions when our study commenced. As a consequence, virtually all respondents complained about current firm renewal activities being limited to internally driven, technical innovations only, with an external focus lacking. That is, a strong 'inward orientation' among employees was observed. Opportunity exploration, in the sense of identifying new businesses or new business approaches, was reported as almost non-existent in currently defined process activities. While the CEO of the SP new setup was highly supportive of the process organisation in general, as captured in his previous quote, he also observed this drawback:

> I think the processes cause inward rather than outward thinking.
>
> [John Davis, CEO of SP new setup]

Our findings identified two distinct clusters of thinking and activity, as shown in Table 4.1: a dominant and prevailing 'inward' orientation focussed on internal structures and policies, and a desired 'outward' orientation focussed on looking for new markets and new products, and thus related to new venturing. As summarised in Table 4.1, the inward orientation that prevailed in Siemens Fire Safety focussed on the exploitation of established businesses, was primarily limited to incremental product innovation, and was driven by well-structured and comprehensive Product Lifecycle Management and Supply Chain Management processes. These were explicitly aimed at achieving a maximum of independence in how the tasks are carried out from the personal capabilities, orientations, ambitions, and emotions of employees, and which embraced tight control. Such an inward orientation was previously reported by comparable studies for large and rather bureaucratic organisations (Miller, 1986, 1996; Sathe, 2003; Christensen, 2005) that are driven

Table 4.1 Inward and outward orientations

	Cluster of aspects of a 'company inward' focus	*Cluster of aspects of an 'outward' focus*
Predominant step of the entrepreneurial process	**Exploitation** of established business	**Exploration** and **evaluation** of new business
Innovation aspect	**Incremental** innovation only (existing products, existing markets)	**Disruptive** innovation (new products, new markets)
Process maturity	**Comprehensive** processes definitions in Product Lifecycle Management (PLM) and Supply Chain Management (SCM)	**Undefined** Management Process, **weakly defined** Customer Relationship Management (CRM) process
Dependence of how activities are carried out on **personal** capabilities, orientations, and ambitions of involved employees	**Low person-dependence** • employees in R&D manufacturing • product managers	**High person-dependence** • sales / key customer relations • entrepreneurs / top management

by business managers primarily adhering to internal policies, structure, and plans (Reynierse, 1997; Zahra, Hayton, and Salvato, 2004; Chell, 2008; Brettel, Engelen, and Heinemann, 2009).

In contrast, an 'outward' focus would comprise the exploration and evaluation of new business primarily based on disruptive innovation aimed at new markets, thus seeing the entire organisation from a market perspective (Drucker, 1954). It would rely on rather lean process definitions and accept significant dependence on personal orientations, ambitions, capabilities, and the free will of employees. Here, a Management Process comprising a definition for business field analysis or business plan derivation simply did not exist in Siemens entities, and only outlines were defined for the Customer Relationship Management process. Research participants lamented the maturity of the 'inward' activities in the researched Siemens entities to the neglect of 'outward' aspects, with reference to the incremental and technical nature of innovations and absence of a customer and market focus. For example:

> Regarding business innovations, nobody cares about, I mean, we concentrate on technical innovation part [. . .]
>
> [Hans Meier, Global Head of FS Human Resources]

> I think one of the things we missed: we put it all around the technology. [. . .] A lot of what our customers need are [is] pioneering processes to make life easy for them.
>
> [Keiko Safaia, Chief Marketing Officer BT]

> At the moment we give awards for certain projects, certain technical innovations, etc., but [. . .] entrepreneurial activity is exploiting an opportunity in a market, rather than just doing a [. . .] new technical design or something like this.
>
> [Robert Schmid, Head of Product Line within SP new setup]

The dominant inward orientation was also seen as being reflected in planning processes and, specifically, the yearly innovation review meetings of Building Technologies division. Every May, business unit CEOs must present all planned activities for entry into new business fields, product portfolios, and so on for coming years to the Building Technologies CEO. In December, a shorter update of activities to date and potential new product developments is presented. Together with the Strategy Review – on which key elements of the Innovation Review are based – these are the most important long-term planning activities. Nonetheless:

> [. . .] frankly to say, this year's Innovation Review, in my view [. . .] was more a review of R&D programmes. Hardly one or two topics which were really [. . .] innovative topics. There is a gap.
>
> [Keiko Safaia, Chief Marketing Officer BT]

The importance of outward-oriented, interpersonal relationships heightens the potential value of human capital and related discretionary behaviours. These typically cannot be fully encapsulated in formal business processes, and that which could be captured can be easily lost. The Shinwha case is particularly instructive in this regard. In 2011, three years after the acquisition, there was consensus among the Fire Safety management that Shinwha's dramatic drop in sales was primarily due to the neglect of personal customer relationships by Shinwha's sales force. As it transpired, there was neither a detailed identification of key customer relationship owners nor a subsequent transfer of these relationships from sales managers – a significant number of whom left following the acquisition – to internal successors. As noted, Customer Relationship Management process definitions were barely implemented in Fire Safety at the time of our study. Notably, a post-integration assessment was carried out by Building Technologies' Mergers & Acquisitions head office in July 2010 in Seoul. The Siemens assessment questionnaire used to judge the Shinwha integration process contained 77 detailed questions about internal processes, IT infrastructure, tools, and organisational structures – but not even one question asked about the customer relations of top and middle management at Siemens Shinwha, key account management, or related market activities. Nor did a customer focus emerge in the official audit of the firm integration – despite its reported importance:

> [. . .] our local business is based on relationship. [. . .] long term relationship [is] very, very important for the local business in Korea.
>
> [CFO BT Korea]

> [. . .] on competences I think we have a massive, massive gap, between what we need, going forward as an organisation, and what we have today. [W]e are trying to see the world based on the solutions which we are comfortable delivering – not so much [. . .] we don't see the customer [. . .] from his point of view, what is it that he needs, end to end.
>
> [Chief Marketing Officer BT]

This lament was not limited to Korean operations. For example:

> I know that every one of my bosses that I've had since I am being in, [. . .] very few of them actually went to see any of my customers. Now that is not entrepreneurial!
>
> [John Davis, CEO of SP new setup]

Indeed, throughout all case studies customer relationships are reported as highly person-specific and requiring many years of investment before becoming effective in the selling of products and solutions. The absence of specific processes designed to capture the key knowledge and opportunities that can be derived through customer networks and, indeed, to transfer the network relationships themselves, led to a loss of deep knowledge of the subsidiary's internal and external context necessary for ongoing opportunity identification and exploitation.

More broadly, the recognition (or creation) of entrepreneurial opportunities and their subsequent evaluation and exploitation represent core elements of entrepreneurship (Casson, 1982; Hills, Lumpkin, and Singh, 1997; Venkataraman, 1997; Zahra, 2008; Alvarez, Barney, and Anderson, 2013) and the entrepreneurial process, shown earlier in Figure 1.1 of Chapter 1. Opportunity recognition, in the sense of identifying new businesses – or new business approaches in existing businesses – was not, however, represented by any defined process activity at Siemens Building Technologies division. Further, only innovation teams concerned with technical innovation based on internal research existed as recognised components in the organisational structure of Siemens Fire Safety at the time of our study. Activities such as venture groups, task forces, strategic business units, freedom to engage in projects of one's own undertaking, and unofficial projects (e.g. bootlegging, skunkworks) could be undertaken to strengthen entrepreneurial activity (Brazeal, 1993). However, Siemens is running all its activities as part of the comprehensive Reference Process House framework that is highly stable over time, and the organisational setup is driven by requirements resulting from the process definitions rather than vice versa. Therefore, in strengthening entrepreneurship it seems more promising for an organisation such as Siemens to pursue actions towards business opportunity recognition and exploration that are in accord with a process perspective. Interestingly, a majority of interviewees agreed on the applicability of the generic process of entrepreneurial activity described in Chapter 1, but nonetheless expected serious difficulties in mapping detailed entrepreneurship-oriented behaviours into defined process steps due to its highly personal, idiosyncratic nature. However, the field research revealed that no attempts to define such process elements have been made so far at Building Technologies, and the entire Management Process element in the Siemens Reference Process House was found to be still undefined.

Notably, in 2010 Building Technologies management decided to expand the definitions of the existing Product Lifecycle Management (PLM) process towards the 'front end' by the end of 2011, covering aspects such as potential new fields of activity for the business, related business planning, and proposed product portfolio activities (representing the 'Plan' and 'Product Portfolio Planning' activities of PLM in Figure 4.1). The fields of activity – as the starting point for such analysis on a PLM level – are mainly defined in the yearly business strategy paper updates and derived from various sources such as trend monitoring, subsequent scenario analyses, or the review of developments in adjacent businesses within Siemens. Rather accidentally, specific business field analyses that include the composition of various forms of business plans are then carried out, driven by these action field definitions, or sometimes by quite spontaneous decisions in board meetings. As such, neither the procedure used nor the expected final deliveries were standardised, since neither a respective process nor reporting templates were yet defined.

Within Fire Safety, it was decided in early 2011 that a working group to define the strategic aspects in the Management Process linked to the Product Lifecycle Management activities should be established. This decision was based on the findings from the field research presented here (which were reported to Fire Safety Management in the first quarter of 2011), the intended expansion of the Product Lifecycle Management process definition with an interface to a defined Management Process, and the first author's membership in the Fire Safety Business Excellence team (responsible for the business unit strategy, as well as being the new owner of the Management Process definition in the Reference Process House from the start of 2011). At the time, the Building Technologies process house definition merely contained the activities 'define action fields', 'analyse external environment', 'analyse internal strengths and weaknesses', 'develop strategy', 'implement strategy', 'control strategy', and 'enable strategic planning and controlling' as part of the overall strategic planning and controlling activity, as shown in Figure 4.2. These definitions were not further elaborated, even though implementations of these elements by detailed description already existed in other Siemens divisions.

Planned key deliveries by the end of 2011 were a defined approach of how to analyse and subsequently report on potential opportunities for Siemens in a new business field, and how to propose related business plans for potential implementation. This process definition, including the proposal templates, was also a necessary prerequisite to formally request new business proposals from subsidiaries, which is an activity others have suggested to foster entrepreneurial activity in subsidiaries (e.g. Birkinshaw and Hood, 1998, 2001). Additionally, it was proposed that the required process steps leading to the identification of such new fields of activity needed to be defined to achieve maximal comprehensiveness in business opportunity recognition. As shown in Figure 4.2, key

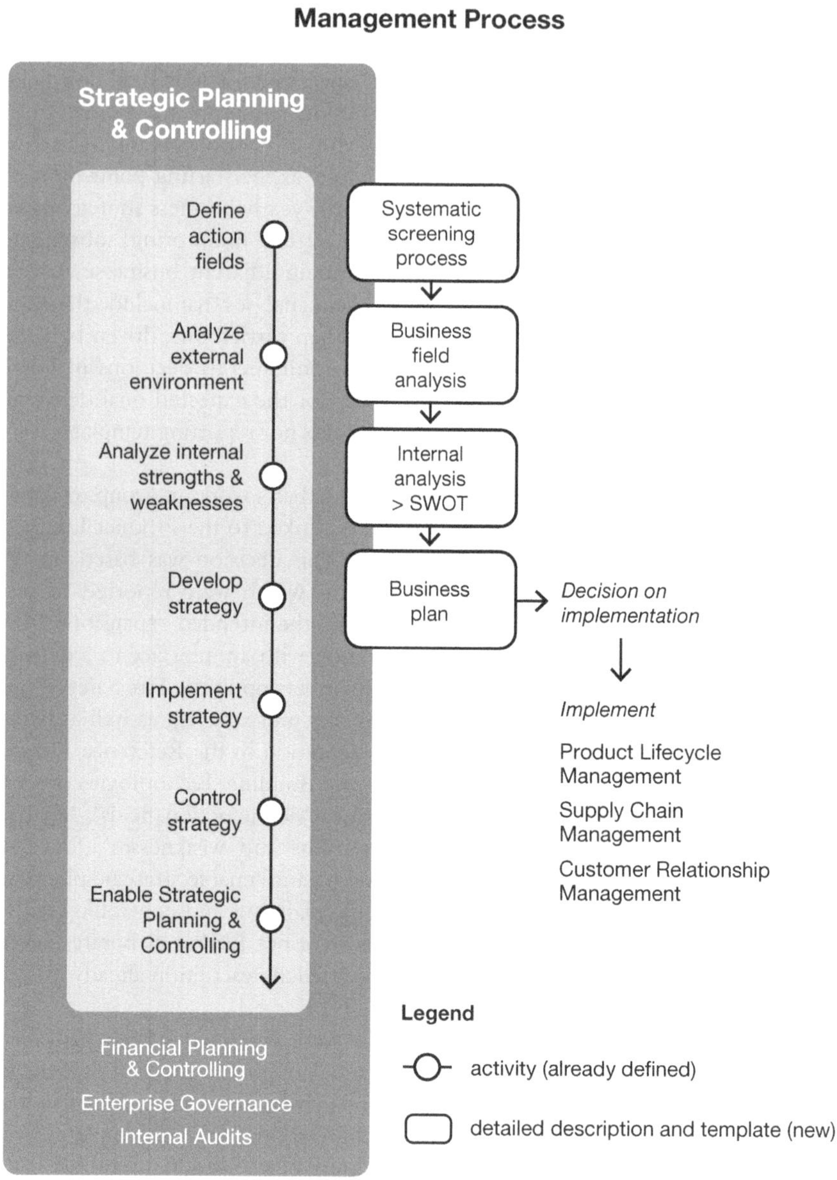

Figure 4.2 Proposed management process expansion

elements on the process definition side include a systematic screening process for new business opportunities based on trend monitoring in respective markets, technologies, regulations, and so on, leading to identification of potential action fields and subsequent business field analysis within these action fields, followed by an internal analysis of one's strengths and weaknesses and a derived SWOT analysis (i.e. the combination of strengths and weaknesses, and market opportunities and threats), and a subsequent business plan proposal. With a positive decision to develop the proposed new business, implementations have to be started in all affected business processes, linking to the Siemens process model. One benefit of working along a defined entrepreneurial process that outlines clear roles is that tasks of opportunity recognition are assigned to identifiable people, since it "is necessary to eliminate organisational structures that obscure personal responsibility and homogenise individual actions" (Menzel, Aaltio, and Ulijn, 2007, p. 740).

Compliance processes, culture, and trust

The huge bribery scandal Siemens went through in recent years had an enormous impact on perceptions of trust and related entrepreneurial endeavours. Siemens used a slush fund of more than €1.3 billion to win overseas contracts in telecom and power business from 2001 to 2007. By the end of 2008 the case was settled with the relevant authorities, with a total cost by mid 2013 estimated by the CEO as €1.3 billion (US$ 3.3 billion).[3] The case was the biggest business bribery scandal in history. This scandal and its aftermath led to a redefined company: vision, changed core values and guiding principles, the creation of new compliance processes and structures, and highly elaborate training on such matters for all employees. For example, in 2006 there were 86 employees worldwide for whom compliance was only a part of their responsibility. By the end of FY 2008, 621 employees were responsible for compliance, including employees in projects for introducing compliance programmes. Similarly, the total number of participants in online and face-to-face compliance training courses was 0 in 2006, 32,000 in 2007, and 175,000 worldwide in FY 2008.[4] A worldwide regulation now defines in detail what activities and behaviours are permissible in the interactions with all groups of relevant stakeholders. Spending for customer events and gifts, for example, is clearly limited and needs specific approval from superiors. Compliance officers check the ongoing business and must be actively consulted in any case of uncertainty.

While there was a general consensus among interviewees that entrepreneurship is *not* linked to non-compliant business, the perception of the effects of these compliance rules on Siemens' business was highly controversial. Headquarter representatives insisted that the rules were not hindering the business, whereas employees in Asia saw a significant impact on sales activities. Former Shinwha employees, as well as exponents from Fire Safety China, saw two "layers of reality": the official world of Siemens rules of conduct and compliance guidelines, and the real world of making business in many regions of the world. Korean business, in particular, was reported as highly dependent on personal relationships and 'give-and-take' customs:

> German culture is more [. . .] logical [. . .] and then based on [. . .] contract [. . .] very logical. Korean culture: less logical, less contraction, but more emotion, more based on [. . .] human relationship. [. . .] I believe you, you become my friend [. . .] this happens naturally [. . .] but Western [. . .] cannot understand it!
>
> [HW Kim, CFO BT Korea]

There was a severe gap perceivable between these two worlds, which was not officially addressed. As one respondent remarked:

> I think, especially in the environment like China, Russia, I cannot imagine: if we are 100 per cent compliant [. . .] we cannot make business.

The Head of Fire Safety in Korea and former CEO of the Shinwha Fire Protection business estimated a loss of ten to fifteen per cent of projects in Korea following the Siemens compliance rules. The building of personal relationships in the conduct of business was linked to significant spending for luxurious dinners and subsequent visits in bars, or invitations to the golf course. But with the establishment of the new compliance rules, such spending is now drastically limited – the spending limit for a dinner invitation was reported to be only US$ 25 per person. Hence, people in Far East entities simply expected to lose these business opportunities to the competition. At the same time, the Global Corruption Index 2010 of Transparency International[5] confirmed an increased corruption worldwide over the previous three years, with six out of ten respondents reporting an increased rate of bribery required to get personal services (linked to health, education, tax, etc.), and overall governmental structures and political parties perceived as behaving in increasingly corrupt ways. Siemens' compliance training and information provided through internal newsletters and emails did not make note of these trends.

While nobody expected any room for change in the target of 'making only clean business', how to achieve such clean business was clearly disputed. In the shorter term, a majority of respondents saw room for process simplifications to reduce the additional workload for employees. Even after a first stage of simplifying the original 104-step Siemens compliance tool in Fire Safety entities, there was consent that further simplifications would be necessary:

> I fully agree, we need the compliance regulations, we need the business ethics, but, but, the issue: how we do that!
>
> [HW Kim, CFO BT Korea]

> This is just too extreme, too extreme!
>
> [Yao Wang, Head of Product Management at FS China]

Respondents also saw the more fundamental issue of either going for a rule and control-based approach, or relying more on trust in the employees:

> Siemens [. . .] has a rule based culture, and not a value based culture, because you can achieve the integrity and compliance also by living it. By trust. Sure, we have as Siemens, we have completely screwed up the subject, and we have to go along now with a rule based approach, but there is no fundamental inheritance that you have to do it that way. You can do it much more value based.
>
> [Jan Traber, Integration Manager iMetrex, 15 September 2010]

> Siemens policy, is very simple: don't trust the employee, don't trust the customer. This is their principle! Based on this principle [is] how we do the business. But we can do the compliance in another arrangement. We trust the people, we trust the customer, we trust the officials' behaviour [. . . .] It is not trust based. I can say: many people are demotivated; most people.
>
> [HW Kim, CFO BT Korea]

This perceived lack of trust in employees within Siemens entities was not only a consequence of the huge bribery scandal that Siemens experienced, but was also an effect of a current culture that prioritised applying comprehensive processes and tight controls. It was identified by respondents as a factor significantly limiting the entrepreneurial behaviour of employees. Trust, as the "psychological state comprising the intention to accept vulnerability based upon positive expectations of the intentions or behaviour of another", is a complex concept (Rousseau, Sitkin, Burt, and Camerer, 1998, pp. 393–395). It has been researched among individuals, groups, and many types of organisations, and can be interpreted as a cause, an effect, or a moderator of action. In the Siemens context, trust underpinned by shared values is reported as increasingly replaced by rules and regulations. Yet relational trust has been found "a powerful ingredient for fostering activities needed for successful new business creation" in established companies, and is especially apt to overcome problems associated with social complexity, causal ambiguity, problems of informational asymmetry, and political tensions that may arise during new business creation (Zahra, Yavuz, and Ucbasaran, 2006, p. 555). At the same time, excessive relational trust could translate to an over-readiness to accept new venture proposals from a trusted source, ad hoc or incomplete controls that lead to incomplete information needed to ensure effective implementation of entrepreneurial plans or take corrective action, or the sabotage of venture ideas of members outside the trusted sphere (Zahra et al., 2006). Trust can have a dark side.

Several significant obstacles hindered a change in Siemens from a business based on detailed rules, regulations, and controlling to one based more – albeit not exclusively – on trust, as advocated by several respondents. In the aftermath of the financial crisis of 2007, the trend towards stronger regulations and legislation accelerated, with Siemens AG being listed in the United States as well as in

Europe – and even operating its own bank facility since December 2010 – and hence required to follow all the related standards.[6] On the level of the building technologies industry, the amount of standardisation in processes – requiring detailed definitions, permanent controlling, and recurring audits – is increasing rather than decreasing. Even if granting trust for new business venturing is not directly linked to these regulations, the overall climate is hardly supportive of such a value change. To ask for the definition of 'trust' as a (new) Siemens core value could therefore not be expected to help much towards achieving the intended goal, and could even create the risk that employees become cynical about the firm's espoused values not reflecting (perceived) reality.

Indeed, the change programme Fire Safety and Siemens more broadly commenced in the aftermath of the bribery scandal could easily lead to cynicism that undermines trust (Buchanan, Claydon, and Doyle, 1999; Cutler, 2000; Wanous, Reichers, and Austin, 2000; Bommer, Rich, and Rubin, 2005; Watt and Piotrowski, 2008). Furthermore, the lay-offs caused by restructuring Shinwha manufacturing and the SP new setup led to negative perceptions in two ways. In the case of the SP new setup, the survival of the former top managers – all of whom secured new jobs within Building Technologies, whilst significant cuts were made throughout the 'ordinary' workforce – sparked many cynical comments from employees. For Shinwha employees, the lay-offs were perceived as contract breaches (Andersson, 1996; Johnson and O'Leary-Kelly, 2003), since Siemens management had declared at deal closing that no lay-offs would take place. Perceived violation of a contract obviously undermines trust in the management. However, these incidents seem somewhat dependent on the specific persons and circumstances involved, as no similar events on a broader scale could be identified throughout the Building Technologies organisation at the time of our study.

Process and organisational complexity

By the end of 2010 more than 600 guidelines for all the different aspects of the business processes could be found within the Building Technologies division. This in itself was a world of complexity that resists a full implementation in practice by the sheer amount of process definitions. Although not a view supported in our study by executives responsible for the definitions, the complexity of rules and regulations in Siemens entities was seen by middle management as hindering new entrepreneurial business endeavours. Shared product platforms and architectures were judged as making it difficult or time consuming to change direction in business units, and the new SMART headquarters organisation was expected to add yet another dimension of complexity to the organisation. Interviewees acknowledged the enormity of the Siemens organisation and the pressure on Siemens top management to introduce tight compliance controls in the aftermath of the big bribery scandal as inherent drivers for the resulting complexity. In addition, previous studies confirm the critical role of firm structures of conglomerates (like Siemens) and its divisional entities behaving as 'machine bureaucracies', viewing this as inhibiting corporate entrepreneurship with respect to new business creation (Miller, 1986, 1996; Sathe, 2003, summarised by Christensen, 2005). As a consequence, "bureaucratic barriers to innovation have to be countered" to become a successful corporate entrepreneur (Kuratko, Montagno, and Hornsby, 1990). Highly sophisticated control systems do not always provide the desired control in reality, and can put too much emphasis on how tasks are carried out rather than selecting the right tasks (Pinchot, 2000). The following quotes illustrate concerns over the demotivating effect on employees' willingness to implement entrepreneurial endeavours, even when first joining Siemens with entrepreneurial aspirations and competence:

> I think [. . .] we start with quite good [. . .] motivation topics [. . .] for this entrepreneurial topics, and then we leave this person on his own, and he should find the way how to [. . .] overcome with all the existing rules [. . .] at the end, this good motivation topic becomes a demotivation factor.
>
> [Hans Meier, Global Head of FS Human Resources]

Even more pessimistic was the regional manager for Korea in Fire Safety headquarters:

> I would say we have people with entrepreneurial capabilities, entrepreneurial traits, but I think they are restricted in what they do. I think they lose the motivation to use their skills [. . .T]he true entrepreneur in my opinion would leave our business in order to be able to fly [. . . .] because their wings are clipped here.
>
> [Michael Bosshard, Regional Manager for Korea in FS HQ]

However, he saw also the opportunity to restrict the application of these tight controls just to the operational side of the business:

> [. . .] entrepreneurial behaviour which is [. . .] taking opportunities in the market, seeing them before other people do, and exploiting those opportunities with some sort of solution or offering, [. . .] quite frankly, processes are a distraction, are an internal activity. And they are very important about getting consistent delivery in what we do, but should the entrepreneur be tasked with running them?
>
> [Michael Bosshard, Regional Manager for Korea in FS HQ]

Unfortunately, initial steps of introducing leaner processes at Building Technologies (focussed on PLM and commencing in January 2010) were negatively impacted by the emergence of a severe product safety issue caused by non-observance of mandatory process steps. Specifically, Fire Safety wireless detector gateways were changed without mandatory system tests being carried out or certification authorities notified. By October 2010 the certification authority discovered the change, and identified conditions under which no fire alarms were transmitted any more. Removal of certification was officially announced, creating significant reputational damage for Fire Safety and extensive – and very costly – product replacement efforts. This led to strengthened calls for comprehensive and strict regulation. Evidently, to root tasks of operational excellence in trust instead of precise process definitions and subsequent controlling is inadvisable. Trust as a concept should not be confused with calculated information exchanges based on a deliberate risk analysis and risk management (Welter and Smallbone, 2006). Obviously, the challenge is to capture the potentially positive effects of trust in the context of new business venturing, and not to foster behaviours that ignore calculable and important risks.

While proposed remedies for excessive complexity and rigidities abound, including calls for 'structural freedom' or 'flexible policies and procedures' (Kuratko et al., 1990), such advice can be somewhat vague when one tries to apply them to a specific organisational and industry context. For a huge MNE like Siemens, persistently following a strategy of integrated solutions offered worldwide and under one brand,[7] organisational complexity cannot be reduced to levels possible for conglomerates primarily acting as equity holdings, or for smaller firms. Nonetheless, variation did exist in the levels of process maturity and complexity across the three researched entities in Siemens Fire Safety. Shinwha Ltd, as an entrepreneurial medium-sized firm, used simple process models that covered key aspects of product innovation and supply chain management. With Shinwha's integration into Siemens, it was decided that only a subset of established Siemens processes should be introduced in order not to overstrain the capabilities of the organisation and employees. In contrast, the SMART project must use the established Siemens processes, although it can use simpler versions (e.g. PEP tiny in the Product Lifecycle Management). At the same time, however, requests were launched from the SMART project team members for a significant reduction of process complexity and greater levels of freedom from Siemens' organisational constraints. A proposal arose out of a SMART initiative benchmarking that "internal regulations should be at a minimum level to guarantee a lean, flexible and fast setup".[8] Within the SP new setup organisation, a drastic reduction of the complexity of the established Siemens processes was taking place at the time of the field research in order to gain competiveness prior to being sold off. As explained by the Head of Product line in the SP new setup:

> Process-wise, I think, I am always [. . .] let's say: defending whatever process – PEP – we have. I like the PEP, I think it's good, the PEP, and the only important things is: you must have the authority to customise it to your needs, and this is what we do [. . .] we are quite aggressively customising it to our needs.

The relatively small size of both Shinwha and SP new setup was seen as key to providing sufficient transparency concerning employees' behaviours without installing additional control provisions. For example:

> In the very large company, you always have excuses: 'oh that was not me, it was the other one'. But if you have this 'CEO principle', compliance is down to the person, easily. It is not a matrix [. . .] and therefore I think, the whole

> compliance [. . .] may need to be adapted also for this kind of setup [. . .I]f you are a small company, and everybody has his role, and his position, and everybody knows each other, and everybody can clearly be made responsible for his part of the business, compliance is just part of the normal way of acting. If you are a big matrix [. . .] complex organisation, then for sure, you need everything written, signatures, and [. . . I]t is like quality! I mean, with all these quality control guys, bla bla [. . .] we will not have that! Quality is part of everybody's personal behaviour, and if someone doesn't behave, and this is possible in a small-medium sized company, if someone doesn't behave, he is out.
>
> [Robert Schmid, Head of Product Line within SP new setup]

Concluding remarks

Indications of the extent to which a process orientation can contribute to corporate entrepreneuring in Siemens was mixed. On the one hand, respondents abhorred the suggestion that elements of entrepreneurial activity be added to process definitions, seeing it as highly person-dependent and as such an attempt at a reversion to the 'old Siemens'; process definitions can preclude the discretionary behaviour and 'free will' core to the exploration of entrepreneurial opportunity; strong internal processes in Product Lifecycle and Supply Chain Management (to the neglect of other process areas) lead to a strong 'inward orientation' in Siemens, with a focus on incremental innovations by R&D to the neglect of externally driven innovation and opportunities and reinforced by planning practices; and excessive and universally standard compliance requirements and process complexity destroy trust, hamper business development across diverse regions, and undermine entrepreneurial motivation.

On the other hand, there was no evidence that inclusion of entrepreneurial activities in the established processes had been attempted in recent years, making the effects of the existence of such process definitions – or of the wisdom of rejecting the idea – impossible to assess; strong processes were seen as potentially creating space for idea generation, as the basics for survival were in place, and particularly useful in the exploitation of entrepreneurial opportunities; formal organisational processes may create a *context* for the identification of both incremental and more radical opportunities beyond the direct application of the process itself; and from 2011 there were moves to develop the then absent Management Process definition in business opportunity identification.

The challenge in a process-oriented organisation, then, seems not so much in the existence of numerous process definitions, but their dextrous application in a 'light and responsive manner' selectively to the differing tasks or activities in corporate entrepreneuring. Indeed, the differing degrees of process orientations across the three Siemens case studies – the SMART subsidiary, Shinwha, and SP new setup – highlight efforts towards structural ambidexterity (Benner and Tushman, 2003) in a conglomerate MNE. Structural ambidexterity involves organisational architectures that simultaneously build in loose and tight coupling. That is, the MNE is composed of multiple subunits (e.g. the prototypical Siemens entity with high compliance to defined processes; SMART subsidiaries; Shinwha; SP new setup subsidiaries). Within each, organisational arrangements are relatively consistent and tightly coupled, but across these subunits arrangements differ, and each subunit is only loosely coupled to the others. Nonetheless, what is evident in the continuing calls for an ever lighter touch (in process complexity and requirements for adherence) across our case studies is the difficulty in remaining, or becoming, fully separate from a heritage of highly stable organisational processes that are also sustained by industry characteristics demanding high levels of certification and compliance, and reinforced by the dramatic events of the bribery scandal and product recalls. Abstract, universally touted 'remedies' for the constraints of a process orientation that neglect enduring elements of organisational heritage and the broader context are unlikely to succeed.

Notes

1 Based on internal corporate documents as of 28 October 2010 and Rohloff (2011).
2 "BT process documentation: Idea Management Process (IMP)", 1 April 2007
3 Compare http://www.guardian.co.uk/business/2008/dec/16/regulation-siemens-scandal-bribery; http://www.spiegel.de/international/business/a-german-giant-in-decline-how-siemens-lost-its-way-a-915008.html, 7 August 2013
4 http://www.siemens.com/investor/pool/en/investor_relations/downloadcenter/sustainability_report_2008.pdf, last accessed 4 June 2016
5 The results are based on a capture of experiences and views of more than 91,500 people in 86 countries and territories. For Russia, "significantly increased petty bribery since 2006" is reported. In China, 46 per cent of respondents see an increased rate of corruption (only 25 per cent report a decrease), with the business/private sector as being most affected. Results published in December 2010 on http://www.transparency.org
6 Accounting is done according to IFRS standard as well as US-GAAP / SOX etc.
7 The only exception to the Siemens one-brand strategy is given by Osram Ltd., fully owned by Siemens AG but still applying the previous Osram brand.
8 As documented out of a SMART initiative benchmarking in "Organization Benchmarking – key findings_V5.pdf"

References

Alvarez, S. A., Barney, J. B. and Anderson, P. (2013). Forming and exploiting opportunities: The implications of discovery and creation processes for entrepreneurial and organizational research. *Organization Science, 24*(1), 301–317.

Amberg, J. J. and McGaughey, S. L. (2016). Human resource activities and corporate entrepreneurship in a multinational enterprise. *The International Journal of Human Resource Management, 6*, 1–35. DOI: 10.1080/09585192.2016.1192051

Andersson, L. M. (1996). Employee cynicism: An examination using a contract violation framework. *Human Relations, 49*, 1395–1418.

Benner, M. J. and Tushman, M. L. (2003). Exploitation, exploration, and process management: The productivity dilemma revisited. *The Academy of Management Review, 28*(2), 238–256.

Birkinshaw, J. and Hood, N. (1998). Multinational subsidiary evolution: Capability and charter change in foreign-owned subsidiary companies. *The Academy of Management Review, 23*(4), 773–795.
Birkinshaw, J. and Hood, N. (2001). Unleash innovation in foreign subsidiaries. *Harvard Business Review, 79*, 131–137.
Bommer, W. H., Rich, G. A. and Rubin, R. S. (2005). Changing attitudes about change: Longitudinal effects of transformational leader behavior on employee cynicism about organizational change. *Journal of Organizational Behavior, 26*, 733–753.
Brazeal, D. V. (1993). Organizing for internally developed corporate ventures. *Journal of Business Venturing, 8*, 75–90.
Brettel, M., Engelen, A. and Heinemann, F. (2009). New entrepreneurial ventures in a globalized world: The role of market orientation. *Journal of International Entrepreneurship, 7*, 88–110.
Buchanan, D., Claydon, T. and Doyle, M. (1999). Organisation development and change: The legacy of the nineties. *Human Resource Management Journal, 9*, 20–37.
Casson, M. (1982). *The entrepreneur*. Totwa, NJ: Barnes and Noble Books.
Chadwick, C. and Dabu, A. (2009). Human resources, human resource management and the competitive advantage of firms: Toward a more comprehensive model of causal linkages. *Organization Science, 20*(1), 253–272.
Chell, E. (2008). *The entrepreneurial personality: A social construction*. Hove, East Sussex; New York: Routledge.
Christensen, K. S. (2005). Enabling intrapreneurship: The case of a knowledge-intensive industrial company. *European Journal of Innovation Management, 8*, 305–322.
Clandinin, D. J. and Connelly, F. M. (2000). *Narrative inquiry: Experience and story in qualitative research*. San Francisco, CA: Jossey-Bass.
Cutler, I. (2000). The cynical manager. *Management Learning, 31*, 295–312.
Drucker, P. (1954). *The practice of management*. New York: Harper and Row.
Gupta, A. K., Smith, K. G. and Shalley, C. E. (2006). The interplay between exploration and exploitation. *The Academy of Management Journal, 49*, 693–706.
Hills, G. E., Lumpkin, G. T. and Singh, R. P. (1997). *Opportunity recognition: Perceptions and behaviors of entrepreneurs*. Wellesley, MA: Babson College.
Johnson, J. L. and O'Leary-Kelly, A. M. (2003). The effects of psychological contract breach and organizational cynicism: Not all social exchange violations are created equal. *Journal of Organizational Behavior, 24*, 627–647.
Kohlbacher, M. (2010). The effects of process orientation: A literature review. *Business Process Management Journal, 16*, 135–152.
Kohlbacher, M. and Reijers, H. A. (2013). The effects of process-oriented organizational design on firm performance. *Business Process Management Journal, 19*, 245–262.
Kuratko, D. F., Montagno, R. V. and Hornsby, J. S. (1990). Developing an intrapreneurial assessment instrument for an effective corporate entrepreneurial environment. *Strategic Management Journal (1986–1998), 11*(special issue), 49–58.
March, J. G. (1991). Exploration and exploitation in organizational learning. *Organization Science, 2*, 71–87.
Menzel, H. C., Aaltio, I. and Ulijn, J. M. (2007). On the way to creativity: Engineers as intrapreneurs in organizations. *Technovation, 27*(12), 732–743.

Miller, D. (1986). Configurations of strategy and structure: Towards a synthesis. *Strategic Management Journal, 7*, 233–249.
Miller, D. (1996). Configurations revisited. *Strategic Management Journal, 17*, 505–512.
Pinchot, G. (2000). *Intrapreneuring*. New York: Harper and Row.
Reynierse, J. H. (1997). An MBTI model of entrepreneurism and bureaucracy: The psychological types of business entrepreneurs compared to business managers and executives. *Journal of Psychological Type, 40*, 3–19.
Rohloff, M. (2011). Advances in business process management implementation based on a maturity assessment and best practice exchange. *Information Systems and e-Business Management, 9*, 383–403.
Rousseau, D. M., Sitkin, S. B., Burt, R. S. and Camerer, C. (1998). Not so different after all: A cross-discipline view of trust. *Academy of Management Review, 23*, 393–404.
Sathe, V. (2003). *Corporate entrepreneurship: Top managers and new business creation*. Cambridge: Cambridge University Press.
Venkataraman, S. (1997). The distinctive domain of entrepreneurship research: An editor's perspective. In Katz, J. and Brockhaus, R. (Eds.), *Advances in entrepreneurship, firm emergence and growth*, pp. 119–138. Greenwich, CT: JAI Press.
Wanous, J. P., Reichers, A. E. and Austin, J. T. (2000). Cynicism about organizational change. *Group and Organization Management, 25*, 132–153.
Watt, J. and Piotrowski, C. (2008). Organizational change cynicism: A review of the literature and intervention strategies. *Organization Development Journal, 26*, 23–32.
Welter, F. and Smallbone, D. (2006). Exploring the role of trust in entrepreneurial activity. *Entrepreneurship Theory and Practice, 30*, 465–475.
Wright, P. M., Dunford, B. B. and Snell, S. A. (2001). Human resources and the resource based view of the firm. *Journal of Management, 27*, 701–721.
Wright, P. M. and McMahan, G. C. (2011). Exploring human capital: Putting human back into strategic human resource management. *Human Resource Management Journal, 21*(2), 93–104.
Zahra, S. A. (2008). The virtuous cycle of discovery and creation of entrepreneurial opportunities. *Strategic Entrepreneurship Journal, 2*, 243–257.
Zahra, S. A., Hayton, J. C. and Salvato, C. (2004). Entrepreneurship in family vs. non-family firms: A resource-based analysis of the effect of organizational culture. *Entrepreneurship Theory and Practice, 28*, 363–379.
Zahra, S. A., Yavuz, R. I. and Ucbasaran, D. (2006). How much do you trust me? The dark side of relational trust in new business creation in established companies. *Entrepreneurship Theory and Practice, 30*, 541–559.

5 Subsidiary mandates and initiative

Introduction

In the previous chapter we considered the influence of the Siemens-wide 'process orientation' on entrepreneurial activities of the three entities studied in the Fire Safety business unit of Siemens AG – good and bad. Here we look more closely at how the subsidiary mandates were pursued. Specifically, we ask *what impediments, if any, exist to the realisation of the mandates of the three studied cases within Fire Safety entities?*, and *what limitations exist in the exercise of subsidiary initiatives beyond the immediately prescribed mandate through, for example, subsidiary-driven mandate extensions?* We begin by briefly revisiting the nature of the mandates and describe the strategic context of the entrepreneurial mandate pursued by Fire Safety's China subsidiary in relation to the SMART initiative, the Shinwha acquisition, and the SP new setup, considering multiple levels within the organisation. We then explore the variable impact of organisational elements (e.g. the pervasive exclusive sales rights, indecisiveness in decision-making, and perceptions of risk and failure) on the pursuit of entrepreneurial mandates. Notably, the effect of each varies across the three studied entities, which are subject to very different mandates and commensurately different opportunities for, or impediments to, entrepreneuring.

Strategic context of subsidiary mandates

We discussed the mandates of the three entities in our research in Chapter 2, and so summarise them only briefly here again. First, the SMART initiative was a groundbreaking new approach within Siemens, involving a new global business mandate based on Far East headquarters. It was aimed at the launch of specific new businesses in lower end markets as well as Asia-specific product adaptations and additions (depending on local languages and standards). Global M3 product responsibility was to be delegated to emerging markets, and local entrepreneurship strengthened to increase market penetration, customer loyalty, and local value added. The China subsidiary in Fire Safety was given this mandate.

Second, the acquisition of the highly entrepreneurial and market-leading Shinwha Electronics in South Korea in 2008 was, from the perspective of Siemens headquarters, intended to achieve significant local sales of fire safety solutions and services within Korea, where market penetration had been difficult for Siemens Fire Safety. This meant a significant change to the sales mandate, since the previous (independent) Shinwha organisation was doing both international project business and product business. This acquisition was, however, considered a failure by 2011.

Third, the SP new setup involved a mandate demanding drastic changes. After the search by Building Technologies' management for a potential buyer for the whole Security Products entity in mid 2008 failed, the new mandate assigned in 2009 involved the development and carve-out of the business into an independently run company with almost complete separation from the Siemens corporate world, hopefully to be sold off to external parties. The vision for the SP new setup entity was not formally established at the time of the field investigations and was expected to change again significantly when sold off.

All three mandates were assigned within the context of a prolonged period of business stagnation within Fire Safety and a huge bribery scandal, with Siemens AG top management identifying a severe lack of entrepreneurship in the company as a critical issue. With the appointment of Peter Löscher as CEO, the Siemens AG vision and values were completely reworked. In particular, the term 'pioneer' was introduced, linking the corporate vision to an extensive citing of the founders of Siemens AG and the company's early achievements:[1]

> Siemens is a global powerhouse that looks ahead and takes the lead. And this pioneering spirit has always defined our company. For us, being a pioneer means more than just fostering invention and embarking on new paths. It means forging ahead into uncharted territory by developing, marketing and integrating leading-edge products and solutions tailored to today's requirements. It also involves taking calculated risks to push innovation. This willingness to innovate, coupled with conviction and passion, is what motivates our employees. Only the kind of teamwork that enables all players to give their best, shoulder their responsibilities and leverage their strengths can yield true pioneering achievements, whether in 1847 – the year our company was founded – or today. And it's this pioneering spirit that informs our company's vision of our technologies and tomorrow's key markets.

The new company values were also linked to the past: "Our Values – responsible, excellent and innovative – have been the basis for Siemens' success for over 160 years".[2] In parallel, since around January 2010 top executives (Siemens board members, cluster and division heads) regularly cited the founders of Siemens (Werner von Siemens, Carl Wilhelm Siemens, Carl Heinrich von Siemens) and their entrepreneurial activities in all internal quarterly communications (including printed newspapers and emails).

All in all, this 'back to the future' approach can be seen as the strategic deployment of corporate history as a symbolic resource: current activities are linked to eminent predecessors and historical figures, thereby offering a sense of continuity between past, current, and future behaviours (Suddaby and Greenwood, 2005;

Foster, Suddaby, Minkus, and Wiebe, 2011; McGaughey, 2013). It signalled the crafting of a new identity for Siemens employees by leaving behind the unfortunate issues of the then recent past (e.g. bribery scandals and the closing of many unsuccessful businesses), and by revisiting the pioneering spirit of Siemens in the 19th century. Siemens' CEO Peter Löscher summarised the development in one sentence in his letter to all employees at the end of 2010: "Today, Siemens is again a normal, world-class company".

However, the new definition of the company vision as described was not evident in most of the interviewees' reflections. Only the SMART Initiative's Global Project Lead – being part of the Siemens corporate head office in Munich – saw the Siemens vision in 2010 as being clearly entrepreneurial, relevant, and visible for employees:

> And the corporate entrepreneurship, when you are talking about Siemens, again, there you can see: there is a clear vision, you know: answer the toughest questions, you know, there is a clear [. . .] so this is also for me a kind of entrepreneurship, that the board, and the CEO, that they have a clear vision where this company should go for. [. . .] and a vision is not [. . .] a vision you do not have for the next year, you have a vision for [. . .] what is in five years.
>
> [Ralf Dunkel, Global Project Lead SMART Initiative]

This view was not shared by any other interviewee. Nor could secondary data reveal comprehensive links from the overall vision to the several strategies defined on sector, division, and business unit levels. Nevertheless, the importance of defining and successfully communicating a 'vision' was strongly confirmed, with Siemens Shinwha, especially, being reported as 'feeling lost':

> They don't see the vision what they try to be, and in my opinion, they are feeling a little bit lost.
>
> [Michael Bosshard, Regional Manager for Korea in FS HQ]

> To motivate people, [you] need to give a clear vision to them. [. . .] this is one example to communicate with the people, otherwise they don't understand our way, they don't understand the vision, they don't have their own dream. So we need to communicate the dream [. . .] effectively and based on trust.
>
> [HW Kim, CFO BT KR]

Having a vision was even seen as being fundamental for any entrepreneur:

> An entrepreneur for me is somebody who has a clear vision about the future of whatever he is doing: the project, or the position, or the role he has. An entrepreneur is able to bring this vision across to other people, that they feel part of this mission and vision [. . .] an entrepreneur is a good communicator, so he is [. . .] I mean [. . .] when you try to motivate people then you have also to communicate in a very good way [. . .]
>
> [Ralf Dunkel, Global Project Lead SMART Initiative]

On the next level down in the organisation, the publication in November 2010 of the vision and mission of the Building Technologies division simply stated: "We are the preferred partner for energy efficient, safe and secure buildings and infrastructure", and repeats the three values defined at top level.[3] On the level of the business unit Fire Safety, neither vision nor values were provided. Although Fire Safety reintroduced in 2008 the name "Cerberus" as the new brand name for all product channel offerings worldwide, harkening back to the pioneering heritage of the business units origins (see Chapter 2) and in accord with the corporate revisiting of Siemens' pioneering heritage, the Fire Safety strategy was formulated simply as follows: *"Fire Safety for the World" is based on proven success factors: Global Presence, Experience in Fire Detection, Installed Base, and Migration Competence, Regulation Management.* Unfortunately, this represented the status quo of the business at Fire Safety and poorly reflected the planned strategic initiatives aimed at strengthening business by a greater focus on specific needs in vertical markets (like marine, train, or wind power business) and moving into 'intelligent response' applications which manage incidents from fire safety and security systems in sophisticated and comprehensive ways. Obviously, the newly formulated Siemens vision was still to be adopted and built into the relevant documents and descriptors in subjacent organisational structures. Indeed, the business strategy of Fire Safety headquarters received, somewhat surprisingly, consistently negative feedback, especially from Korean management representatives:

> [T]here is no strategy into a significant increase in non-served markets – like the US developing countries and Asia Pacific as a whole. [. . .I]t's a careful strategy which you can write down as 'return on sales first' – on a yearly basis or even quarterly, and not on maximising the business plan over the potential of the future. [. . .I]t's more like maintaining the status-quo and doing very careful growth initiatives.

Similarly, a senior executive in Siemens Shinwha stated in the interview that "[t]here is no long term business strategy [of Fire Safety]", picked the Fire Safety strategy booklet up from his desk, scanned it shortly, and confirmed: "I cannot find anything for the global strategy". A view was openly expressed by respondents from Fire Safety headquarters as well as Siemens Korea that a key reason for the absence in Fire Safety of strategic growth and renewal perspectives was the high percentage of the Fire Safety profit that was routinely transferred to Building Technologies every year. This was seen as removing the money available at the subsidiary level for significant discretionary investments and treating Fire Safety as the 'cash cow' within Building Technologies. Interestingly, the acquisition of Siemens Shinwha was initiated by the Siemens Korea organisation (not the Fire Safety headquarters executives), but was finally paid by Building Technologies, thus returning some of the profit for growth in the Fire Safety business. This tight control at the divisional or corporate level was also reflected in the origins of the subsidiary mandates.

Origins of subsidiary mandates

Within this strategic context of Siemens AG, and in examining the three investigated cases, there is a recurring pattern – namely, the key source for mandate creation or evolution appears to be from outside the business unit Fire Safety, and is not an outcome of a mandate-creating initiative from within. That is, the mandates assigned to each of the case studies all reflect what Birkinshaw and Hood (1998) term 'parent driven investments'. Setting up a global SMART headquarters in China was primarily pushed by the SMART initiative from the Siemens AG top management. The Shinwha acquisition was mainly driven by the divisional organisation of Building Technologies in Korea, not the management of Fire Safety. The carve-out of the unsuccessful Security Products business was supported and decided by the management of the Building Technology division. In addition, major initiatives around subsidiary certification and a systems-house approach intended to foster entrepreneurial investments (described in 'Absent empowerment and subsidiary certification') were driven by divisional headquarters. It is thus evident that the main push for entrepreneurial activity was coming from superior levels in the Siemens organisation, and not from the Fire Safety business unit and its management, as illustrated in Figure 5.1.

Impediments to subsidiary initiatives

In light of clearly entrepreneurial mandates supplied from higher organisational levels outside of Fire Safety, what impediments, if any, exist to the realisation or these mandates by the Fire Safety entities? Further, what limitations exist in the exercise of subsidiary initiatives beyond the immediately prescribed mandate through, for example, subsidiary-driven mandate extensions? Here we explore these questions.

Intra-MNE relationships: exclusive sales rights and the new collaboration model

Mechanisms of coordination and control within large MNEs, while often essential, can also serve as impediments to subsidiary initiatives. The global Siemens sales organisation is based on country-specific sales offices owning, typically, the exclusive sales rights for all products and services within their territory (please see Chapter 2 for an overview of Siemens' structure). The main drivers for such an arrangement were reported to be: (1) the required coordination of all offerings in a country to avoid competing Siemens offers to customers, (2) the concentration of the country-specific market knowledge, and (3) the achievement of a synergistic organisation by unified offices, common tools, and services. However, product portfolios and business strategies are driven from the respective global headquarters. All divisional and business unit headquarters still resided in Germany at the time of our study – with the exception of the Building Technologies division, which was located in Zug, Switzerland. The field research revealed three

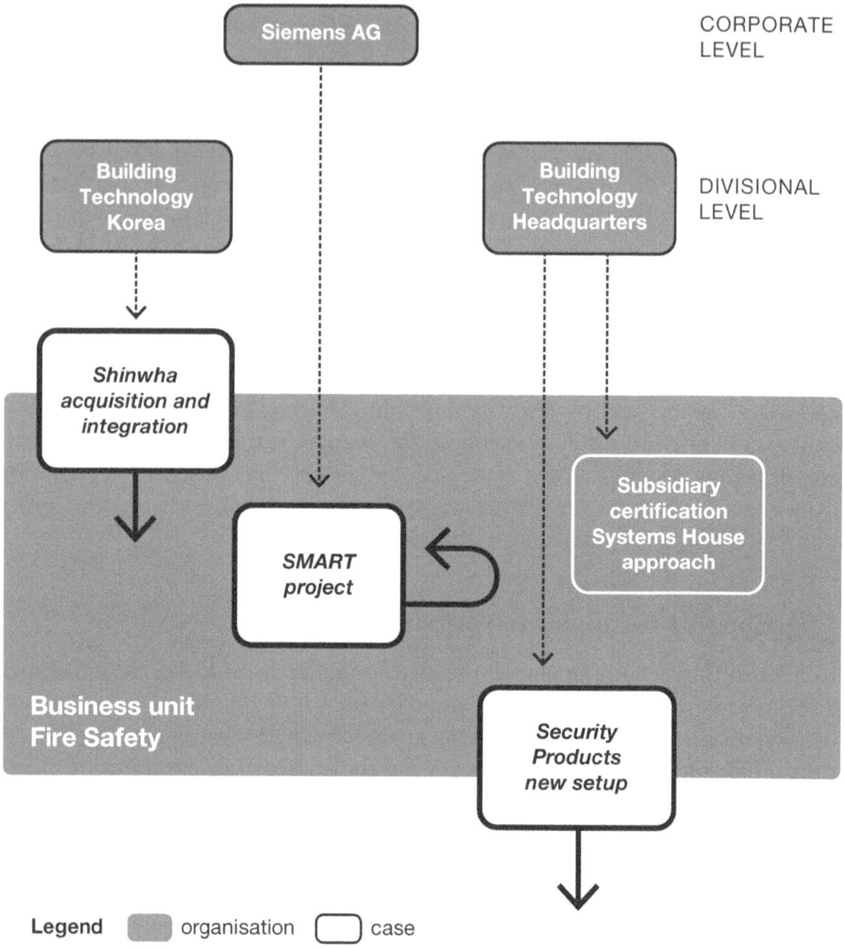

Figure 5.1 Drivers of entrepreneurial activity

specific contexts where significant conflicts arose in this arrangement: (1) difficult negotiation situations when a customer must be served in several countries or even globally, (2) projects in target countries where no representation of the specific business in the Siemens organisation exists, and (3) a lack of local support for businesses which create negligible turnovers in that host country. The limiting effects of the existing process definitions and controls on cross-border entrepreneurial activity were even confirmed by the Fire Safety CEO:

> So I would consider overall – for all regional activities – exclusive sales rights are always limiting entrepreneurial behavior.
>
> [Peter Mueller, CEO BT FS]

The imposition of exclusive sales rights was particularly problematic for entrepreneurial behaviour in the Shinwha case. The former Shinwha organisation achieved around twenty per cent of its turnover – and an over-proportional part of its profit – with solution projects outside Korea. After the integration into Siemens, two big projects were lost in Vietnam (i.e. Nohn Track Power Plant and Hanoi Land Mark Tower in Vietnam) due to the internal effects of competence conflicts, delays in submitting the offers, and the loss of competitive pricing by margin stacking. Out of these conflicts, a set of rules derived at the end of 2009 defined five distinct business cases and clear competences and responsibilities within Fire Safety Korea for business conducted internationally. However, no steps were taken by Fire Safety headquarters or Building Technologies headquarters to create a global guideline from this definition. In parallel and independently, Siemens Corporate Finance worked out a New Collaboration Model.[4] This defined in detail all aspects of international projects regarding legal and accounting matters, attempting to overcome the tremendous difficulties in international solution projects. But to apply the guideline in practice at the Fire Safety business unit, further adaptations were seen as required by Building Technologies division.

A simplification and clarification of responsibilities and ownerships, with an enhancement of business mandates, would significantly and positively impact the willingness and ability of subsidiaries to go for such business opportunities, even beyond markets addressed today. In the case of the SP new setup, the fundamental Siemens concept of 'exclusive sales rights' was simply abandoned. This, along with closing one of the three product lines and moving the headquarters from Switzerland and Germany to Sweden, impacted the subsidiary mandate in several ways. In particular, profitability to be achieved by the stand-alone operation became key, and considerations of doing combined business together with Fire Safety – a main reason for many delays and compromises in the past – were now gone. A further consequence of this decoupling was that local Siemens organisations had to apply for delivery contracts with the new SP organisation in the same way that was required for third party customers. In most countries, delivery to Siemens ceased. However, the SP new setup demonstrated the possibility of having setups without exclusive sales rights, and local Siemens country heads became aware of the need to nurture local businesses or to risk losing them completely. However, this uncoupling of the SP entity from Siemens was only accepted within Siemens under the goal of selling the new firm, and cannot be interpreted as representing a new type of somewhat loose integration considered by top management for other existing entities. The circumstances of the failure of the old setup of SP revealed significant limitations of the Siemens 'full integration' model practice: smaller entities, operating in product markets and being far away from market leadership, are almost 'strangulated' by the requirements of integration, and thus experience severe limitations in pursuing new initiatives or subsidiary-driven extensions to existing mandates. The most important effects cited in this context were decision processes being slowed down by complex compliance rules and organisational setup,[5] and by 'base costs' for infrastructure and tools, especially in IT (with ERP and HR systems based on SAP), that were far too high.

Finally, the SMART project was just entering the phase of starting international sales (in Russia and Brazil) at the time the field research took place. Within the SMART project, the overall business mandate was translated into a set of guiding principles,[6] which were further elaborated into detailed definitions along 9 'use-cases', defining a total of 32 activities. A use-case is a methodology used to clarify and organise the interactions of all involved actors in a specific environment and is related to a particular goal. The description of use-case number three – "Defining business plans for product developments" – shall serve here as the illustration of the approach taken. Figure 5.2 summarises the use-case, including actors, activities, and roles.[7]

First, the use-case detailed four related activities: 'drive market transparency', 'develop and prioritise product developments', 'create business plan', and 'review / approve business plan'. The roles were defined for all actors involved – the new M3 headquarters executives (M3 HQ), the global product management (Global PM), the local Siemens country management (Country), the executives from Fire Safety global headquarters (FS SYS CEO and CFO), and the regional managers in headquarters (REM). The role definition was standardised into four aspects: being responsible (R), being accountable (A), required to be consulted (C), and to be informed (I). The understanding of these role definitions was again described in detail in the 'guiding principles' document.

This approach was seen by the respondents as 'best practice' for formally defining mandates in a way that is understandable for all parties involved. However,

ACTORS	Drive market transparency	Develop and prioritise product developments	Create business plan	Review/approve business plan
M3 HQ	A	R	R	A
Global PM	I	I		C
Country	R	C	C	I
FS SYS CEO and CFO	A			A
REM	C	I	C	I

R Responsible for   A Accountable for   C Consulted   I Informed

Figure 5.2 SMART use-case definition

the most crucial point – selling the products on a global scale – has just started at the time of our study. Early feedback indicated challenges in aligning the three involved parties – the new SMART headquarters in China, the global Fire Safety headquarters in Switzerland, and the local sales organisation – in relation to the market strategy and respective product portfolio definition. The headquarters responsible appreciated the local market knowledge and support regarding tools and infrastructure, but tried to put in place their own understanding of the Siemens M1 to M3 market segmentation. As explained by the Head of Product Management at Fire Safety China:

> [F]or us we get a clear mandate; we can go everywhere, but how to synchronise with regional managers, and how to synchronise all these portfolios? And in each country [. . .] for example, if you go to each country, and [. . .] our ECO [the product name of the new lower end product portfolio targeted at M3 markets] will be sold in M3 for sure, and what is going to be sold in M2 and M1? And how to synchronise with all these activities with the regional managers? Here I think it is not clear, we need really to define this part!
>
> [Yao Wang, Head of Product Management at FS China]

Furthermore, organisational aspects seemed not to be defined clearly enough:

> There are simple questions: who is building up the sales channels: is it the Russia organisation, or is it Beijing?
>
> [Paul Amstutz, Regional Coordinator for Korea and China]

In headquarters, there were some doubts about a sufficient knowledge within the Fire Safety China product management team regarding foreign target markets:

> Whenever you do a product definition, nobody from China has ever been in Russia to get all these requirements.
>
> [Hans Meier, Global Head of FS Human Resources]

So, this new approach of having SMART headquarters in Asia with global responsibility in M3 markets adds yet another dimension of complexity to the organisation: namely the distributed nature of product portfolio decision-making, since the responsibility for M1 and M2 markets and products will remain in European headquarters. This is unlikely to make it easier for potential intrapreneurs trying to develop emerging M3 markets, since they are still also required to align their activities with the headquarters' functions, managing the higher end portfolios and all the sales activities in the market countries. Indeed, the existing multimatrix organisation of Siemens – with European-based headquarters responsible for business-specific R&D, manufacturing, and overall business success, country-specific organisations integrating sales throughout all Siemens business domains, and cluster offices being responsible for the sales in whole regions again – was not synchronised with the new SMART entities working as world entrepreneurs.

Initial feedback from the Siemens SMART initiative indicated responsibility conflicts in sales that resulted from this structure and unresolved product portfolio planning conflicts between the established headquarter functions and the new 'world entrepreneurs'.

Overall, when asking the interview participants about potential fields for improvement regarding subsidiary mandates, the top priority was the need for clearer definitions that were better aligned with the current strategy and other granted mandates, written up in appropriate forms such as the clear use-cases of the SMART initiative, and communicated to a broader group of involved people than today:

> [T]he headquarters management must give the clear definition over the role for each part, and made the deadline. [. . .M]ost of the big topics, there is no driver, only passengers, no driver.
>
> [HW Kim, CFO BT Korea]

> Clear and cascaded communication; so it is not sufficient only to go to top management, you also need to address the next level and the very next level [. . .]
>
> [Peter Mueller, CEO BT FS]

> And whenever you make this mandate for these entrepreneurship tasks, with this [. . .] with wanted responsibility in their organisation, and another responsibility on the other side, and [if] this is not synchronised, you get into chaos. And at the moment, we are on the best way to get into these troubles, because we keep this responsibility unclear.
>
> [Hans Meier, Global Head of FS Human Resources]

Indecision, failure forgiveness, and subsidiary-driven mandate extensions

Even with clear communication and explicitly assigned responsibilities, subsidiary roles can evolve. For example, subsidiaries need not always simply follow headquarter assigned mandates, but may engage in conscious efforts to seek out new business opportunities or to build new competencies, with or without parent company involvement (Birkinshaw and Hood, 1998). The experiences recounted by the management within Fire Safety Korea and Shinwha, and directly observed by the first author during his executive roles within Fire Safety, are illustrative of impediments to such initiatives. In particular, the importance of 'decisiveness' – in the sense of making decisions frequently and in a short time frame – by those implementing, extending, or enabling subsidiary mandates was a strong theme that emerged from our data collection and analysis. The Chief Marketing Officer of Building Technologies, who happened to be a highly successful former (independent) entrepreneur and the main owner of iMetrex, put it quite simply:

> First of all there has to be a culture of taking decisions, and taking ownership, this has to be broadened. [. . .] For me, entrepreneurship – without even

> thinking – would be a bias for decision. [. . .] [I]n a year, in a given business year, you may have ten opportunities to make decisions, let's say. Important decisions I mean, of a weight which is substantial. And if you only make one decision, or two decisions, your success on what you get out of it is limited by the impact of those two decisions. But if you were able to make ten decisions, or nine decisions out of the ten, yes sure, one or two will go bad, but at least you got six or seven positive out of [. . .] and in the balance, it is better for the company.
>
> [Keiko Safaia, Chief Marketing Officer BT]

This view was shared by the Integration Manager of iMetrix – "I am not only responsible for what I do, but I am also responsible for what I am not doing" – and, interestingly, by the CEO of Fire Safety, although he had never acted as an independent entrepreneur before: "Entrepreneurship is [. . .] being successful with the 80 per cent approach [. . . .] meaning: a fast decision is better than no decision". Nevertheless, interviewees were rather sceptical that such a culture of entrepreneurial decisiveness related to mandate implementation or extension exists at all in Siemens.

At the time of the Shinwha acquisition, the sales funnel of Fire Safety Korea contained around twenty international project endeavours in various maturity states, from 'first idea' to 'deal closed'. Since the acquisition was accepted on the basis of a significant growth of turnovers year by year, these international projects were not abandoned, but also not especially supported by Fire Safety headquarters in Switzerland. As a consequence, several international projects were lost to competition (see also 'Intra-MNE relationships: exclusive sales rights and the new collaboration model' regarding exclusive sales rights). For example, Fire Safety Korea developed a version of its domestic HomeSmoke product for the Japanese market. HomeSmokes are stand-alone fire detectors also sold in retail outlets such as shopping centres. The first product delivery was ready for shipment mid 2010, and the customer was urgently awaiting the delivery. However, by 2011 selling was still not allowed since Fire Safety Korea was waiting to be granted sales rights for Japan by Fire Safety headquarters in Zug. As it turned out, they never did receive permission and lost the whole business.

Fire Safety Korea management also proposed to set up a competence centre for Fire Extinguishing products and solutions in Seoul for the whole Far East area. Fire Extinguishing represented more than 50 per cent of turnover and up to 70 per cent of profits in the international business. This proposal thus extended an already well-established business, and would significantly support headquarters in Zug to develop this business with its global products. Again, there was neither an acceptance nor a denial of the proposal, and even 30 months after the acquisition there was no decision for or against setting up such a competence centre.

This pattern of simply 'not deciding' also took place in relation to the subsidiary's R&D role in Korea. As outlined in Chapter 2 and previously, the intention of Siemens was simply to "buy the fire safety market in Korea" by the acquisition of Shinwha Ltd. In reality, it was the addition of a whole new subsidiary, covering virtually all aspects of the value chain, to Fire Safety, since Shinwha was also running its own significant R&D and manufacturing. After the acquisition the manufacturing plant was closed, and its function – and most of the previous employees – merged with the already existing production plant of Building Technologies Korea. Dealing with the integration of the R&D side, however, proved to be much more complex due to a vast product portfolio that existed, the need to be compliant to strong local regulations (defined in Korean language, content-wise unfamiliar to Fire Safety headquarters, and not simply replaceable with existing Fire Safety products), and a major language gap caused by having all requirements and documentation in Korean.

To facilitate considerations of developing a more adequate mandate for the Korean R&D unit, mapping of the global Fire Safety R&D sites was first required. This was undertaken by the first author as part of his role as an integration manager for the Shinwha acquisition. Prior to this work, no explicit 'site concept' that defined clear mandates for the Fire Safety R&D locations existed. To develop such a site concept, the R&D locations in Switzerland (CH), Germany (DE), Italy (IT), France (FR), the United States (US), China (CN), and Korea (KR) were positioned relative to each other along two dimensions: (1) the strategic importance of the local environment, and (2) the subsidiary level of local resources and capabilities, as proposed by Bartlett and Ghoshal (2002). This helped define past, present, and potential future roles, as shown in Figure 5.3.

Specifically, Figure 5.3 shows the past (1997), the then present (2008), and the future (i.e. 2012) positioning of the internal R&D locations, as planned by Fire Safety headquarters management. The movement in placements between 1997 and 2008 summarises the subsidiary developments by planned and unplanned effects, whereas the proposed changes between 2008 to 2012 reflect the proposals for the evolution of the subsidiary positioning. Sites in Germany and France were to be restructured and reduced, the Switzerland and United States sites expanded, the main site in China consolidated, and the Italian site's responsibility moved to the business unit CPS.[8] This mapping helped in planning and visualising the developments of all previously existing sites and received appreciative feedback from the involved Fire Safety headquarters management. As of end of business year 2011, however, this mapping had not led to a more clearly defined role or mandate for the R&D of Fire Safety Korea. As in other examples discussed in this chapter, even more than two years after the deal closing no decisions beyond 'keeping the status quo' had been taken.

The then low speed in decision-making in Siemens entities was also acknowledged outside of Shinwha and at all levels within the organisation, but with no easy solution. For example:

> [. . .] entrepreneur[ship] I think has very much to do with timing, that we are on speed, that we are faster to the market [. . .We know] from our own experience, that decisions, in the past, sometimes have [. . .] took too long to get the things moving, and only once you have agreed everything, than really you can drive it forward. And of course the question would be: what

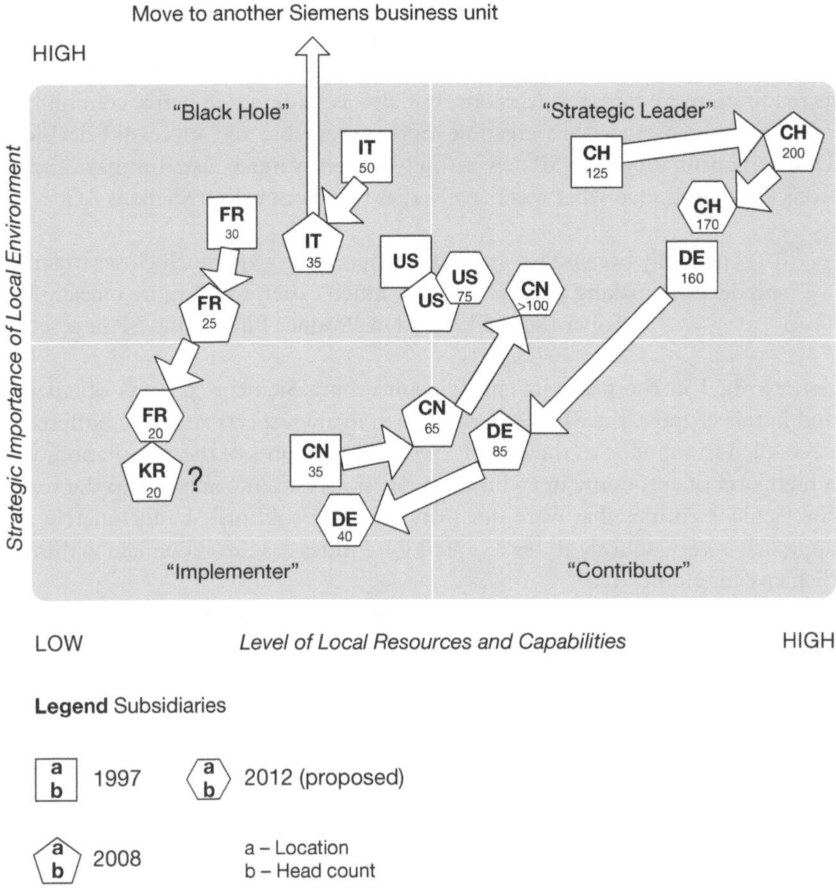

Figure 5.3 Past, present, and potential Fire Safety R&D locations

> could we do to speed up these decisions? [. . .] I think we somehow could improve on the speed without compromising on the success rate. How to do it [. . .] of course that [. . .] this is a hundred-million-dollar question [. . .]
> [Ralf Dunkel, Global Project Lead SMART Initiative]

Calls to take decisions faster in business fields with fast-paced innovation cycles, like security products, were also strong:

> That does involve timing issues [. . .] it also needs faster decision cycles, because you may miss a window of opportunity simply because you think too long about it. If you have asked everybody which has to be involved within this [. . .]
> [Jan Traber, Integration Manager iMetrex]

Decision-making towards entrepreneurial endeavours in the formerly independent Shinwha and iMetrex entities was primarily done by the top management. For the SP new setup, a new culture of making decisions based on the more comprehensive involvement of all stakeholders was reported. This approach was seen as requiring more time for decisions, but also as leading to a better commitment of all relevant parties, thus creating more sustainable and successful decisions. Despite consultation, the SP new setup was seen as much faster in making decisions and acting than what was perceived as the norm within Siemens AG:

> [. . .] not only because we are smaller, but also we are much closer together, and decision making process is much, much easier, much more efficient.
>
> [Robert Schmid, Head of Product Line within SP new setup]

As described in the previous chapter concerning Siemens' process orientation and in this chapter, the SP new setup was in many respects an entity buffered or decoupled from much of the complexity and constraints of the corporation, with a high level of autonomy in its business decisions (when compared to the rest of the Siemens entities that were not planned to be sold off). Unfortunately, this approach is very unlikely to be accepted for entities that are to remain within the Siemens conglomerate.

To foster entrepreneurship within other entities of Siemens Fire Safety, respondents saw the need to overcome this severe lack of decisiveness within Siemens, which was also strongly linked to a perceived absence of 'failure forgiveness' and lack of empowerment:

> And if you try to be entrepreneurial, that means: doing decisions based on your own understanding what is right and wrong, you are quite often [. . .] you are stopped, and halted by other people, who feel: oh this is too fast, I was not involved [. . .] by [. . .] whatever, by BAs [business administrators], or by compliance, or by whatever rules [. . .]
>
> [Robert Schmid, Head of Product Line within SP new setup]

> Nobody wants to make a decision, because as soon as he does a decision, and it might be that this decision is wrong, we have the culture that [. . .] he needs to be punished. [. . .] Therefore, it is better to ask first, first the top management before I am doing a bigger [. . .] decision. Or whenever you need to make a decision, to do this decision in such a way, that the decision maker has at least the possibility to find somebody who can be blamed.
>
> [Hans Meier, Global Head of FS Human Resources]

The concept of such "collective" decisions instead of having empowerment and accountability with single persons was perceived as a legacy of the Siemens culture:

> [. . .] if you look at the fact that we needed a Peter Löscher coming into the organisation and changing the organisation and structure to ensure accountability, that

> shows you that we are from a cultural history rather used to taking decisions together, so that in the end nobody is responsible. So I think we need to create [. . .] or allow, for examples, even if that failed to be successful, so that people feel that they are actually allowed to decide, and they are wanting to decide. [. . .] I think that they are very closely linked, the decisiveness and the risk-aversion [. . .]
> [Sandra Amrein, Management Development at Siemens Corporate Office]

But these collective decisions are also seen as an inherent effect of larger corporations:

> [. . .] it is a collective decision, there is [. . .] obviously more stakeholders, but you end up creating an opportunity for people to make decisions, because by default, the bias for decision making is rather low in a corporate environment. This is given. And therefore, if anybody is able to demystify the issues, and take a better assurance on the success, and also take the responsibility for those decisions, then you again have [. . .] that ability to move forward.
> [Connie Clark, Global Head of Product Line Intrusion (before SP new setup)]

So, good communication skills to "demystify planned entrepreneurial endeavours" seem to be required to get a positive decision. But even if decisions are taken at last,

> They are not properly documented, nor afterwards is the implementation of this decision communicated. [. . .] Meaning: we can go out of a meeting, three of us, and three of us will have understood something slightly different. And nobody then will write down then the minutes, and say: this means this for Joe, this means this for Susanne, and this means this for person X. So the way they are documented, and the way they are followed up is fuzzy. And therefore, they are not stuck to, not meaning that people are really trying to work against the decision, I don't think that anybody is really trying to work against decisions, I think sometimes they are just not properly communicated.
> [Connie Clark, Global Head of Product Line Intrusion (before SP new setup)]

Absent empowerment and subsidiary certification

As these quotes allude to, it is not only a matter of indecision but also a lack of empowerment impeding entrepreneurial initiatives. An episode in Building Technologies headquarters, observed in August 2010, confirmed an often cited phenomenon within the company with a clear example: the tendency of micromanagement even from top management levels, instead of granting comprehensive responsibilities and using management by objectives. The CEO of the

Building Technologies division (and thus head of around 42,000 employees, and responsible for a turnover of around €8 billion in 2009), decided to go for an investment of €350,000. This investment was planned and approved long before as part of the yearly budget, and could easily be paid from cash due to the highly successful running of the business (EBIT was around ten per cent of turnover, and far above targets). Nevertheless, the divisional CEO had to ask the Siemens top management board, again, for permission to be allowed to invest the money.

> [T]he management style of the board, they have a very detail-oriented management style. So that's rather a trust issue, and there we are back again to leadership. [. . .] However, I live in doubt and in hope that the management board knows what they are doing, [. . .] the effect I am afraid of that by this lengthy process: we might miss opportunities.
>
> [Management Development at Siemens Corporate Office]

Within the business units and divisions, new venture ideas are usually discussed in very small top management circles only, and typically just when required by superior organisations to provide an updated business strategy. The Siemens management board is clearly not perceived as providing meaningful mandates based on trust, which would involve a focus on achieved targets instead of "interfering" (as it was seen by some) in daily business. Taking all these obstacles into account, the proposed approach of the Integration Manager of iMetrix was simply to decide, even without having a granted mandate, respective rights or responsibility:

> I just took the decision, I didn't have the mandate, I didn't have the right, I didn't have the responsibility; I took a decision! Very simple [. . .] And that goes back: every morning, be ready to get fired. Because you may have made a mistake. Sorry, I have taken many decisions without competence, and so far nobody has shot me for that.
>
> [Jan Traber, Integration Manager iMetrex]

Notably, a key reason for the SMART mandate being given to the China subsidiary was the importance of empowering the local entrepreneurs:

> [T]his is also a reason why we will have a headquarters [. . .] a real headquarters for M3 in China, being responsible globally [. . .] I mean, this goes back to the empowerment; find the people who are driving it, who are really passionate about this, to make really a business out of it, so it is also [. . .] a criteria for entrepreneurship is passion, that you have the passion for something, and then: empower them! And 'empower them' in our case means: yeah, give them the freedom to decide things without asking always [. . .] and getting then a decision from the headquarters here.
>
> [Global Head of Fire Safety Security Solutions]

In the context of granting more comprehensive mandates with more local autonomy towards new business venturing, Building Technologies CEO Johannes

Milde presented at the Global Management Conference in May 2010 the idea of turning Building Technologies into a 'global systems house', and having the 'branches' (as subsidiaries were called within Building Technologies division) and their employees certified. A systems house provides customer-specific solutions and turnkey systems typically integrating different disciplines (e.g. Fire Safety, Security, Heating, Ventilation, and Air Conditioning). Such an approach commenced in 2007 in Fire Extinguishing by Fire Safety as a pilot project, and was perceived as quite successful. It sought to achieve three specific goals: (1) to "effectively make qualified investments in Building Technologies business growth opportunities", (2) to "manage existing financial and reputational risks", and (3) to "secure the needed (solution) experts with the right qualifications".[9] Granted branch certification levels (Blue, Silver, Gold) would be highly dependent on delivered business performance (growth and profit) and process maturity to manage quality and risk. Similarly, employees were to be certified by using the three levels: professional, advanced, and expert, as shown in Figure 5.4.[10]

By the end of 2010, a branch certification manager at Building Technologies divisional level had been appointed to implement this initiative. This certification process approach received quite positive feedback:

> Milde's initiative sends that message: Do your internal stuff well, and I give you more freedom on your external. [. . .] And I think that this is a great platform for launching [. . .] or, not launching, but fostering entrepreneurial behaviour. And I think it will attract different people to our business, to lead branches. I think they will aspire to get 'Gold' status, so that they get the freedom to do what they believe is right to run their business.
>
> [Michael Bosshard, Regional Manager for Korea in FS HQ]

The extent to which employee competencies matched the requirements of this Systems House approach and more entrepreneurial ventures remained in doubt:

> [. . .] on competences I think we have a massive, massive gap, between what we need, going forward as an organisation, and what we have today. [W]e trying to see the world based on the solutions which we are comfortable delivering – not so much [. . .] we don't see the customer [. . .] from his point of view, what is it that he needs, end to end.
>
> [Keiko Safaia, Chief Marketing Officer BT]

This again confirmed the prevailing inward orientation of employees on firm internal structures and policies at the time of our study, as described in Chapter 4. Nonetheless, as of May 2013, 34 branches and areas in Building Technologies had been certified. According to a staff magazine of Building Technologies that celebrated the achievement of fourteen new certifications, three of which were Gold, Gold branches are "exemplary in the management of their local operations" and give the signal that they are on standby "to help shape the future of Building Technologies", seeking to "be the first choice when Business Technologies pilots

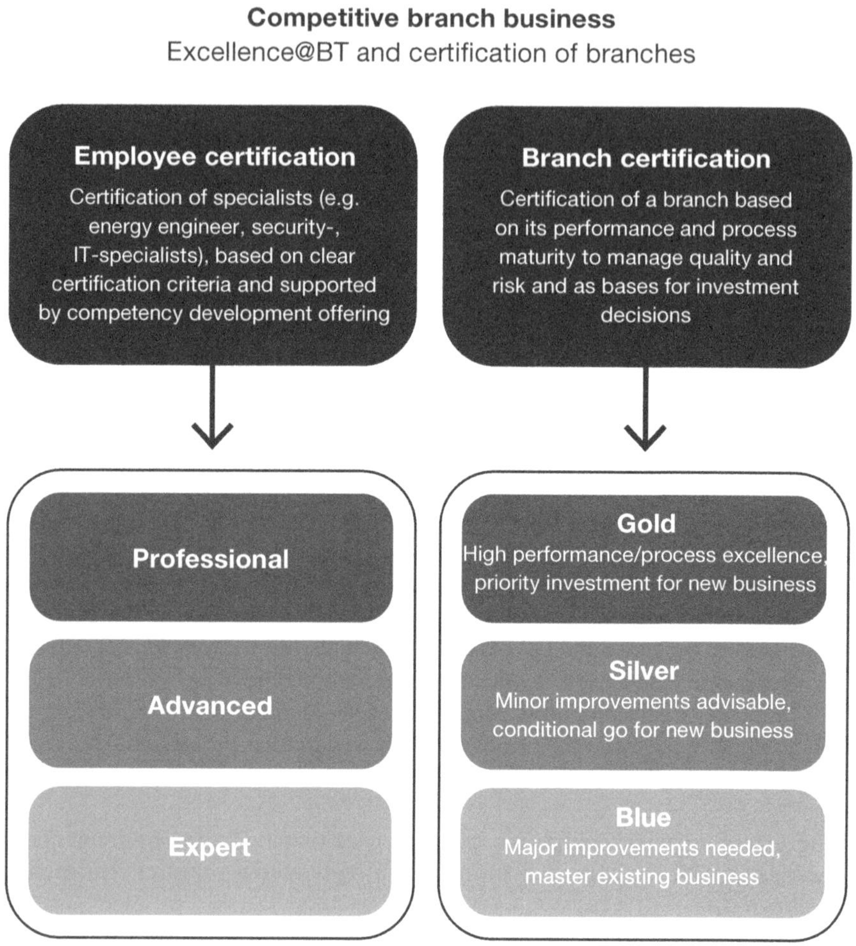

Figure 5.4 Certification concept for branches and employees

new concepts".[11] Notably, the award of certification levels had a less obvious but important effect: it signalled recognition, with the resultant greater autonomy seen as a reward. Recognition signals the importance of entrepreneurial values to the organisation and creates legitimacy for such endeavours (Hayton, 2005), and non-financial rewards such as recognition by praise and granting certificates have been found important to support an entrepreneurial culture in previous studies (Block and Ornati, 1987; Sykes, 1992; Brazeal, 1993; Hornsby, Kuratko, and Montango, 1999; Chandler, Keller, and Lyon, 2000). If successful, these competence-based certifications of subsidiaries and individuals may help foster positive feedback loops, leading to higher competencies for entrepreneuring and the pursuit of such initiatives.

The approach of Johannes Milde for turning Building Technologies into a "global systems house", and having defined competencies and thus roles of branches based on achieved certification levels, could be seen as comprehensively applicable to all major value chain elements. From a headquarters perspective, however, global alignments were still expected in the areas of R&D and manufacturing, since positive economy-of-scale effects on a minimal number of locations carrying out these tasks were expected. Additionally, the potential autonomy of subsidiaries *vis-á-vis* reusing created cash for new entrepreneurial endeavours may be impeded by high targets set for transferring created profits to the owners and a yearly investment budget process still tightly controlled by headquarters. At the time of our study, decisions about how and where to use created cash for investments were predominantly taken outside the subsidiary. This missing autonomy negatively affects the entrepreneurial orientation of the subsidiary management due to the rather cumbersome process to gain such investment approvals (as identified in the pilot study).

Concluding remarks

The subsidiary mandates assigned to each of the case studies reflect 'parent driven investments' originating outside Fire Safety at higher levels of the Siemens organisation, rather than being subsidiary-driven charter extensions or reinforcement (Birkinshaw and Hood, 1998). Both the implementation of these mandates and the pursuit of new subsidiary initiatives were seen to be impeded by a strategic vision for Siemens as a whole and within lower levels (i.e. division and business unit) that is not seen as prioritising corporate entrepreneuring, despite a return to early pioneering values: organisational processes are seen to be overly complex and reflect an absence of trust (see, also, Chapter 4); rules restrict new venturing across borders (e.g. exclusive sales rights); and slow decision-making and indecisiveness is in part fuelled by a perceived culture of blame and low levels of forgiveness for failed ventures. The situation of unclear or reportedly poorly communicated subsidiary mandates could also be seen as an effect of headquarters management perceiving the necessity – but lacking the concrete process definitions or organisational architecture – for the transition towards a world of more decentralised responsibilities (Paterson and Brock, 2002), as reflected in the challenges for 'world entrepreneurs' in the multi-matrix organisation of Siemens.

A lack of empowerment and local autonomy, perhaps based on a lack of trust, was also seen to be an impediment to subsidiary initiatives. The certification process of subsidiaries and experts was, however, seen as a potentially good means of creating trust in people and organisations in a well-defined and replicable approach. Trust based on previous education, examination, and recurring achievement of objectives represents a very 'Siemens-like' process approach, thus implying ready acceptance of this approach and ultimately greater autonomy for local entities. To foster entrepreneurship in local entities of MNEs, Mahnke, Venzin, and Zahra (2007, p. 1293) stressed the importance of co-locating decision rights. The SP new setup largely overcame difficulties around a lack of autonomy due to the nature of its mandate (leading ultimately to divestment), which enabled a decoupling of its operations from those of the broader Siemens organisation. The SMART initiative also fosters autonomy, with the Siemens top management simply enforcing such an empowerment of local entities to seek global new business by themselves, even against the opposition – or at least lacking the support – of the CEOs of respective business units, divisions, or country organisations.

However, the evolution of subsidiary roles is further influenced by the strategy of the respective business units and division, the relationships and rivalries between such subsidiaries, and the accessibility of resources and markets (Birkinshaw and Hood, 1998, 2000). Recent research acknowledges the complex processes of sensemaking and sensegiving micro-political bargaining processes in the co-construction and evolution of specific subsidiary mandates (Dörrenbächer and Gammelgaard, 2006; Alfoldi, Clegg, and McGaughey, 2012; Alfoldi, McGaughey, and Clegg, 2016). Facilitating mechanisms on the level of business units and divisions (e.g. sales rights and collaboration rules in international projects) thus require development of a shared understanding among diverse units: a simple command from Siemens top management will not be sufficient in the end. Furthermore, the role of a subsidiary in the international context can be different for each element of the value chain: Siemens Shinwha, for example, uses a mixture of local and global foci when looking at R&D, manufacturing, and sales. So the concept of granted mandates must be defined for each element of the value chain (Rugman, Verbeke, and Yuan, 2011), with the SMART initiative primarily an example of how to grant world mandates on the sales side.

Notes

1 Source: http://www.siemens.com/annual/10/_pdf/Siemens_AR2010_Vision.pdf, page 64, last accessed 2010–12–31
2 Source: http://www.siemens.com/about/en/index/values.htm, last accessed 2010–12–31.
3 As defined in a respective presentation published in November 2010 on BT intranet as https://workspace.sbt.siemens.com/content/00000013/intranet_docs/GC%20Documents/division_presentation_bt_en.pdf
4 Document "Siemens RPS New Collaboration Model NCM Guideline / Version 7 / Sep 2010", 170 pages
5 Just as two examples for simplifications in the SP new setup, SAP has been replaced by Excel sheets, and the compliance officer has been removed.
6 Last accessed version: I BT FS M3 HQ Guiding Principles – V19 of 2010–06–15.pdf
7 Based on interviews and last accessed version for the use-cases discussed here: I BT FS M3 Headquarters Definition – 2010–06–16.pdf
8 Most of this took place, especially the reduction in Germany and the build-up in China. The whole R&D organisations of FS and CPS were merged 2012/2013, including headquarters.
9 Management presentation, slide 5, published as "Competency-Excellence master presentation.pdf" on https://workspace.sbt.siemens.com/content/00001002/lcm/competence_excellence, last accessed 2011–11–28

10 Adapted from a presentation by Johannes Milde (BT CEO) at the Global Management Conference in May 2010.
11 Building Up. Das Mitarbeitermagazin der Building Technologies Division April / Mai 2013. Siemens. Available at: http://vcsc.ch/Informationen/Building-up/Building_up_AprilMai_de.pdf, last accessed 2016-05-06. Translation by the authors.

References

Alfoldi, E., Clegg, L. J. and McGaughey, S. L. (2012). Coordination at the edge of the empire: Subsidiary regional management mandates in the multinational enterprise. *Journal of International Management, 18*, 276–292.

Alfoldi, E., McGaughey, S. L. and Clegg, L. J. (2016). Neighbours or bosses? The ambiguity and co-construction of MNE regional management mandates. Paper presented at *Journal of Management Studies Special Issue Workshop*, WU Vienna, 28–29 January.

Bartlett, C. and Ghoshal, S. (2002). *Managing across borders: The transnational solution (2nd edition)*. Boston, MA: Harvard Business School Press.

Birkinshaw, J. and Hood, N. (1998). Multinational subsidiary evolution: Capability and charter change in foreign-owned subsidiary companies. *The Academy of Management Review, 23*(4), 773–795.

Birkinshaw, J. and Hood, N. (2000). Characteristics of foreign subsidiaries in industry clusters. *Journal of International Business Studies, 31*, 141–154.

Block, Z. and Ornati, O. A. (1987). Compensating corporate venture managers. *Journal of Business Venturing, 2*, 41–51.

Brazeal, D. V. (1993). Organizing for internally developed corporate ventures. *Journal of Business Venturing, 8*, 75–90.

Chandler, G. N., Keller, C. and Lyon, D. W. (2000). Unravelling the determinants and consequences of an innovation-supportive organizational culture. *Entrepreneurship Theory and Practice, 25*, 59–76.

Dörrenbächer, C. and Gammelgaard, J. (2006). Subsidiary role development: The effect of micro-political headquarters-subsidiary negotiations on the product, market and value-added scope of foreign-owned subsidiaries. *Journal of International Management, 12*, 266–283.

Foster, W. M., Suddaby, R., Minkus, A. and Wiebe, E. (2011). History as social memory assets: The example of Tim Hortons. *Management and Organizational History, 6*(1), 101–120.

Hayton, J. C. (2005). Promoting corporate entrepreneurship through human resource management practices: A review of empirical research. *Human Resource Management Review, 15*, 21–41.

Hornsby, J. S., Kuratko, D. F. and Montagno, R. V. (1999). Perception of internal factors for corporate entrepreneurship: A comparison of Canadian and U.S. managers. *Entrepreneurship Theory and Practice, 24*, 9–24.

Mahnke, V., Venzin, M. and Zahra, S. A. (2007). Governing entrepreneurial opportunity recognition in MNEs: Aligning interests and cognition under uncertainty. *Journal of Management Studies, 44*, 1278–1298.

McGaughey, S. L. (2013). Institutional entrepreneurship in North American lightning protection standards: Rhetorical history and unintended consequences of failure. *Business History, 55*(1–2), 73–97.

Paterson, S. L. and Brock, D. M. (2002). The development of subsidiary-management research: Review and theoretical analysis. *International Business Review, 11*, 139–163.

Rugman, A., Verbeke, A. and Yuan, W. (2011). Re-conceptualizing Bartlett and Ghoshal's classification of national subsidiary roles in the multinational enterprise. *Journal of Management Studies, 48*, 253–277.

Suddaby, R. and Greenwood, R. (2005). Rhetorical strategies of legitimacy. *Administrative Science Quarterly, 50*, 35–67.

Sykes, H. B. (1992). Incentive compensation for corporate venture personnel. *Journal of Business Venturing, 7*, 253–265.

6 Managing human resources

Introduction

We observed in Chapter 1 that human resource management (HRM) – with its emphasis on human capital development and related firm-specific capabilities (Wright, Dunford, and Snell, 2001; Wright and McMahon, 1992, 2011) – is core to the success of entrepreneurial endeavours. Sets of formal HRM activities can guide knowledge generation, coordination, and utilisation within the firm for entrepreneurial endeavours. HRM activities can also be used to build up intra-organisational contexts favourable to coordinating and utilising the dispersed knowledge held by employees for CE. Thus, HRM activities – whether undertaken by a formal HRM department or elsewhere – function as part of the firm's strategic infrastructure by helping to generate and leverage the entrepreneurial knowledge needed to sustain a firm's competitive advantage over time, and contribute significantly to 'managerial entrepreneurship' (Chadwick and Dabu, 2009). The preceding two chapters have already touched on HRM's contribution to managerial entrepreneurship. In Chapter 4, for example, we explored the implications of a process orientation for corporate entrepreneuring, including the implications of 'person independence' arising from 'process maturity'. In Chapter 5 we alluded to attributes or capabilities of human resources when considering the importance of 'decisiveness' and decision-making processes for corporate entrepreneuring, as well as subsidiary and employee certifications. In this chapter we more explicitly focus on the management of people within Siemens Fire Safety, and ask *how do the formal and informal human resource management policies and practices shape the nature and extent of corporate entrepreneuring within Siemens Fire Safety?* In particular, we explore the links between the Siemens people excellence initiative and the long-term orientation needed for corporate entrepreneuring, the capabilities measured and fostered under the Siemens Leadership Framework, and HRM's role in fostering ambidexterity and a tolerance for risk (or otherwise) in entrepreneuring, and the nature of rewards and recognition. We thus consider not only the role of the formal HRM department, but also people management more broadly.

The *top talent* programme and long-term orientation

Part of the Siemens people excellence initiative is the 'top talent program', whereby specific guidelines and processes are defined to identify and develop certain individuals towards executive positions. A key selection criterion is the expected potential for the individual to climb the Siemens hierarchy ladder by at least two functional levels within five to seven years. Specific coaches, typically serving in the positions targeted (i.e. two levels higher than the coached person selected), are provided to top talents. Additionally, customised seminar programmes are run for junior top talents (typically limited to a participant age of 40), allowing them to develop direct contacts with top executives and providing educational seminars organised by human resource functions. Top talents must sign their consent to be ready to move to any work place in the world in order to be allowed to participate in the program. Furthermore, a top talent is required to have served in at least two completely different areas of the business covered by Siemens to be promoted to an executive function in the end. It is usual, therefore, to send top talents as time-limited delegates (typically two and not more than three years) into key functions abroad.

Limitations of short tenure

Length of tenure in an executive position was viewed as impacting corporate entrepreneurial behaviour and endeavours. The CEOs of the acquired Shinwha Electronics and iMetrex served, or rather acted, as independent entrepreneurs for ten years and more. In contrast, within Siemens Building Technologies and Fire Safety the CEOs on the level of business units or country organisations typically stay for two to three years and then move on. Daniel Bertok, a German and the initiator of the Shinwha acquisition, left his job as the CEO of Building Technologies Korea after three years. Sander Herden (a German) was his successor – based, again, on a delegation limited to the maximum of three years. John Davis was appointed as the CEO of SP new setup for two years, with the clear goal of finding a buyer for the entity towards the end of his term. Top talents typically fill these executive positions and must show such a development to the next highest level in order to maintain their status.

These two- to three-year stays in a specific executive position were highly controversial within Siemens Fire Safety, with almost all those interviewed judging the current service periods as clearly too short. Indeed, they were seen to be inconsistent with a 'long-term orientation' – the tendency to prioritise the long-range implications and impact of decisions and actions that come to fruition after an extended time period (Lumpkin, Brigham, and Moss, 2010) – which has long been linked to successful corporate entrepreneuring (Fry, 1987; Zhara and Covin, 1995; Hitt, Nixon, Hoskisson, and Kochhar, 1999; Ling, Simsek, Lubatkin, and Veiga, 2008; Morris, Kuratko, and Covin, 2008). Fry (1987, p. 4); for example, said the intrapreneurs of the highly successful 3M: "[. . .] they want to change things, spend money, think long term [. . .]". An important area in which the top talent career model of changing positions every two to three years was viewed as undermining CE was in the development of deep, domain-specific business knowledge that was deemed essential in the identification and evaluation of entrepreneurial opportunities. This deep domain knowledge is a precondition to an 'entrepreneurial alertness' to changed conditions or to overlooked possibilities (Kirzner, 2009), and relates to not only technologies, but also industry characteristics and long-term relationships with, for example, customers:

> Because domain knowledge in Building Technologies doesn't get built in months, it takes years [. . . I'm] not so convinced about the model of [. . .] rotation [. . .] it is maybe fine from an individual's career point of view, but from a business point of view, not to have domain experts serving functions over time, and growing within a domain is a big loss for the organisation. [. . .]Building Technologies needs to hire more people from competition, and not so much from internal [. . .] found within Siemens [. . .] let's not take away the fact, that the more knowledgeable you are [. . .] you will actually be able to make more entrepreneurial decisions.
>
> [Keiko Safaia, Chief Marketing Officer BT]

Related, the internal rotations of the top talents also held consequences for the 'inward orientation' described in Chapter 4: "We breed this kind of person to be internally focussed, and then we expect them to be called an entrepreneur" [Michael Bosshard, Regional Manager for Korea in FS HQ]. Perceptions of the inward orientation among top talents were supported by the provenance of Siemens top talents. When Peter Löscher took over the Siemens CEO position, he requested an overview of the specific business process areas from which the top talents came. The data delivered drew attention to the quite famous formula of "11–6–3": with every 11 top talents coming from R&D, there are 6 from purchasing, and only 3 come from product management and sales.[1]

Overall and across all cases, periods of service of top executives in a specific position were found to vary significantly, with Siemens managers only staying for two to three years on average, whereas the leaders of the independent entities served for ten years and more. The significant entrepreneurial activity of the owners of Shinwha and iMetrex, who were also the long-term executives, was reflected by the high growth rates of their business and confirmed by interviewee feedback. Key staff members in R&D, manufacturing, and sales were found in the respective due diligence investigations as having already served for five and more years. Indeed, a majority of respondents advocated five-year periods on average, arguing that otherwise achievements could not be properly judged. Furthermore – and linked to the business domains of Building Technologies – it was brought forward that it would take years to build up the specific business domain knowledge. Thus, interviewees were not only asking for longer stays, but also for appointments of executive successors from within the respective industry environment, instead of promoting internal Siemens top talents coming from different industries. Nevertheless, only two respondents claimed an undoubted existence of a direct relation between length of service and delivered business results. Periods of service of ten years and more were generally seen as negative and leading to a standstill regarding new ventures within Siemens Fire Safety.

There are, inevitably, both pros and cons to shorter stays. For example, shorter stays may limit the possibility of identifying new business opportunities due to a lack of deep business domain knowledge needed for new combinations of knowledge. At the same time, however, shorter rotations may have the benefit of minimising blindness to new opportunities arising from not having experienced other business domains. Interestingly, interviewees saw benefit in exchanging managers primarily on the CxO level after three to five years, whereas at the level of middle management and experts longer stays were clearly seen as a required prerequisite for successfully identifying entrepreneurial opportunities. Even so, perhaps reflecting the entrepreneurial acumen of the owner-entrepreneurs of Shinwha and iMetrix, variation in personal inclinations towards entrepreneurial endeavours and the entrepreneurial capabilities of individuals was viewed as a more powerful determinant of entreprenerurial behaviour than were the years of service alone.

Performance measurement and career-making

Zahra and Covin (1995, p. 44) long ago observed that "CE should not be viewed as a short-term 'fix', but as a long-term strategy for achieving superior financial performance. [. . .] CE activities may take many years to fully pay off". The shorter stays were, however, tightly coupled with how performance is typically measured within the Building Technologies Division, with KPIs and planning cycles emphasising yearly (and quarterly) performance measures for business units, and annual performance measures for individuals. This inevitably impacted the pursuit of entrepreneurial mandates. Several interviewees proposed a significant expansion of the judgment periods:

> I really think that long-term orientation is one of the key aspects that we have lost over the years [. . .] If you define what long term is: [. . .] five years and above, and when it comes to that kind of planning, it is not particularly visible, I know that we do it, but it is not visible [. . .]
>
> [Management Development at Siemens Corporate Office]

> [. . .] we focus on the next year performance, short term performance, but [. . .] in order to create and find new business, we need a certain investment in a certain period, but without any activity [. . .] results, then I think, the working level, they don't like to invest their time for new businesses, because that [. . .] they measure their current performance – that is the conflict. Then the manager, the leader, should compensate that, because they [. . .] maybe through the target settings, they minimise the conflict, more invest for the new market, new business, long term [. . .]
>
> [SH Wong, Head of R&D and Manufacturing at FS Korea]

The short-term orientation was exacerbated by a career-making tendency that was seen as endemic among 'top talents'. This is hardly surprising: to join the 'top talent' programme is a declaration of the intent to climb the corporate hierarchy. Such career-making in the context of Siemens was not, however, seen as consistent with entrepreneurial endeavours, where the impact of decisions and actions often only come to fruition after an extended time period (Lumpkin et al., 2010):

> [I]f you have only career making people, [. . .] they are the wrong ones [. . .] trying to be an entrepreneur is stopped by those guys at any time. [. . . Y]ou must really shape the people into a different culture to really have this more entrepreneurial thing [. . .] and you don't need to hire people who want to make careers.
>
> [Robert Schmid, Head of Product Line within SP new setup]

> Most people are thinking about going up the ladder, rather than creating something as a real legacy for the business that they are managing right now. [. . .] I don't think the succession planning is very effective within Siemens, and I don't think that rewards entrepreneurship as well [. . . . T]here is not enough emphasis placed on creating and being entrepreneurial. This structure is backed by KPIs.
>
> [John Davis, CEO of SP new setup]

Indeed, 'career-makers' were seen as primarily entrepreneurial in the sense of managing their own personal advancement:

> [. . .] they only live for that, and whatever they do, and whatever actions they take, is just for supporting their career, they don't care at all about products, or people, or whatever; they just look for themselves, and if you have these kind of people, anyone want [. . .] or trying to be an entrepreneur is stopped by those guys at any time.
>
> [Robert Schmid, Head of Product Line within SP new setup]

This effect seems so widely spread that Keiko Safaia – after being only a few months in the company – stated:

> I think, the biggest gap I see is: there is too much room for expectation management. And this I see is a [. . .] failure in translating our ideas to reality, because it's not so much about how best we can exploit an opportunity. It's pretty much about: what is your perception, and how do I keep your perception in a framework that I can outperform, and then everybody is happy. [. . .] I find it quite surprising that we allow this.
>
> [Keiko Safaia, Chief Marketing Officer BT]

Employee cynicism

Related to "too much room for expectation management", the selection of the top talents was perceived to be too dependent on direct superiors, opening up the purposeful push of friends to create "rope teams". Indeed, it was perceived by many that belonging to a rope team was a prerequisite to be promoted into the top talent program, and further career steps were not seen as primarily based on delivered business performance. However, employees took these mechanisms somewhat for granted and as a commonly known "unwritten law", thus leaving it to the employee to either accept it or to leave the company. Not surprisingly, employee cynicism towards Siemens organisation or management was explicitly noted in interviews in the context of the top talent programme and respective employee promotions:

> People are quite cynical about people development, and therefore entrepreneurship.
>
> [John Davis, CEO of Security Products (SP) new setup]

Research on cynicism of employees towards their management and work environment has evolved in recent years (Bommer, Rich, and Rubin, 2005; Stanley, Meyer, and Topolnytsky, 2005; Urbany, 2005; Wu, Neubert, and Yi, 2007; Watt and Piotrowski, 2008). "Many employees are highly cynical about the effectiveness of management and view large, bureaucratic organisations with disdain and contempt" (Feldman, 2000, p. 1286). Cynicism is defined as "an attitude characterised by frustration, hopelessness, and disillusionment, as well as contempt toward and distrust of business organisations, executives, and other objects in the workplace" (Andersson, 1996, p. 1395). Some articles use popular Dilbert comics (Feldman, 2000) or even the metaphor of "dementors"[2] to visualise cynical management and other employees and their deeds (Denton and Campbell, 2009). Such organisational cynicism is seen as a complex attitude including affective, cognitive, and behavioural aspects caused by lost trust in the management and the organisation, the feeling of being treated unfairly, and frustrated expectations (Bommer et al., 2005; Watt and Piotrowski, 2008). Change situations have been found to cause higher levels of cynicism, and employees' cynicism has been found consistently to be negatively related to engagement[3] with the firm (Watt and Piotrowski, 2008), with higher levels of absenteeism, fluctuation, and number of labour grievances filed (Wanous, Reichers, and Austin, 2000). Employees with a disposition that results in low engagement towards the firm can hardly be expected to act as inspiring corporate entrepreneurs undertaking new ventures.[4] As a consequence, the corporate human resource office was instructed to start a re-evaluation of all Siemens top talents based on a standardised measurement and judgments to be carried out by independent experts unrelated to the respective business unit or division. These activities were started in January 2010 but had not yet emerged within the Building Technologies division at the time of our study.

Siemens Leadership Framework and entrepreneurial capabilities

Individual capabilities, also referred to here as competencies, are aggregates of the knowledge required to achieve a desired outcome, the skills to use that knowledge, and the personal characteristics needed to motivate the use of this knowledge and skills (Hayton and Kelly, 2006). The competencies of individual employees that they deploy in the pursuit of corporate entrepreneurship are fundamental to a company's ability to nurture and sustain innovation, corporate renewal, and new venture creation. For example, Hayton and Kelly (2006, p. 415) describe four key competencies for corporate entrepreneuring. An 'innovative competence' in CE requires an ability to identify new market, organisational, or technological opportunities, and is a function of domain-specific knowledge, cognitive ability, and creativity. Whereas more traditional task-oriented job-analytic tools are highly specific to a given job, and differences rather than commonalities across a job are identified, a competence-based approach instead emphasises the generic behaviours rather than the specific tasks and technologies involved. Similarly, while traditional forms of job analysis are based on a given job context, a competency-based approach is more linked to the organisational context. Hayton and Kelly (2006) thus argue that a competency-based approach to entrepreneuring is superior for a variety of reasons. Only the broad behavioural requirements for corporate entrepreneuring are knowable in advance; it is difficult to identify who in an organisation will identify new opportunities, and entrepreneurial activities are likely to occur erratically and infrequently and may thus be missed by traditional methods of job analysis. In effect, their argument points to the uncertainty inherent in explorative learning. The Siemens Leadership Framework to some extent attempted a competence- or capability-based approach, but with poor support for corporate entrepreneuring.

Capability judgements

To define the required set of employee capabilities as well as current levels of individual capabilities, Siemens used the Siemens Leadership Framework.[5] This framework outlined, primarily, nine specific capabilities used for job reference profile definitions and respective measurements – or judgments – of candidates and employees: Business Results Orientation, Strategic-Innovative Orientation, Customer Orientation, Change Management, Collaboration and Influencing, Intercultural Sensitivity, Leadership, Team Development, and Value Orientation. The latest update of the framework at the time of our study was introduced in March 2010. It reduced the number of capability dimensions from eighteen to nine, and elaborated seven levels of expertise per capability in detailed textual descriptions. However, none of the terms 'entrepreneurship', 'intrapreneurship', 'venturing', or 'uncertainty' can be found in the extensive description, and 'risk' appears primarily in the context of controlling risk.

Based on the Siemens Leadership Framework dimensions, reference profiles of typical jobs were defined and introduced, as illustrated in Figure 6.1. The seven levels of capability maturity were, unfortunately, primarily linked with the hierarchical position of the job within the company. Thus, a divisional CEO position ends up with capability levels of four to five, whereas senior consultants (as an example of low-ranked employees) only reach levels of two for all capabilities

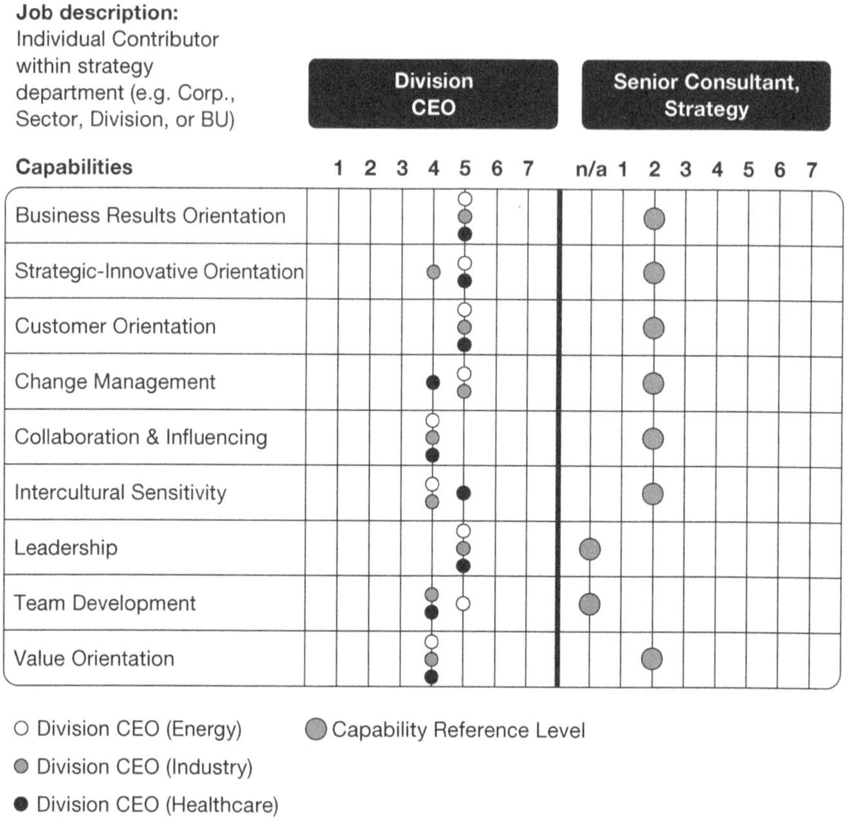

Figure 6.1 Indicative capability reference profiles

(and leadership and team development capabilities are even declared as "non-applicable"). Internal rumours reported levels five to six for sector CEOs, and six to seven for the overall CEO, but respective profiles were never disclosed. The initial capability ranking of employees was completed by the end of 2010, with these target definitions linking capabilities to levels in organisational hierarchy. Top management instructed the line management to do judgements of the employees in such a way that the average result was "compliant" with these predefined values. Massive protests ensued, with employees objecting to the judgements made about them. Employees saw these judgments as having little to do with their real capabilities, and much to do with predefined results. The reference profiles were thus withdrawn and completely deleted from the Siemens intranet, and any capability judgments were declared voluntary for employees in 2010 and 2011.

Of course, in a process-driven organisation where people independence is seen as a measure of process maturity (see Chapter 4), individual capabilities may be more readily disregarded. In our study, two respondents advocated the reduction of people dependence in corporate entrepreneuring by good processes, allowing the short-term exchange of employees without impairing the firm's performance. This perception – which might well be applicable in routine jobs on the business exploitation side – was strongly rejected by most. If processes cannot be devised to make CE people independent, selection criteria based on individual capabilities take on elevated importance:

> [. . .] no matter how you change this backwards and forwards, people are the key factor [. . .], because there is no machine that can invent something new. [. . .] Even though there might be a process to do so, without the right people living those processes, you have no chance for future success.
>
> [Management Development at Siemens Corporate Office]

The recruitment and selection of new employees was based on job descriptions that refer to more generic job profiles built from 'required capabilities', as defined along the dimensions given in the Siemens Leadership Framework. By adding entrepreneurial capabilities to these definitions, such selection criteria could be applied to job descriptions – and thus employee selection – without introducing new procedures or adding to organisational complexity. The proposed changes in the top talent selection process described here – namely, the deployment of independent experts to avoid 'rope team' effects, and the placing of more emphasis on promoting candidates from sales and product management instead of R&D – should also provide support for a shift towards more entrepreneurial capabilities within Siemens Fire Safety.

In addition to recruitment and selection, training and development plays a vital role in the development of entrepreneurial capabilities of individuals. Siemens enjoys highly developed internal education structures, offering a vast set of training opportunities that draw on internal and external teachers. However, at the time of our study entrepreneurship was only addressed at a short session of the two-day branch manager training. There was clearly scope for further sessions that broach entrepreneurial thinking to be added to existing training for project managers, product management, sales forces, and so on.

Managerial support, sponsoring CE, and decisiveness

The case study findings revealed the importance of managerial support for entrepreneurial endeavours. The SMART project was perceived in interviewee responses as a successful and positive example of explicit top management support, whereas Siemens entities in general seem to lack such backing. The relevance of such support for fostering entrepreneurial behaviour has been confirmed by several previous studies (Fry, 1987; Kuratko et al., 1990; Antoncic and Hisrich, 2001; Menzel, Aaltio, and Ulijin, 2007), and is seen by some authors as one of the "main five activities"[6] from a HRM perspective (Hornsby, Kuratko, and Montango, 1999; Hayton, 2005; Kuratko, Hornsby, and Bishop, 2005a, 2005b; Marvel, Griffin, Hebda, and Vojak, 2007). Coaching has been identified as a key ingredient: "[. . .] both would-be and active intrapreneurs need advocates. These are key stakeholders – not necessarily direct superiors – who support intrapreneurs with their broad experience in conducting projects, corporate politics, and professional knowledge. Their main task should thus be coaching the intrapreneur" (Menzel et al., 2007, p. 741). "Managing" the entrepreneurial aspirations of subordinates in the sense of controlling has not been confirmed as a useful concept in the well-known 3M intrapreneurship example: "Be sure management sponsors the concept. [. . .] Give intrapreneurs freedom: a lot of rope. Sponsor, do not manage their program" (Fry, 1987, p. 9). Employee development through, for example, coaching was also seen as desirable. In the Siemens context, formal coaching (or mentoring) of employees only exists for 'top talents'. Since the top talent programme has high visibility, and initiatives within it have a signalling effect to all employees, the inclusion of coaching for entrepreneurial ideas and subsequent endeavours in the top talent career concept could be a significant cornerstone for establishing such a culture. Additionally, coaching for entrepreneurial ideas of employees and related behaviours could be linked to the expansion of the Siemens capability model (proposed in 'Capability judgements').

Hayton and Kelley (2006) too identified sponsoring as an important competence for fostering corporate entrepreneurship. Sponsoring involves helping entrepreneurs gain access to resources they need to pursue opportunities identified and providing advice and guidance. While a 'champion' identifies and selects projects deserving support, sponsors ensure the necessary resource availability. Hayton and Kelly (2006) argue that executive sponsors bridge the technological innovator and the firm's owner/founders. Importantly, sponsors create the context in which the exploitation of an opportunity is possible, and thereby act as the bridge between exploration and exploitation.

The key characteristics underlying a sponsoring competence for CE include deep business and technological knowledge that allows the "business insight necessary for making risky or even uncertain investments" (discussed previously) and "a willingness to accept risk" (see later on), as well as "transformational leadership" and "tenacity" (Hayton and Kelly, 2006, p. 418). Our findings suggest, however, that *decisiveness* is also a central ingredient. In Chapter 5 a strong capability-oriented theme that emerged from our data collection and analysis was the importance of 'decisiveness'. The need for decisiveness – that is, taking decisions frequently and in a short time frame – is evident in studies of individual entrepreneurs (Miner, 1997, 2000; Hisrich, Langan-Fox, and Grant, 2007). As Floyd and Woolridge (1999) observe, speed, flexibility, and decisiveness are central to entrepreneurship. Yet decisiveness does not feature as an important ingredient in the corporate entrepreneurship literature. Our findings suggest, however, that it is an important (yet unrecognised) characteristic underlying the 'competence in sponsoring CE' identified by Hayton and Kelly (2006).

Decisiveness does not necessarily imply a greater tolerance for risk and uncertainty. On the contrary, Eisenhardt (1989) found that fast decision-making was associated with more information, rather than less, and more information can serve to either increase or decrease perceptions of calculable risk or genuine uncertainty. That is, 'risk tolerance' is not a conceptual substitute for decisiveness. A willingness to make fast decisions often can also signal confidence on the part of the executive. Confidence (even over-confidence) may in turn attract the support and commitment of others (Hayward, Forster, Saravathy, and Fredrickson, 2010). Hence, executive sponsors who are decisive are more likely to attract support and resources for a new venture, even where they do not have direct authority over those resources. Of course, decisiveness may not always result in the pursuit of a new venture, but could also lead to a withdrawal of sponsorship and thereby release resources to pursue alternative opportunities. Either way, a decision made in a timely manner about whether or not to sponsor a new venture is arguably the foundation stone in the bridge between exploration and exploitation. That is, decisiveness is conceptually distinct from a tolerance for risk or uncertainty, and an essential characteristic underpinning a competence in sponsoring CE.

From a human resource management perspective, it was proposed within Siemens that higher levels of decisiveness could be achieved by appropriate people selection and a changed attitude in management:

> [I]n the recruiting process: to have more people who really are [. . .] willing to make this decision and have the capabilities to do it. And at the end, I mean [. . .] this cultural change, we can as well try to influence the line management in order to go more in this direction [. . .] with all the limits HR has. I think we could as well [. . .] from our daily business, or daily behaviour, support the line management on saying: OK, let's try [. . .] let's do the decision, we are sure, we know it [. . .] and bring this attitude into the organisation.
>
> [Hans Meier, Global Head of FS Human Resources]

A closely linked aspect – seen as relevant by six respondents in the case studies, but perceived as far from being satisfactorily done at the time of our study – is a strengthened empowerment of entrepreneurially minded employees through having more responsibility, taking ownership, and being accountable for actions and outcomes. As Mintzberg (1996, p. 633) observed, "What empowerment really means is stopping the disempowering of people. But that just brings us back to hierarchy, because hierarchy is precisely what empowerment reinforces". That is, one is only *granted* decision rights and autonomy because a hierarchy exists. To avoid this effect, Mintzberg proposed to see – and run – the firm like a beehive: the queen (the top manager) should just "exude a chemical substance that holds the system together" (providing primarily the spirit or vision of the firm), while "worker bees are adults, so to speak, who know exactly what they have to do". In the Siemens context of our study, this would require a dramatic step back from the tight controls and processes focussed on how things are done at the time of our study, supporting more decisiveness in setting goals, clearer priorities and thus focus, and significantly enlarged competences of those responsible for achieving these goals. Such a change would also require significantly higher levels of trust for employees than perceived to exist – a development which will only take place over a long period of time. Nevertheless, people empowerment based on clear decisions on goals and respective appointments of goal owners – in fact, a strengthened application of the well-known concept of management by objectives – as well as ensuring appropriate competencies are in place is a potential activity to foster entrepreneurship behaviour. The branch certifications based on subsidiary and employee competencies described in Chapter 5 is a move in this direction at the unit and individual level.

Knowledge exploration and exploitation

HRM takes on strategic significance by supporting the "accretion, coordination and exploitation of knowledge" within firms in a process Chadwick and Dabu (2009, p. 254) called 'managerial entrepreneurship'. The generation of entrepreneurial rents requires complex and idiosyncratic coordination and deployment mechanisms concerning the generation and exploitation of knowledge held by the unique community of actors comprising the firm. A central challenge here is how to respond to apparent needs for organisational ambidexterity – that is, the simultaneous exploration and exploitation of entrepreneurial opportunity, as previously discussed – and the contribution of human resource management to resolving this dilemma.

Roles and ambidexterity

In the absence of comparable process definition within Siemens, interview participants were introduced to the process model of entrepreneurial opportunity recognition and exploitation derived from literature and based somewhat on a 'practitioner perspective', as discussed in Chapter 1 and depicted in the entrepreneurial process of Figure 1.1. Reflecting on this model, ambidexterity management – exploiting established business in parallel to new business exploration activities – was seen by respondents to be one of the main challenges to entrepreneurial activity:

> I think that's [. . .] especially where we need entrepreneurs to really balance this trade-off.
>
> [Ralf Dunkel, Global Project Lead SMART Initiative]

A majority interpreted this task as a general management activity leading primarily to budget planning, and product managers were seen as having to live with daily ambidexterity conflicts:

> I think PM [product management] is a typical job to experience these conflicts.
>
> [Yao Wang, Head of Product Management at FS China]

Table 6.1 summarises respondents' views on the challenges related to the pursuit of ambidexterity and possible solutions within Siemens Fire Safety. Notably, the limitations in exploration activities were seen less in the amount of resources (reflecting given budgets) than in the capabilities of the employees – a view which was (perhaps unsurprisingly) most popular among headquarters executives. A majority of interviewees preferred a separation of people doing exploration and evaluation:

> [. . .] have dedicated resources, at least for a start-up, if you have a new business idea, put people together [. . .] in best: a very diverse group, with different business backgrounds, different histories, different knowledge; and let them work out the strategy, the concept, in a kind of project [. . .] or [a] competence centre approach. And once you have achieved the first level of maturity, you should bring it back into the normal organization.
>
> [Peter Mueller, CEO BT FS]

Benner and Tushman (2015) argue that structural separation of exploratory efforts from exploitative efforts is crucial to buffering experimental activity from inertial efficiency requirements of exploitation. When the exploratory efforts achieve sufficient customer and strategic legitimacy, they are less susceptible to being destroyed by the corporate immune system and can be brought back into the main organisation. Gibson and Birkinshaw (2004) suggest that contextual ambidexterity may take the place of structural ambidexterity with, for example, employees being given the discretion to decide how they divide their time between exploration and exploitation. Within Siemens, even if it was acknowledged by respondents that there could be mutual benefits of having some people doing both activities, a continuation of structural separation (in roles, if not separate subunits) was justified as creating clear priorities for the employees:

> [. . .] if one person has to do both, he has to set priorities [. . .] I assume both of the businesses are not part time jobs, so you end up with a 200 per cent job, or, you have to set priorities, which means one [job] is behind the other one – but if you want to drive both [jobs] successfully, you need full attention.
>
> [Paul Amstutz, Regional Coordinator for Korea and China]

At the time the field research took place, a separate team existed only for technology innovation at Fire Safety, and the investigation of potential new endeavours was set up as an ad hoc project not following defined processes. Indeed, the only such endeavour was the Intelligent Response project, tasked with identifying additional business opportunities in mass notification applications. On the level of the worldwide Building Technologies organisation, at the end of 2009 Keiko Safaia, as the new Chief Marketing Officer, started specific working groups in the fields of energy efficiencies, safety and security to address new business opportunities. This build-up of business domain specific working

Table 6.1 Perceived challenges in achieving ambidexterity

		Shinwha – FS KR	*SMART*	*SP*	*Siemens in general*
CEO / CFO / PL	**in headquarters**		RD 1 entrepreneurs are the balancers of the trade-off of exploration – exploitation 2 risk-averse German culture is limiting on the side of exploration 3 we could do more on exploration side resource-wise 4 clear impact of the financial crisis to the budget cuts on the exploration side	KS 1 “I don’t think you have manager who are equally good in both.” 2 separate operational excellence via a COO etc. 3 too few resources on exploration side due to short term goals	PM 1 there is a tendency to hide behind what you are used to do, and continuing, because there is some uncertainty of doing something different → hinders the organisation to be faster in establishing and exploiting new businesses 2 it needs different people with different knowledge for exploration / exploitation; set up projects, or centre of competences for exploration 3 we have to improve and faster adapt the competences in exploration 4 SP too small resources, FS: investing takes place despite the crisis HM 1 previous Cerberus setup with having the same people and organisation doing all was not successful 2 another approach in a former company – with completely separated teams – did not work either

					3 you need some oddballs upfront to have new ideas out side the box – but then come down to reality to have any result in the end 4 some people – willing and capable of – can work over the whole process 5 real innovation, business innovation is missing today, we are focussed on incremental technical innovation 6 I doubt if we have the right entrepreneurial climate today
	in entities	HWK 1 FS KR is in restructuring due to missing profit, we are short term oriented now 2 one key aspect is to switch from make to buy – frees up resources and improves profitability → go for exploration again 3 mutual doing of exploration and exploitation can only take place as far as the knowledge and experience is there	KH 1 clear target conflict 2 keep the things separate (own rooms etc.) for people doing exploration 3 be aware of the risks of cannibalizing the own existing business → get over internal resistance to do that, otherwise competition will cannibalize you!	JD 1 there are many mutual benefits: apply customer feedbacks, have shared knowledge, mutual learning 2 exploring activities cannot just be "hung at the end of an employee's job description"	

(*Continued*)

Table 6.1 (Continued)

		Shinwha – FS KR	*SMART*	*SP*	*Siemens in general*
		4 existing people are just repeating what they have already done -> we need to inject new ideas, and partially replace managers 5 amount of resources for exploration is OK, quality is not -> capabilities, going for new business, for service business, even English skills	4 requires more empowerment on the side of exploration 5 limitations on exploration side is given by the quality of people, and decisiveness of the management. . .	3 doing significant exploring is more a question of clear goals and priorities than the absolute level of resources 4 running the exploitation properly – especially by having good processes – is an important prerequisite to go for successful exploration	
Middle management	**in headquarters**	MB 1 there should be no handover. The idea should be exploited by the same people 2 ambidexterity problems –caused by HQ - are avoided in the countries by not revealing the activities (stealth operations)	PA 1 on the recognition side we have difficulty in understanding the customer, especially in M3 which is new for us 2 in M3, you need local people who understand local needs, local customers 3 exploration and exploitation cannot be done by the same people, because a. they will get lost in setting priorities	CC 1 "on a level of a BU or segment leader, [entrepreneurs] would probably die or suffocate in this environment, because I don't think the framework is given to support that kind of behaviour."	SA 1 has to be split by capabilities 2 big limitation in missing exchange of knowledge throughout the whole Siemens 3 exploration limited by the (old) Siemens culture – not really feeling as innovators, pioneers 4 entrepreneurs have also to match with the respective national cultures

		3 many new opportunities are coming from customers in the regional companies → they will never reach HQ (see 2) – we have a significant regional companies-HQ problem here 4 discussions with HQ are avoided by regional companies – too slow, too hindering 5 HQ does not recognize all the creativity existing in the regional companies 6 to overcome this: “system house approach as proposed by Milde	b. you need different people capabilities 4 amount of resources is OK, it is more about setting the right priorities 5 limitation is in the organisation set-up and the way Siemens is managed	2 SP: missing decisions / priorities between exploration and exploitation activities 3 SP: key issues especially in the evaluation/ decision phase – no decisions 4 there can be one overall manager, but you need specific groups working on the issues 5 mutual benefit is knowledge exchange, but separation has to take place in the broad work	

(*Continued*)

Table 6.1 (Continued)

		Shinwha – FS KR	*SMART*	*SP*	*Siemens in general*
	in entities	SHW 1 short term orientation – due to performance measuring, bonus, incentives – clearly limits exploration → no investment in long term activities, including customer relationships ! 2 risk aversion clearly limits exploration 3 missing knowledge about products and customers limits the recognition of new opportunities	YW 1 PM is typical job to experience these conflicts; exploitation problems – like quality leaks – are always priority one and will stop the exploration tasks 2 same management doing both is OK, same resources underneath is a problem → one person cannot do both, working with priorities does not really work 3 we do not have enough resources for exploration at the moment (FS China scope) 4 even on a technology side we do not have enough activities today – even from HQ side	JT 1 this conflict clearly exists 2 I would see some think tank upfront for exploration. But you have to have people there who are not just coming from university, who have real experience 3 for disruptive innovation, think even of separate start-ups like Intel is doing – and then integrate if it gets successful 4 smaller innovation steps can be done by existing own people RS 1 huge struggle with getting the resources on the exploration side 2 missing support on the exploration side from the established way of setting yearly targets, and measure target fulfilment 3 room for exploitation tremendously depends on the prosperity of you running the business 4 doing exploitation and exploration with the same people puts them out of their "comfort zone" 5 BT overall: enough resources for exploration, but not focussed enough, no convincing results 6 SP: very tight resources currently	

groups at Building Technologies level from the end of 2009 involved longer serving experts and intrapreneurs (some of them already worked for the previously independent companies now forming the Building Technologies entity),[7] who met regularly to propel new business ventures, and in the process generated trust and mutual goals. This was akin to the building of entrepreneurial 'clans' throughout the MNE to foster opportunity exploration (Mahnke, Venzin, and Zahra, 2007). Clans depend, however, on continuing communication and close relations among their members (Alvarez and Barney, 2005). Here again the Siemens career model of changing positions within two to three years undermines the persistence of clans over time. On the positive side, tradition as one of the informal requirements in clan constructs (Ouchi, 1980) was getting significantly higher attention in recent years at Building Technologies, as well as in the overall company, by top management. As described in Chapter 3, Fire Safety reintroduced in 2008 the name "Cerberus" as the new brand name for all product channel offerings worldwide, and since early 2010 Siemens top executives regularly cited the pioneering founders of Siemens and their activities in internal communications: so some preconditions were emerging to foster such a 'clan type' approach towards easing new opportunity recognition, although other impediments persisted.

Nonetheless, here again the problem of having tasks from exploitation and exploration in parallel occurred:

> I think we are making some progress in this approach of creating working groups. But even the working groups [. . .] also have to be staffed with some more commitment, [. . .] you need some real work on these topics, to go deep dive, or do some research, analysis about options, and come up with value proposals, because you can't do it part time, so the project taken now in the working group to have two people, two or three people coming to a dedicated full time [. . .] for a few weeks, to come up with more details on a certain topic. And we have to look on our ideas a little more, to see how we can have a structure, have a process where we get some dedication into this [. . .]
>
> [Keiko Safaia, Chief Marketing Officer BT]

Interestingly, this statement of Keiko Safaia could be seen as a clear contradiction to his disapproval of having processes guiding entrepreneurial activity, as stated earlier (Chapter 4). The reality of suffering from the effects of priority conflicts created by the ambidextrous situation of opportunity exploration and exploration in parallel, along with the enduring process orientation within Siemens perhaps made him call for a respective process definition to "get dedication to" the exploration tasks.

'Slack' in human resources

To support innovative activities and firm renewal, and to absorb any potential failures of such endeavours, a degree of organisational slack is often required

(Rosner, 1968; Bourgeois III, 1981; Sharfman, Wolf, Chase, and Tansik, 1988; Nohria and Gulati, 1995; Tan and Peng, 2003; Herold, Jayaraman, and Narayanasamy, 2006). Such slack constitutes "the pool of resources in an organisation that is in excess of the minimum necessary to produce a given level of organisational output" (Nohria and Gulati, 1996, p. 1246). By assigning defined roles to people, such resource spending is explicitly stipulated. As part of these 'budgeted' slack resources, business developers, product portfolio managers, or the members of the technical innovation team can explore new businesses as defined by their job descriptions.

The existence of organisational slack within Fire Safety was hard to identify, since a classical approach of allowing all employees to apply a certain ratio of working time for thinking about potential new businesses – like 15 per cent at 3M, or 20 per cent at Wella (Menzel et al., 2007) – does not exist in Siemens. There was also no granted 'patient money' (Pinchot, 1985) at the potential intrapreneurs' disposal to support their endeavours. Since Siemens is primarily focussed on technical innovations, Siemens management measures investments into innovation by the ratio of the R&D spending to the total turnover, and the number of (mainly technical) patents filed each year. In 2009, for example, Siemens spent €3.9 billion (5.1 per cent of turnover) on R&D and held 56,000 active patents (ranked #2 in Europe, and #12 in US).[8] There are significant amounts invested in these innovation endeavours already, and so it is perhaps unrealistic to introduce a general ratio of slack resources for all employees of the firm, due to the significant additional cost. Indeed, the case findings overall do not indicate a general shortage in resources, including human resources, as a main obstacle to entrepreneurial behaviour – at least in innovation. Furthermore, several studies confirm the relationship of slack and resulting firm performance as curvilinear: a certain amount of slack resources creates an optimum resulting performance via created innovation and firm renewal, whereas no, or even too much, slack provides weaker results (Bourgeois III, 1981; Sharfman et al., 1988; Nohria and Gulati, 1995; Tan and Peng, 2003; Herold, Jayaraman, and Narayanaswamy, 2006).

Nevertheless, those interviewed advocated that free time to think about new external opportunities could be granted specifically in relation to the function and length of service of employees (implying a correlation between the amount of domain knowledge gained and periods of service), with these options added to concrete job descriptions and yearly targets. In addition, Siemens grants three sabbatical days per year for middle to upper management (i.e. "Funktionsstufen", residing at functional levels 1–5) to be used for training purposes related to one's current position. These sabbatical days could be used for entrepreneurial activities within the firm or related training. The strongly process-oriented culture of Siemens emphasises compliance to guidelines and rules, thereby granting would-be intrapreneurs little freedom when walking the "fine line between clever resourcefulness and outright rule breaking" (Kuratko and Goldsby, 2004, p. 13). However, such a defined and structured approach of providing resources would be consistent with this process orientation, while still better at fostering possibilities for individual discretion in entrepreneurial behaviour.

Tolerance for risk

The pursuit of new ventures, firm renewal, or subsidiary mandate extensions inevitably involves some degree of risk. Indeed, a willingness to bear risk was seen by many respondents as a core attribute of entrepreneurial behaviour, as described in Chapter 3 and captured in the thoughts of the regional coordinator for Korea and China in Fire Safety R&D (HQ) when reflecting on the nature of entrepreneurship:

> Clear business responsibility, to have the freedom to take risks – allowed to take risks, and forced to take risks, and to make decisions. In the end, it is also – from the commercial [aspect] – P&L [profit and loss] responsibility.

However, several respondents observed a dominant "culture of taking zero risk" in the investigated Siemens entities:

> I think, to be recognised that it is OK to take a risk is important, is very, very important [. . . but] the current recognition is for zero risk! Nobody is motivated to give you a new idea, because there is always a risk. [. . .I]f you say: I have taken a risk – it's a bad thing in Siemens! [. . .] So if you are the leader in a business unit, at the moment the culture is: not to show that you taking risk!
> [Michael Bosshard, Regional Manager for Korea in FS HQ]

> I don't think that there are enough [. . .] what shall I say [. . .] the culture of bringing to table topics which will give longer term value and taking risks, or taking responsibility for bringing such [. . .] investing in such areas, this needs to come.
> [Keiko Safaia, Chief Marketing Officer BT]

Risk avoidance was especially seen as linked to 'career-making' behaviours described previously and a desire to not endanger one's own career by endeavours that may fail. The short stays in Siemens top talent career model was, somewhat cynically, seen to foster risk aversion, such that any failure would not become apparent until after the next promotion was secured and one had already left the failing venture. In turn, such risk-averse behaviour was reinforced by a perceived lack of forgiveness for such 'failures' and little expectation of receiving significant recognition for success (discussed below):

> [W]e lack the culture of trial and error, and we don't want to get punished for doing something wrong, and [. . .] rather following the rules than trying something new; and entrepreneurial: try something, take the risk.
> [Jan Traber, Integration Manager iMetrex]

Low levels of risk taking in the researched Siemens entities were seen by interviewees as directly related to the still dominant role of German managers, again fostered by the top talent career concept. It was also claimed that the appointment of more executives coming from the specific region would represent a much better embedding of the firm in the local culture and language and thereby foster local entrepreneurship. Looking at the formerly independent and entrepreneurial Shinwha and iMetrex entities, both companies were dominated by the respective Korean and Indian culture, having almost 100 per cent domestic staff (i.e. a polycentric staffing approach). Low tolerance for risk does not appear attributable to cultural diversity per se, but was attributed more so to a specific cultural group:

> [. . .] you would find more risk takers in other cultures than in Germany [. . .] The German culture per definition is not particularly risk taking.
> [Sandra Amrein, Management Development at Siemens Corporate Office]

> I think, in terms of risk taking, German people are typically quite risk-aware, so [. . .] also we at Siemens have certainly a tendency to more focus on the short term things, on the existing things, other people are much more open to take risks, and they are also willing to invest at them [. . .]
> [Ralf Dunkel, Global Project Lead SMART Initiative]

The efforts in strengthening diversity at Siemens in recent years were not reflected in interview feedback as having been successful, and most key executive positions at Building Technologies were still held by German nationals. As a contrast, middle management in the regions – typically representing local nationalities – was seen as having entrepreneurial drive but currently being hindered in pursuing such endeavours:

> [. . .] if given the opportunity, they were able to exercise some entrepreneurial spirit. It means us taking a risk, it means us being willing to take risks in certain regions, and accepting that entrepreneurial activity generally means that one in however many ideas really flies, and a number of them fail, and not persecuting people for failure. [. . .] Because at the moment we have a tendency to say: "I told you so", rather than say: "at least we tried" [. . .A]t the moment, there is nothing there that gives the people the opportunity to invest in an idea [. . .]
> [Michael Bosshard, Regional Manager for Korea]

Menzel and colleagues (2007) argue that top management must encourage successful intrapreneurship by rewarding engineers for intrapreneurial action, irrespective of a possible failure, using the slogan *Never a shot, always a miss.* Forgiveness and even freedom to fail was cited early on as a key ingredient of a successful entrepreneurial culture (e.g. Hisrich and Peters, 1986; Fry, 1987), and its importance has been confirmed by more recent studies (Hornsby, Kuratko, and Zahra, 2002; Shepherd, Covin, and Kuratko, 2009). To see more entrepreneurial activity, Michael Bosshard (Regional Manager for Korea in FS HQ) simply proposed: "[. . .] remove the penalties for failed attempts at being entrepreneurial".

However, there seem to be fundamental and systematic mechanisms leading to a higher risk aversion in established and large firms when compared to start-ups and small companies led by the owners:

> [T]he people who are most impacted by the risk [in small companies], are very close to the risk itself, and therefore you know, whether you can cut the losses, and move into a different direction, to gain time. Whereas in a large organisation, this is fundamentally not possible, because the man impaired by the risk is not even seen, and therefore everybody has to justify to another layer, and therefore the time taken to really come up to a decision, that, yeah, we made up a wrong choice, in a particular technology, or a particular hardware architecture, or a particular approach, to re-change, to redefine a course, can really be hard [. . .]
>
> [Keiko Safaia, Chief Marketing Officer BT]

So, the former Shinwha and iMetrex entities represented small and independent companies with the owners judging and taking the risks of entrepreneurial endeavours directly. Proposed new businesses were reported to be typically discussed directly with the owners as the acting key executives. In contrast, the many layers of agents in Siemens entities to whom new entrepreneurial ideas must be justified – with the principal (or owner) not being visible at all – significantly changes the environment for taking risks or being risk averse. Furthermore, the complexity of involved organisations, processes, and especially technology (including shared product platforms and architectures) can make it more difficult or time consuming to change direction.

In recommending how to overcome excessive risk aversion hampering entrepreneurial behaviour, the specific firm context needs due consideration. The large MNE in itself represents a certain culture, defined by Hofstede as being entirely distinct from national cultures, since "[. . .] organisational cultures are the collective programming of the mind that distinguishes the members of one organisation from another" (2001, p. 391). The widespread culture at Siemens of seeing business risk expositions as something negative coincides with reported low levels of failure forgiveness, leading to career-making primarily based on short-term goal achievements by the exploitation of established business and personal 'zero-failure tracks'. On an individual level "[. . .] the only certain thing about behaviour leading to CE is the need on the part of the individual to accept risk and uncertainty" (Hayton, 2005, p. 37). Hayton's review of empirical studies of HRM activities towards fostering CE in established firms leads to specific recommendations: the human resource management (HRM) function should encourage risk taking and the acceptance of failures. However, the proposition to primarily achieve that by fostering "intra- and inter-organisational relationships" among employees seems of less direct relevance in the Siemens context. The HR function was quite a lean organisation at the time of our study, strongly focussed on the core HRM tasks (e.g. employee recruitment, target setting mechanisms, training, benefits and compensation, leave management, and legal aspects of employment) and not involved in business decision processes or activities such as the setup of focus groups and best practice sharing.

More convincing in the Siemens context is the proposal of Peris-Ortiz to apply "personnel selection and control" (2009, p. 475). Within Siemens, HRM is always involved in the selection of new employees and acts as the owner of the Siemens Leadership Framework (described previously). To foster entrepreneurship, capabilities could be reworked towards explicit mentioning of new business venturing and renewal and a respective mapping of required capabilities undertaken. Taking account of each individuals' actual capabilities rather than predefining individuals' capabilities top down in accord with their position and role would help to avoid a repeat of the massive demotivation of employees resulting from an earlier attempt at deploying the Siemens Leadership Framework and related capability profiles. Beyond the formal HRM systems, however, there is tremendous scope for fostering entrepreneurial behaviour and appropriate levels of risk taking through, for example, executives developing a competence in sponsoring CE (Hayton and Kelly, 2006), described previously.

Rewards and recognition

The entrepreneurship literature has long identified rewards and incentive systems as a critical dimension of environments that foster corporate entrepreneurship, including the KPI systems that were applied for calculating the rewards granted (Durand, 1974; Durand and Shea, 1974; Fry, 1987; Brazeal, 1993; Chandler, Keller, and Lyon, 2000; Shane, Locke, and Collins, 2003; Hayton, 2005; Locke and Baum, 2007; Menzel et al., 2007; Monsen, Patzelt, and Saxton, 2010; de Villiers-Scheepers, 2012): "[R]eward is one part of motivation" [Jan Traber, Integration Manager iMetrex]. The relevance of incentive systems in shaping entrepreneurial behaviour in the Siemens organisation was confirmed by several respondents as consistent with Siemens' broader culture:

> Target setting, incentives [. . .] is for me still [. . .] we are all humans, and if we have a smart system pushing that for everybody, every individual, I am pretty sure this helps a lot. [. . .I]f I am looking at the Siemens' [. . .] environment here, it is the only way of really bringing it forward, because everything works over rewards and [. . .] incentives.
>
> [Robert Schmid, Head of Product Line within SP new setup]

There was seen to be a certain 'justice' in monetary rewards:

> If I have come up with a new idea, the senior executives in this business have got a bonus from it because it has made us more money, then it is only fair that those who have worked on developing that idea are rewarded.
>
> [Michael Bosshard, Regional Manager for Korea in FS HQ]

Nonetheless, the effect of financial incentives on motivating appropriate entrepreneuring is not straightforward. For example, Monsen et al. (2010) propose that a higher probability of a new venture's success enhances the motivating effect of financial incentives (e.g. profit sharing, bonuses, or promotions leading to higher salaries), whereas higher pay risk, job risk, and greater work effort required diminishes this effect. In a huge enterprise like Siemens, only insignificant stakes of the firm could be provided to all the potential corporate entrepreneurs, which would hardly create noticeable financial rewards out of the success of a specific entrepreneurial endeavour. Looking for implementations that are also feasible for lower management ranks, experts, and 'normal' employees, it comes down to established incentive mechanisms: the dependence of the payout of a certain amount of the planned total yearly compensation on achieving predefined goals. Based on his analysis of related empirical studies, Hayton (2005) advocated performance evaluations and incentives to promote risk-taking behaviours necessary to foster new corporate venture activities, but saw these as more relevant where there is a high degree of technical innovation and environmental complexity, and during rather early stages in business life-cycles (thus representing higher levels of risk and uncertainty). Measuring Siemens AG against these dimensions, environmental complexity and a high-tech innovation environment can be seen as given, whereas many stages in life-cycles exist in parallel for all the different businesses involved. Since an incentive system already exists in Siemens for all employees,[9] the challenge perhaps lies more in a dexterous definition of respective entrepreneurial goals and rewarding schemes than the 'technical' implementation of such a process.

In prior studies, non-financial rewards such as achievement recognition by praise and granting certificates are found equally important to supporting an entrepreneurial culture (Block and Ornati, 1987; Sykes, 1992; Brazeal, 1993; Hornsby et al., 1999; Chandler et al., 2000; Hayton, 2005). Recognition signals the importance of entrepreneurial values to the organisation, creates legitimacy for such endeavours and those involved (Hayton, 2005), and increases resulting job satisfaction (Kuratko et al., 2005a). Indeed, extrinsic rewards such as financial incentives may "inhibit creativity by limiting the benefit of its intrinsic rewards" (Hayton, 2005, p. 37). There was a strong sense among Siemens' respondents that financial incentives could complement but not *substitute* for intrinsic motivation, or compensate for a lack thereof, and significant importance was placed on a broader and somewhat public recognition of achievement within the Siemens organisation:

> To be part of a successful team, I would expect this is already motivation enough [. . .] of course, at the end it is always a bit about the money, but [. . .] I am not coming because of [that] [. . .] intrinsic motivation; that is mandatory.
>
> [PM, Regional Coordinator for Korea and China]

> I think: recognition before reward! [. . .] [M]ake sure that our management sees that there is personal recognition for this kind of thinking. [. . .] I think the message, the benefit is more significant to the rest of the organisation, to see that the guys who worked on the idea were rewarded [. . .] is more motivation of the rest to the organisation.
>
> [Michael Bosshard, Regional Manager for Korea in FS HQ]

On the level of Siemens-wide initiatives, neither the Top+ awards nor the "3i" initiative (described in Chapter 3) were viewed by respondents as especially fostering entrepreneurial activity. However, Top+ awards were cited as a good mechanism to show a broad audience that

> [. . .] a team has really made a difference that can be measured, and they are then afterwards put up on stage, and they get a reward, and they are even in newsletters and things like that, [. . .] it is not just a creative idea, it's gonna go through the whole chain, [. . .] it is approved to be successful.
>
> [Connie Clark, Global Head of Product Line Intrusion (before SP new setup)]

For the formerly independent Shinwha and iMetrex entities, no explicit mechanisms of entrepreneurial achievement recognition or related rewards and incentives for employees could be identified. In both companies top management shared ownership of the firms, thus primarily participating in an increased value of the firm and higher dividends created by successful endeavours. In the SP new setup, no new approaches towards achievement recognition and related rewards or incentives were reported. Arguably, a potentially different culture was yet to be developed – and this may require legal independence from Siemens first.

In general, the established recognition and reward mechanisms and existing KPI systems in the researched Siemens entities were perceived to concentrate on short-term goals, reinforced low risk taking (also reinforced by elements of the top talent programme and Siemens Leadership Framework described earlier in this Chapter), and were intolerant of unsuccessful new business ventures:

> [. . .] the behaviours rewarded [today] are not necessarily in line with the behaviours of entrepreneurship. I have seen in some of the people that manage me in Siemens that rather tick a box then that they have achieved something, rather than actually going to create something new [. . .] what they do first of all is: tick the easy wins, that will get them a good job review, and there is not enough emphasis placed on creating and being entrepreneurial. This structure is backed by KPIs.
>
> [John Davis, CEO of SP new setup]

Concluding remarks

A variety of recommendations about how HRM and people management activities could better foster entrepreneuring in Siemens were proposed. This included a change in KPIs to include the measurement of the 'filling level' of the innovation pipeline, aimed at increasing the decisiveness of executives to canvass and act upon new business fields and to limit missed business opportunities. In acting upon these opportunities more supervisory support in their specific innovative and entrepreneurial endeavours, and an 'open door' policy towards new ideas and coaching in entrepreneuring was also requested. Similarly, a significant expansion of the judgment period for financial returns from new ventures in order to foster a longer-term orientation and, relatedly, changed incentive programmes of executives to remove inappropriate short-term thinking was advocated. Siemens' employee goal achievement levels are currently almost completely based on 'metric' definitions, and typically consider only one business year term. But assessment of whether entrepreneurial targets have been achieved must be done with time horizons that extend beyond one year and be based on judgments that include entrepreneurial activity rather than unsatisfying attempts to 'measure' entrepreneurship by new KPIs. In fact, the mention of a potential introduction of entrepreneurial KPIs was met with clear resistance in the interviews. Interviewees simply did not believe that an applicable metric KPI scheme could exist. Longer-term targets – whether metric or behavioural – could be broken down to yearly scopes using appropriate milestone definitions (Block and Ornati, 1987; Sykes, 1992). Here the well-established mechanism of the yearly 'round tables' (already held for all employees to review achievements and further potential) at Siemens could be expanded by including an evaluation of the entrepreneurial behaviour of a specific employee.

Respondents also sought more corporate entrepreneuring competencies to be recognised and embedded into selection processes. The nine capability dimensions with detailed level descriptions – adapted accordingly as proposed previously – may serve as the unified scale for both judging performance and recruitment and selection. From a human resource management perspective it was proposed that higher levels of decisiveness, for example, could be achieved by appropriate people selection and a consequent changed attitude in management. By reusing already existing mechanisms, stifling entrepreneurial creativity by adding further to an already highly formalised 'bureaucratic' and mechanistic structure (Miller, 1986, 1996; Chandler et al., 2000; Morris et al., 2008) could perhaps be avoided.

Long-term oriented KPIs also necessitated extending the average periods of service of executives from three to five years by adaptations of the top talent programme and delegation rules. Respondents asked for more weight to be given to specific domain knowledge, longer stays that would allow for a build-up of deep business domain knowledge, and the creation of working groups akin to the building of entrepreneurial clans, which in turn is expected to foster new knowledge recombinations (Chadwick and Dabu, 2009). The hiring of externals from the industry (rather than internal top talents) would also bring in additional domain expertise. In a similar vein, the extensive expatriation of German managers to executive jobs worldwide was challenged by a perceived need for more appointments of candidates from geographical regions in order to create a better 'cultural fit' with, and local sensitivity by, the local entity. An executive staffing policy that is more polycentric (i.e. prioritising host country nationals) or regiocentric (i.e. drawing executives from the region) might also encourage longer stays in executive positions and help address the need to reduce the perceived aversion to risk taking that was linked to the dominance of German nationals in executive positions. In bringing about such changes, however, mechanisms of reward and recognition also need to be brought into alignment to create positive reinforcement of desired behaviours and outcomes.

Notes

1 As discussed with Prof. Dr. Jörg Sauerbrey, CD S SD ST, on 2009-11-19
2 "A Dementor is a Dark creature, considered one of the foulest to inhabit the world. Dementors feed off human happiness, and thus cause depression and despair to anyone near them. [. . .] ". In: *Harry Potter* by J.K. Rowling. Source: http://harrypotter.wikia.com/wiki/Dementor, last accessed 2011-01-08
3 Kahn (1990, p. 700) defined personal engagement as "the simultaneous employment and expression of a person's 'preferred self' in task behaviours that promote connections to work and to others, personal presence (physical, cognitive, and emotional), and active, full role performances".
4 More severely, organisational changes arising from entrepreneurial endeavours themselves can be expected to increase levels of cynicism in employees (Connell and Waring, 2002).
5 As defined in a comprehensive presentation (41 pages) on https://intranet.cd.siemens.com/cms/cde/en/default/Documents/SLF_CapabilitiesInDetail_en.pdf, last accessed 2010-12-12
6 Cited in (Marvel et al., 2007, p. 753) as "rewards, management support, resources including time, organizational structures (at the macro level), and risk acceptance".
7 Landis & Gyr AG and Cerberus AG; see Chapter 2.
8 Source: http://www.siemens.com/innovation/pool/en/2010/innovation_at_siemens_10_08_2010_e.pdf, last accessed 2010-12-29. Another significant investment in business renewal can be seen in the amounts invested in respective mergers and acquisitions.
9 The stake of incentives or bonuses depends on the individual function level of the employee, starting with stakes below ten per cent of yearly compensation, depending on overall performance of the respective business unit, up to major stakes of compensation fully dependent on individual target achievements and overall firm performance.

References

Alvarez, S. A. and Barney, J. B. (2005). How do entrepreneurs organize firms under conditions of uncertainty? *Journal of Management, 31*, 776–793.

Andersson, L. M. (1996). Employee cynicism: An examination using a contract violation framework. *Human Relations, 49*, 1395–1418.

Antoncic, B. and Hisrich, R. D. (2001). Intrapreneurship: Construct refinement and cross cultural validation. *Journal of Business Venturing, 16*, 495–527.

Benner, M. J. and Tushman, M. L. (2015). Reflections on the 2013 decade award – "exploitation, exploration, and process management: The productivity dilemma revisited" ten years later. *Academy of Management Review, 40*(4), 497–514.

Block, Z. and Ornati, O. A. (1987). Compensating corporate venture managers. *Journal of Business Venturing, 2*, 41–51.

Bommer, W. H., Rich, G. A. and Rubin, R. S. (2005). Changing attitudes about change: Longitudinal effects of transformational leader behavior on employee cynicism about organizational change. *Journal of Organizational Behavior, 26*, 733–753.

Bourgeois III, L. J. (1981). On the measurement of organizational slack. *Academy of Management. The Academy of Management Review, 6*, 29–39.
Brazeal, D. V. (1993). Organizing for internally developed corporate ventures. *Journal of Business Venturing, 8*, 75–90.
Chadwick, C. and Dabu, A. (2009). Human resources, human resource management, and the competitive advantage of firms: Toward a more comprehensive model of causal linkages. *Organization Science, 20*, 253–272.
Chandler, G. N., Keller, C. and Lyon, D. W. (2000). Unraveling the determinants and consequences of an innovation-supportive organizational culture. *Entrepreneurship Theory and Practice, 25*, 59–76.
Connell, J. and Waring, P. (2002). The BOHICA syndrome: A symptom of cynicism towards change initiatives? *Strategic Change, 11*, 347–356.
Denton, L. and Campbell, C. (2009). Dementors in our midst: Managing the highly productive but morale-killing employee. *Journal of Applied Management and Entrepreneurship, 14*, 3–25.
Durand, D. E. (1974). Training and development of entrepreneurs: A comparison of motivation and skill approaches. *Journal of Small Business Management (pre-1986), 12*, 23–26.
Durand, D. E. and Shea, D. (1974). Entrepreneurial activity as a function of achievement motivation and reinforcement control. *Journal of Psychology: Interdisciplinary and Applied, 88*, 57–63.
Eisenhardt, K. M. (1989). Making fast strategic decisions in high-velocity environments. *Academy of Management Journal, 32*, 543–576.
Feldman, D. C. (2000). The Dilbert syndrome: How employee cynicism about ineffective management is changing the nature of careers in organizations. *The American Behavioral Scientist, 43*, 1286–1300.
Floyd, S. W. and Woolridge, B. (1999). Knowledge creation and social networks in corporate entrepreneurship: The renewal of organizational capability. *Entrepreneurship Theory and Practice, 23*, 123–143.
Fry, A. (1987). The post-it note: An intrapreneurial success. *S.A.M. Advanced Management Journal, 52*, 4–9.
Gibson, C. B. and Birkinshaw, J. (2004). The antecedents, consequences and mediating role of organizational ambidexterity. *Academy of Management Journal, 47*(2), 209–226.
Hayton, J. C. (2005). Promoting corporate entrepreneurship through human resource management practices: A review of empirical research. *Human Resource Management Review, 15*, 21–41.
Hayton, J. C. and Kelley, D. J. (2006). A competency-based framework for promoting corporate entrepreneurship. *Human Resource Management, 45*, 407–427.
Hayward, M. L. A., Forster, W. R., Saravathy, S. D. and Frederikson, B. L. (2010). Beyond hubris: How highly confident entrepreneurs rebound to venture again. *Journal of Business Venturing, 25*, 569–578.
Herold, D. M., Jayaraman, N. and Narayanaswamy, C. R. (2006). What is the relationship between organizational slack and innovation? *Journal of Managerial Issues, 18*(3), 372–392.
Hisrich, R. D., Langan-Fox, J. and Grant, S. (2007). Entrepreneurship research and practice: A call to action for psychology. *American Psychologist, 62*, 575–589.
Hisrich, R. D. and Peters, M. P. (1986). Establishing a new business venture unit within a firm. *Journal of Business Venturing, 1*(3), 307–322.

Hitt, M. A., Nixon, R. D., Hoskisson, R. E. and Kochhar, R. (1999). Corporate entrepreneurship and cross-functional fertilization: Activation, process and disintegration of a new product design team. *Entrepreneurship Theory and Practice, 23*, 145–167.

Hofstede, G. H. (2001). *Culture's consequences: Comparing values, behaviors, institutions, and organizations across nations.* London: Sage.

Hornsby, J. S., Kuratko, D. F. and Montagno, R. V. (1999). Perception of internal factors for corporate entrepreneurship: A comparison of Canadian and U.S. managers. *Entrepreneurship Theory and Practice, 24*, 9–24.

Hornsby, J. S., Kuratko, D. F. and Zahra, S. A. (2002). Middle managers' perception of the internal environment for corporate entrepreneurship: Assessing a measurement scale. *Journal of Business Venturing, 17*, 253–273.

Johanna de Villiers-Scheepers, M. (2012). Antecedents of strategic corporate entrepreneurship. *European Business Review, 24*(5), 400–424.

Kahn, W. A. (1990). Psychological conditions of personal engagement and disengagement at work. *Academy of Management Journal, 33*, 692–724.

Kirzner, I. M. (2009). The alert and creative entrepreneur: A clarification. *Small Business Economics, 32*(2), 145–152.

Kuratko, D. F. and Goldsby, M. G. (2004). Corporate entrepreneurs or rogue middle managers? A framework for ethical corporate entrepreneurship. *Journal of Business Ethics, 55*, 13–30.

Kuratko, D. F., Hornsby, J. S. and Bishop, J. W. (2005a). Managers' Corporate Entrepreneurial Actions and Job Satisfaction. *International Entrepreneurship and Management Journal, 1*, 275–291.

Kuratko, D. F., Ireland, R. D., Covin, J. G. and Hornsby, J. S. (2005b). A model of middle-level managers' entrepreneurial behavior. *Entrepreneurship Theory and Practice, 29*, 699–716.

Kuratko, D. F., Montagno, R. V. and Hornsby, J. S. (1990). Developing an intrapreneurial assessment instrument for an effective corporate entrepreneurial environment. *Strategic Management Journal, 11*, 49–58.

Ling, Y., Simsek, Z., Lubatkin, M. and Veiga, J. (2008). Transformational leadership's role in promoting corporate entrepreneurship: Examining the CEO–TMT interface. *Academy of Management Journal, 51*, 557–576.

Locke, E. A. and Baum, J. R. (2007). Entrepreneurial motivation. In Baum, J. R., Frese, M. and Baron, R. A. (Eds.), *The psychology of entrepreneurship, the organizational frontiers.* Mahwah, NJ: Lawrence Erlbaum, pp. 93–112.

Lumpkin, G., Brigham, K. and Moss, T. (2010). Long-term orientation: Implications for the entrepreneurial orientation and performance of family businesses. *Entrepreneurship and Regional Development, 22*, 241–264.

Mahnke, V., Venzin, M. and Zahra, S. A. (2007). Governing entrepreneurial opportunity recognition in MNEs: Aligning interests and cognition under uncertainty. *Journal of Management Studies, 44*, 1278–1298.

Marvel, M. R., Griffin, A., Hebda, J. and Vojak, B. (2007). Examining the technical corporate entrepreneurs' motivation: Voices from the field. *Entrepreneurship Theory and Practice, 31*, 753–768.

Menzel, H. C., Aaltio, I. and Ulijn, J. M. (2007). On the way to creativity: Engineers as intrapreneurs in organizations. *Technovation, 27*(12), 732–743.

Miller, D. (1986). Configurations of strategy and structure: Towards a synthesis. *Strategic Management Journal, 7*, 233–249.

Miller, D. (1996). Configurations revisited. *Strategic Management Journal, 17*, 505–512.
Miner, J. B. (1997). *A psychological typology of successful entrepreneurs*. Westport, CT: Quorum Books.
Miner, J. B. (2000). Testing a psychological typology of entrepreneurship using business founders. *The Journal of Applied Behavioral Science, 36*, 43–69.
Mintzberg, H. (1996). Musings on management. *Harvard Business Review, 74*(4), 61–67.
Monsen, E., Patzelt, H. and Saxton, T. (2010). Beyond simple utility: Incentive design and trade-offs for corporate employee-entrepreneurs. *Entrepreneurship: Theory and Practice, 34*(1), 105–130.
Morris, M. H., Kuratko, D. F. and Covin, J. G. (2008). *Corporate entrepreneurship and innovation*. Mason, OH: South Western Cengage Learning.
Nohria, N. and Gulati, R. (1995). What is the optimum amount of organizational slack? A study of the relationship between slack and innovation in multinational firms. *European Management Journal, 15*(6), 603–611.
Nohria, N. and Gulati, R. (1996). Is slack good or bad for innovation? *Academy of Management Journal, 39*, 1245–1264.
Ouchi, W. G. (1980). Markets, bureaucracies and clans. *Administrative Science Quarterly, 25*, 129–141.
Peris-Ortiz, M. (2009). An analytical model for human resource management as an enabler of organizational renewal: A framework for corporate entrepreneurship. *International Entrepreneurship and Management Journal, 5*, 461–479.
Pinchot, G., III. (1985). Introducing the 'Intrapreneur'. *IEEE Spectrum, 22*, 74–79.
Rosner, M. M. (1968). Economic Determinants of Organizational Innovation. *Administrative Science Quarterly, 12*, 614–625.
Shane, S., Locke, E. A. and Collins, C. J. (2003). Entrepreneurial motivation. *Human Resource Management Review, 13*, 257–279.
Sharfman, M. P., Wolf, G., Chase, R. B. and Tansik, D. A. (1988). Antecedents of organizational slack. *Academy of Management Review, 13*, 601–614.
Shepherd, D. A., Covin, J. G. and Kuratko, D. F. (2009). Project failure from corporate entrepreneurship: Managing the grief process. *Journal of Business Venturing, 24*, 588–600.
Stanley, D. J., Meyer, J. P. and Topolnytsky, L. (2005). Employee cynicism and resistance to organizational change. *Journal of Business and Psychology, 19*, 429–459.
Sykes, H. B. (1992). Incentive compensation for corporate venture personnel. *Journal of Business Venturing, 7*, 253–265.
Tan, J. and Peng, M. W. (2003). Organizational slack and firm performance during economic transitions: Two studies from an emerging economy. *Strategic Management Journal, 24*, 1249–1263.
Urbany, J. E. (2005). Inspiration and cynicism in values statements. *Journal of Business Ethics, 62*, 169–182.
Wanous, J. P., Reichers, A. E. and Austin, J. T. (2000). Cynicism about organizational change. *Group and Organization Management, 25*, 132–153.
Watt, J. and Piotrowski, C. (2008). Organizational change cynicism: A review of the literature and intervention strategies. *Organization Development Journal, 26*, 23–32.
Wright, P. M., Dunford, B. B. and Snell, S. A. (2001). Human resources and the resource based view of the firm. *Journal of Management, 27*, 701–721.

Wright, P. M. and McMahan, G. C. (1992). Theoretical perspectives on strategic human resource management. *Journal of Management, 18*, 295–320.

Wright, P. M. and McMahan, G. C. (2011). Exploring human capital: Putting human back into strategic human resource management. *Human Resource Management Journal, 21*, 93–104.

Wu, C., Neubert, M. J. and Yi, X. (2007). Transformational leadership, cohesion perceptions, and employee cynicism about organizational change: The mediating role of justice perceptions. *The Journal of Applied Behavioral Science, 43*, 327–351.

Zahra, S. A. and Covin, J. G. (1995). Contextual influences on the corporate entrepreneurship-performance relationship: A longitudinal analysis. *Journal of Business Venturing, 10*, 43–58.

7 Sustained inertia in corporate entrepreneuring

Introduction

What explains the continuing apparently low level of, or lack of success in, corporate entrepreneuring within Siemens Fire Safety? Does corporate entrpreneuring manifest differently within the business unit, and if so, why and with what consequences?

How might 'local entrepreneurship' be strengthened in the organisational and industry context of Siemens Fire Safety? These are the questions that guided our study as we sought a deeper understanding of sustained low levels of corporate entrepreneurship.

Established in 1847, Siemens is one of the oldest players among the global top 500. With the average life expectancy of multinational enterprises estimated at around 40 to 50 years only (De Geus, 1997), the age of Siemens AG already implies significant activities in firm renewal as an explanation for its long-term survival. Siemens is also highly innovative when measured by filed patents (in FY 2010, Siemens announced 8,800 new inventions and listed 4,300 new patents) and R&D spending (Fire Safety, for example, had been investing an almost constant amount of five per cent of its turnover in R&D activities for the ten years up to 2009). Yet much of this innovation within Fire Safety was incremental, whereby old products were replaced with implementations that had comparable characteristics. Indeed, in the five years prior to our study Siemens AG showed significant symptoms of business stagnation and severe shortcomings in company guidance, as indicated by weak business performance, failed acquisitions, and a huge bribery scandal. Our initial pilot study of the acquisition of Shinwha Electronics in South Korea highlighted the relevance of entrepreneurial activity for achieving improved firm performance in the Fire Safety business unit, in contrast to the 'normal way' in Siemens Fire Safety. Independent of our study, Siemens top management identified at the start of 2009 a severe lack of entrepreneurship in the company as an important issue, and defined the strengthening of 'local entrepreneurship' as a new key action item in the strategic planning of Siemens AG. The SMART initiative was a central element of this strategy, with explicit top management support. The SP new setup emerged in response to the limitations to corporate entrepreneurship within the Siemens Fire Safety context and pointed to possibilities for an alternative model.

We thus sought to explore the challenges and opportunities for corporate entrepreneuring within a business unit of a large conglomerate MNE, in all its real-world complexity. A novelty of our study is our attempt to better understand the extended period of *business stagnation*, rather than the more common focus on *success*. This dominant focus on success can lead to a cumulative bias (McGaughey, 2013) in our understanding of how to foster sustained corporate entrepreneuring. Throughout the presentation of our findings in previous chapters, we have sought to acknowledge different perspectives of respondents from across the case studies and corporate headquarters, employing extensive verbatim quoting to share the role of authorship with organisational members (Martin, 1995). Our hope was to avoid the 'narrative smoothing' (Clandinin and Connelly, 2000) that can homogenise diverse contexts and perspectives within large, complex organisations and that can lead to overestimation of the causal fabric of experience.

In this concluding chapter we pull together the findings of our preceding chapters. We make three main points: first, we argue that a pattern or configuration of critical, interdependent organisational and individual elements residing at multiple levels within the Siemens Fire Safety business unit mutually reinforce each other and sustain inertia in *low* levels of corporate entrepreneurship. Redressing such inertia thus entails initiatives that not only target isolated elements, but also recognise the recursive, mutually reinforcing relationships between key elements at individual and organisational (business unit, division, and corporate) levels. Second, we summarise both the challenges to and recommendations for managerial entrepreneurship arising from our study in the context of Siemens Fire Safety. We invite all readers – scholars, corporate executives, policy makers, students, and the curious individual – to reflect on their own experiences, knowledge, and assumptions in relation to these challenges and recommendations. Third, we draw attention to the false promise of universal best practices and the influence of 'embedded agency' on the form that managerial entrepreneurship and CE initiatives may successfully take, highlighting the context specificity of such endeavours. We conclude with some brief thoughts on possible extensions to our research and future directions.

Explaining sustained inertia in low levels of corporate entrepreneuring

Relationships between the various factors identified in Chapters 3 to 6 as important in fostering or impeding entrepreneurial activity across the three cases have been configured into an 'interactions diagram' shown in Figure 7.1. Starting in the top left-hand corner of Figure 7.1, the prevailing process orientation with high maturity levels on the exploitation side, but not in exploration, along with strong industry-driven compliance needs and a dominance of technology-related and incremental innovation were seen as fostering an internal focus by management and employees, somewhat hindering entrepreneurial behaviour. The current top talent career concept was viewed as supporting short-term orientation and risk aversion. Employee selection, driven also in part by the top talent career

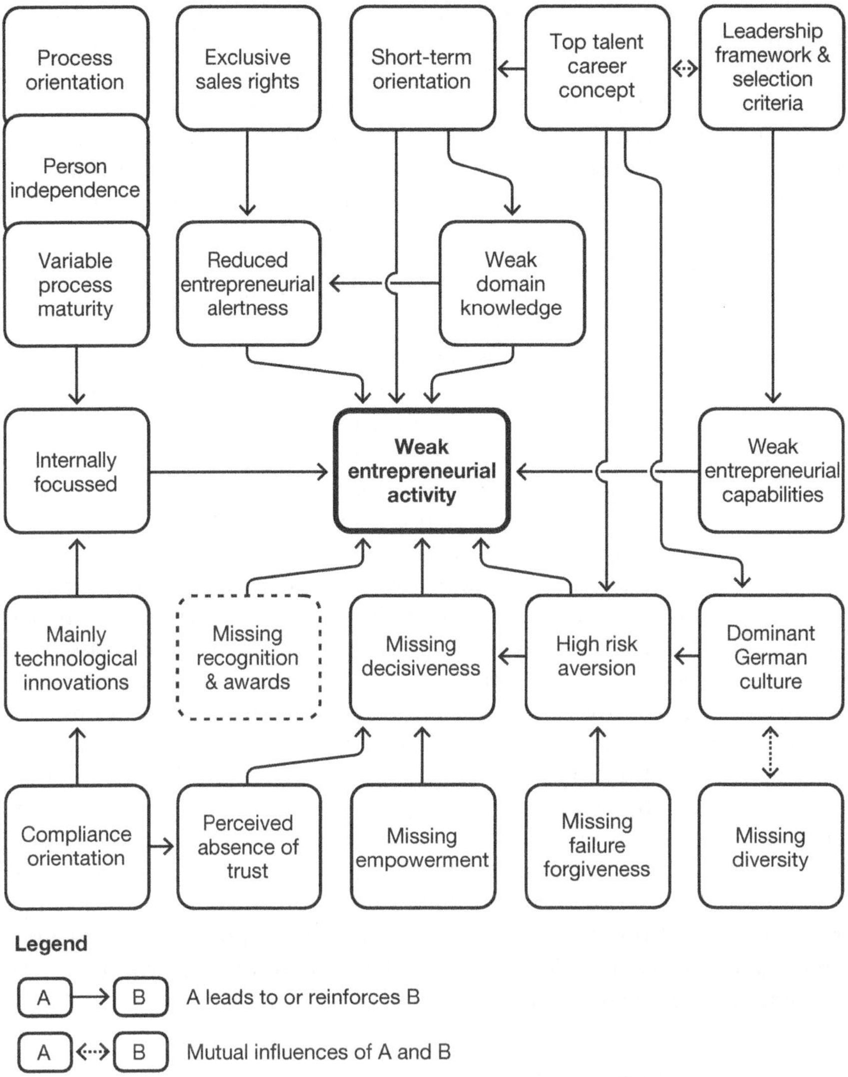

Figure 7.1 Interactions leading to weak entrepreneurial activity

concept, was seen to result in somewhat weak employee capabilities and business domain knowledge in terms of industry and local context domains. All of these negatively impacted entrepreneurial behaviour and activity. Weak business (industry and local context) domain knowledge and the long-standing practice of exclusive sales rights were seen to impede entrepreneurial alertness required in the exploration, in particular, of entrepreneurial opportunities. A reported high level of risk aversion was fostered by the top talent career concept, the absence of failure forgiveness, and a still dominant German culture. This strong Germanic heritage, seemingly reinforced by 'rope teams' related to the top talent career concept, was seen to further promote a lack of national diversity among senior executives at the time of our study, despite the then newly stated intent to foster local entrepreneurship. Last, risk aversion and a lack of empowerment, along with the strong compliance orientation – which was driven by both industry characteristics and then recent scandals – led to a lack of decisiveness among key employees in relation to seeking and acting upon entrepreneurial opportunities. The lack of recognition and granted rewards for entrepreneurial activity was primarily seen as having a direct and negative influence on levels of entrepreneurial activity, largely by diminishing motivation. Of course, these interactions between internal elements are set within a broader strategic and industry context.

Kuratko, Hornsby, and Goldsby (2004) presented a model that recognises the importance of context and highlights, in very broad terms, the critical elements needed for sustained corporate entrepreneurship, including the importance of perceived implementation-output relationships at multiple (individual and organisational) levels. As shown in the top section of Figure 7.2, the model comprises five building blocks: external transformation triggers, the corporate entrepreneurial strategy of the firm, organisational antecedents, individual entrepreneurial behaviour, and the entrepreneurial outcomes. The strategy-outcome relationship, as perceived by decision makers, affects future strategy making for corporate entrepreneurship: the more the CE strategy is seen to lead to desirable outcomes, the stronger will be the motivation to continue with such a strategy. Similarly, if the desired and expected outcomes (i.e. intrinsic and extrinsic rewards) of entrepreneurial behaviour are met or exceeded, an individual is more likely to continue to engage in such behaviour (Kuratko, Ireland, Covin, and Hornsby, 2005). We use this generic model as a 'reference model' to structure our findings in Figure 7.2, distinguishing between external transformational triggers and context (Part A) and interactions between Fire Safety elements (Part B). We also extend the model by identifying, among other things, new recursive relationships that reinforce inertia in corporate entrepreneuring and highlight emerging initiatives that seek to disrupt this inertia – the success of which is as yet unknowable.

Clusters and patterns of critical interactions

Arguably, two key forces can help to achieve significant changes towards entrepreneurial activity. First – and a classic driver – the external environment may exert sufficient pressure to force an entrepreneurial adaptation of the firm in an attempt to overcome its current competitive disadvantages. Second – and specifically applicable in case of larger organisations with hierarchical entity structures similar to the researched Siemens environment – the management of an overlying structure may take such measures as comprehensively changing the strategy and the setup of a subjacent entity. As Ireland, Covin, and Kuratko (2009) observe, top level management shoulders much of the responsibility for promoting entrepreneurial behaviour through the development and communication of a strategic vision and plan.

Siemens top management is actively driving a shared vision, mission, and company culture with the One Siemens vision,[1] a one brand strategy, and integrated Siemens One solutions offerings are also based on shared organisations (described in Chapter 2). A company-wide shared vision is clearly intended by the top management and, arguably, is required to work successfully in shared organisations and integrated projects. With the Annual Report 2010, Siemens published a reworked declaration of its key values regarding vision and mission, and related activities in strategy and operations. As discussed in Chapter 5, a new emphasis in the strategy and executive communications on the term 'pioneer' – most closely representing entrepreneurial behaviour – represents a strategic deployment of corporate history as a symbolic resource. That is, current activities are linked to eminent predecessors and the innovations of historical figures, thereby offering a sense of continuity between the pioneering past and current and future behaviours (Suddaby and Greenwood, 2005; Foster, Suddaby, Minkus, and Wiebe, 2011; McGaughey, 2013). It was, however, only applied in the context of "technology driven markets": innovation was only mentioned in this context of technology and portfolios that seemed to represent only product portfolios, since the service business is mentioned separately. This is not really surprising since our study revealed a significant inward orientation at Siemens. The new strategy and values declaration did, however, also explicitly address a necessary intensification of customer focus. Ideally, the aspect of pioneering in the sense of new venturing would be expanded towards the context of customer-oriented business and related innovations on the sales side (e.g. new business approaches, go-to-market models), and might even lead to entire value chain re-engineering.

Even the new definition of being "a pioneer in technology driven markets" was not, however, of high priority for the main Building Technologies business units of Fire Safety, CPS, and BAU. The Fire Safety business was not primarily driven by substantive technological innovations, but rather by incremental innovation. Hence, as shown in Figure 7.2 the business unit strategy focussed on incremental technical innovations, or "going for organic growth in existing business segments and markets". Indeed, one of the biggest changes for the Building Technologies business around the time of our study was the introduction of the new business model of energy savings performance contracting (ESPC)[2] – a business innovation which was not invented or driven by Siemens. On a broader scale, Siemens healthcare and power sectors were, to a greater degree, dependent on technical innovation (e.g. new medical diagnostic approaches and power generation by wind turbines and solar technology), and the selection of environmentally friendly – or 'green' – portfolios as a key focus area must be appreciated as an entrepreneurial decision in itself. It is not surprising, therefore, that the strategic focus by the business unit on mainly incremental technological innovations resulted in exactly that.

Does that mean that the new corporate emphasis on 'local entrepreneurship' is not relevant or appropriate for the Fire Safety business unit? The industry maturity

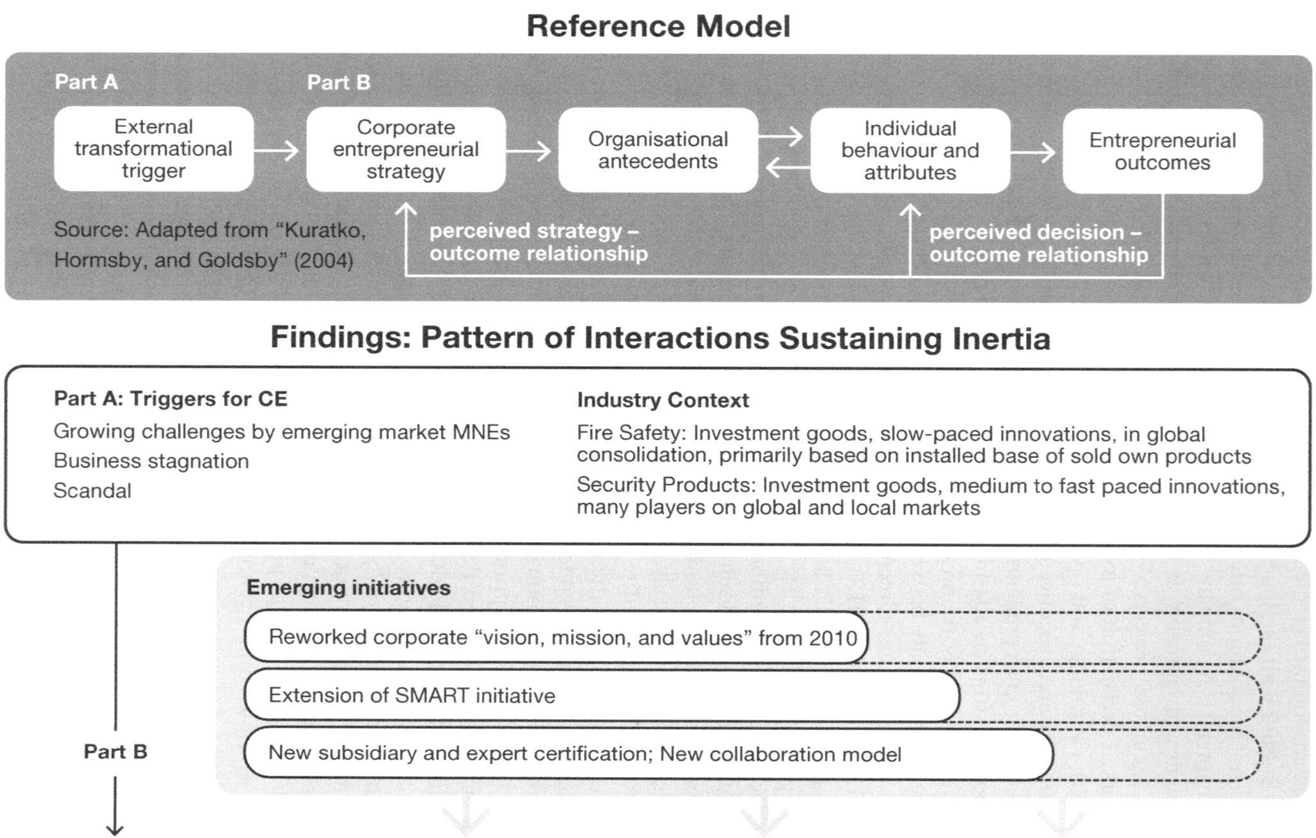
Reference Model
Part A
Part B
External transformational trigger
Corporate entrepreneurial strategy
Organisational antecedents
Individual behaviour and attributes
Entrepreneurial outcomes
Source: Adapted from "Kuratko, Hormsby, and Goldsby" (2004)
perceived strategy – outcome relationship
perceived decision – outcome relationship
Findings: Pattern of Interactions Sustaining Inertia
Part A: Triggers for CE
Growing challenges by emerging market MNEs
Business stagnation
Scandal
Industry Context
Fire Safety: Investment goods, slow-paced innovations, in global consolidation, primarily based on installed base of sold own products
Security Products: Investment goods, medium to fast paced innovations, many players on global and local markets
Emerging initiatives
Reworked corporate "vision, mission, and values" from 2010
Extension of SMART initiative
New subsidiary and expert certification; New collaboration model
Part B

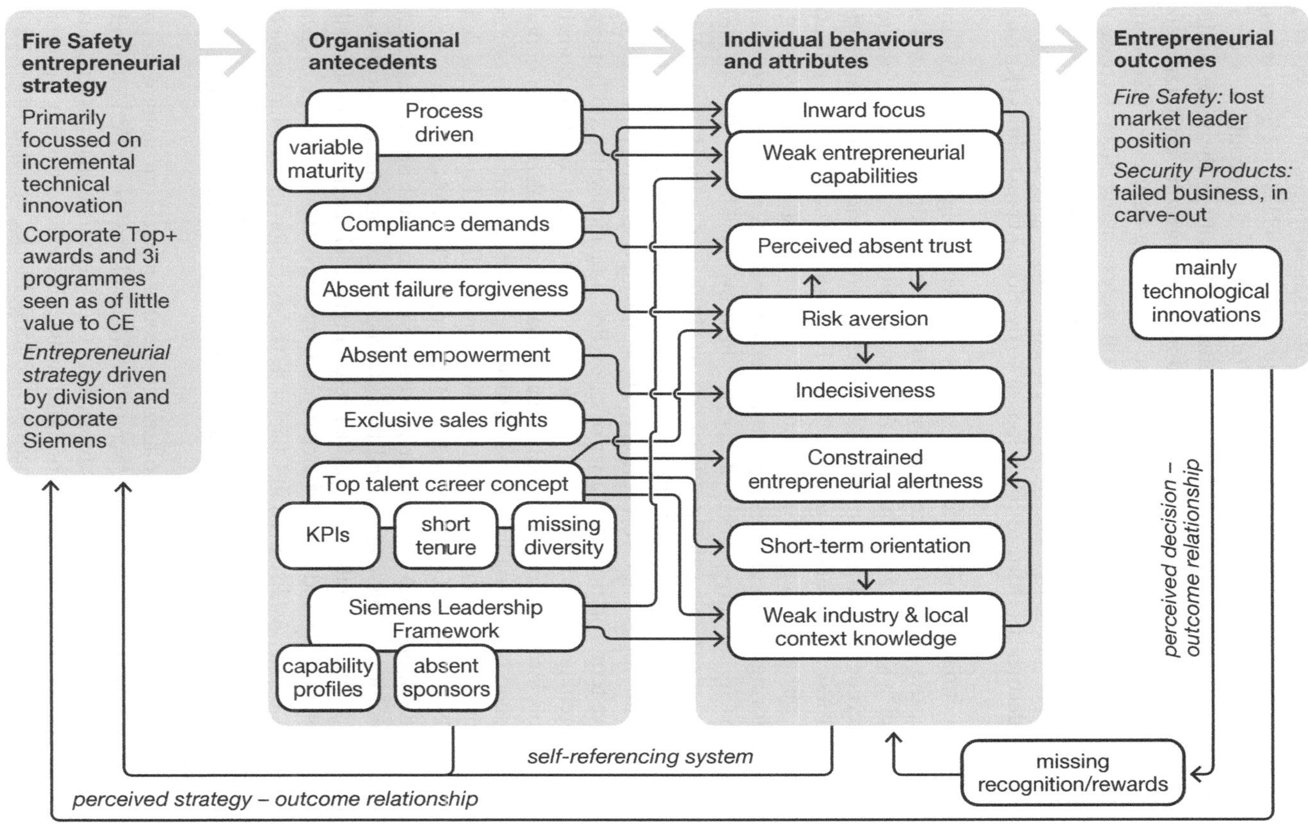

Figure 7.2 Patterns that sustain inertia in low levels of corporate entrepreneuring

of the fire safety business needs to be considered in relation to an appropriate company, divisional, and business unit level vision and strategy. As discussed in Chapter 2, the industry – based on the current business approaches – was considered to be in consolidation, with top competitors like UTC and Tyco having bought many companies in the decade prior to our study. This could be seen as an indicator of limited potential for entrepreneurial activity in the sense of disruptive innovations, and points towards maximising opportunity exploitation by competitive aggressiveness. However, since the underlying business of protecting people and goods against dangers from fires will increase rather than decrease in importance, the maturity of the current business could signal the potential for disruptive new approaches, elevating the potential value of an enhanced entrepreneurial alertness to changed conditions or to overlooked possibilities (Kirzner, 2009).

Entrepreneurial alertness refers to "a sense of what might be 'around the corner,' i.e., the sense to notice that which has hitherto not been suspected of existing at all" (Kirzner, 2009, p. 151). As shown in Figure 7.2, however, organisational antecedents within Siemens undermined both the *capacity* for entrepreneurial alertness and its actual *use* at Siemens Fire Safety. The norm of exclusive sales rights within Siemens AG, for example, directly constrained the possibilities for exploring entrepreneurial opportunities across borders (i.e. the use of an existing capacity for entrepreneurial alertness held by individuals). Two organisational antecedents in particular appear to curtail the development of a capacity for entrepreneurial alertness in the first place. First is the Siemens Leadership Framework and top talent career concept. These, through selection processes that involve short-term rotations and a set of capability judgements that do not capture entrepreneuring capabilities, undermine the development of deep domain (industry and local context) knowledge that enhances one's alertness to opportunities. Second is the variable process maturity in the process orientation of Fire Safety. When our study commenced, there were only well-developed process definitions for Product Lifecycle Management and Supply Chain Management, weak Customer Relationship Management process definitions, and no Management Process definitions. This contributed to a strong inward orientation, as shown in Figure 7.2, and inevitably focussed any entrepreneurial alertness on internally derived opportunities and reduced incentives to develop deep knowledge of local (external) contexts. As discussed in Chapter 4, the extension of the Management Process definition to include opportunity recognition may help to overcome some of these limitations and to ameliorate the dominance of the inward focus at Fire Safety.

Consistent with Kuratko's and colleagues' (2004) model, our findings highlight the interactions *between* the discrete 'building blocks' or critical elements in building sustained CE – for example, between 'organisational antecedents' and the 'attributes and behaviours of individuals'. However, our study not only highlights important relationships between building blocks, but also *within* each of these elements driving entrepreneurial activity. In terms of individual behaviours and attributes, for example, an 'inward focus' and 'weak industry and local context knowledge' both constrain 'entrepreneurial alertness', as described previously. Similarly shown in Figure 7.2, within the domain of individual entrepreneurial behaviour and attributes a short term-orientation fostered a risk aversion to entrepreneurial endeavours, leading to (and also reinforced by) a posture of paralysing indecisiveness.

The interaction between a process-oriented organisational design and human resource management (HRM) policies and practices within 'organisational antecedents' is also significant. Formal business processes structure human activity, with high levels of business process maturity often seeking to secure 'person independence' by (intentionally) limiting discretionary behaviour and, as our study shows, (unintentionally) decreasing motivation for sustained corporate entrepreneuring. While comprehensive reviews of the effects of a process orientation on organisational performance point to benefits for quality, customer satisfaction, cost reductions, and improved financial performance (e.g. Kohlbacher, 2010), its potential effect on CE is often overlooked. Similarly, it is not uncommon for studies linking human resource practices and CE to control for organisational characteristics such as firm age, firm size, ownership, and industry, simply following the lead of previous academic studies (e.g. Kaya, 2006; Tang, Wei, Snape, and Ng, 2015), but ignoring organisational design elements that structure human activity. In a process-oriented organisation, clearly defined and prescribed processes are central to the coordination and deployment of human resources through the designation of tasks, roles, role relationships, and responsibilities. When contributing to competitive advantage, devising and applying these formal business processes is a strategic activity of human resource management and part of managerial entrepreneurship – albeit not necessarily performed by the formal HRM department.

The literature on business process modelling and HRM have, however, developed largely as separate streams of research with seemingly little interaction. Where the two coexist, HRM tends to be cast in a purely operational role, providing performance measurement techniques and job descriptions to help optimisation, with human resources cast as an 'input' to processes (e.g. Glykas, 2011). Some studies stress the importance of teamwork in process-oriented organisations (e.g. Kohlbacher and Gruenwald, 2011; Kohlbacher and Rijers, 2013), but what this means in terms of human resource activities or management is rarely unpacked. Our study within Siemens AG shows that a more critical and nuanced discussion of the interactions between HRM activities and a process-driven orientation as organisational antecedents to corporate entrepreneuring is warranted. Hence, what matters is not only the interactions *between* the 'boxes', explicitly depicted in Figure 7.2, but also those interactions *within* the 'boxes'.

Perceived outcomes and effects

Overall, the critical aspects identified in the researched cases within Siemens Fire Safety can be interpreted as a distinct pattern or configuration (Miller, 1986, 1996) of conditions and influential factors spread over the elements of firm strategy, organisational antecedents, and individual behaviour. Looking at the huge Siemens organisation – with higher organisational levels defining the strategy of the business units and division – the apparent insignificance of the refreshed corporate strategy for many interviewed in the Fire Safety business unit indicates potential limitations of the corporate strategy as a driving force for corporate entrepreneuring.

Looking at the feedback interactions and cycles depicted in Figure 7.2, the elements of 'organisational antecedents' and 'individual entrepreneurial behaviour' mutually influence each other significantly (as also proposed by Kuratko and colleagues). People within organisations operate in a present which is always infused, and which they are further infusing, with recollections of the past and projections or expectations for the future (Richardson, 1990; Munn, 1992). The perceived decision-outcome relationship for individuals – based on past and present experiences and expectations for future outcomes – was found to be greatly influenced by an almost complete absence of recognition and rewards for behaviours that foster sustained entrepreneuring. The case research indicated that this configuration of elements and the absence of recognition and rewards in particular may create additional resistance to changes towards a more entrepreneurial set-up. If the business unit management itself is short-term oriented due to people selection, promotion programmes, and incentive systems, it can hardly be expected that an entrepreneurial – and thus longer-term – corporate, divisional, or business unit level strategy will be actively promoted.

The absence of an entrepreneurial strategy as an accepted driving force for corporate entrepreneuring sets up organisational antecedents and individual entrepreneurial behaviour and attributes as a self-referencing system, with critical elements 'stabilising' each other to a certain extent by mutual interactions. This effect is expected to create an additional hurdle for a desired and necessary change towards more entrepreneurial activity. Unfortunately, little research seems to exist on such specific multifactor interactions, although exceptions exist. Heinonen and Toivonen (2007), for example, acknowledged the existence and relevance of a "two-way interactive and recursive process" in the "co-evolution of managerial and employee behaviour and organisational structures" (p. 165). Further studies of multidimensional models primarily portray interactions as unidirectional and toward one (or only a few) aspects (e.g. Baum, Edwin, and Ken, 2001; Baum and Locke, 2004) rather than recognising the recursive, co-evolutionary dynamics suggested here.

Added complexity in conglomerate MNEs

The researched cases – the SMART subsidiary, Shinwha acquisition and integration, and the SP new setup – revealed the key triggers for entrepreneurial strategy within Siemens' Fire Safety business unit as being derived from higher organisational levels within the Siemens AG, rather than from the external environment of the firm. As noted in Chapter 5, the mandates assigned to each of the case studies all reflect what Birkinshaw and Hood (1998) term 'parent driven investments'.

Establishment of the global SMART headquarter in China was primarily driven by the SMART initiative from the Siemens AG top management. The Shinwha acquisition was pushed by the divisional organisation of Building Technologies in Korea, and not the management of Fire Safety. The carve-out of the unsuccessful Security Products business was supported and decided by the management of the Building Technologies division. Key initiatives around subsidiary certification and a systems-house approach intended to foster entrepreneurial investments were also driven by divisional headquarters.

Given that the impetus for corporate entrepreneuring arose from superior levels within Siemens, how corporate entrepreneuring within Siemens Fire Safety unfolds over time is shaped by interactions between relevant entity layers (here: business unit at the lowest level, division, and sector). As illustrated in Figure 7.3, entrepreneurial strategy and organisational measures are typically discussed and agreed upon between the entity layers, if not just defined top down (1). Entrepreneurial outcomes must be justified to the next higher entity level on a regular basis (2). This highlights the added complexity of corporate entrepreneuring in conglomerates such as Siemens. In fact, the constellation at Siemens is even more complex than depicted in Figure 7.3, since the interactions occur in headquarters' organisations as well as in the organisations in every country containing an active business unit. This arrangement thus indicates the replication of the principal-agent constellation and related challenges (Shleifer and Vishny, 1997; Audretsch, Lehmann, and Plummer, 2009), with a whole chain of such relationships existing in conglomerates.

Much prior research investigates such vertical effects in the context of top management, middle managers and typical employees within one firm (Hornsby, Kuratko, and Zahra, 2002; Kuratko et al., 2004, Kuratko et al., 2005; Ireland et al., 2009). Indeed, models of corporate entrepreneurship typically present simply an abstraction of 'the firm' as a whole (Guth and Ginsberg, 1990; Covin and Slevin, 1991; Lumpkin and Dess, 1996, Paterson and Brock, 2002; Kuratko et al., 2004; Narayanan, Yang, and Zahra, 2009; Behrens and Patzelt, 2016). Conglomerates like Siemens consist of a layered structure of 'firms', characterised as the MNE's internal entities being arranged in tiers or 'divisions' (Miller, 1986, 1996; Morris, Kuratko, and Covin, 2008). Paraphrasing Edith Penrose, Nason, McKelvie, and Luumpkin (2015) observe that accumulating knowledge about the nature of CE activities across firms of different sizes may be akin to comparing caterpillars and butterflies. The extension of existing models to capture more complex organisation setups would facilitate further explanations of entrepreneurial inertia at the lowest layer of the conglomerate structure, perhaps by linking it to the research of similar structures in large governmental organisations, and especially by investigating aspects of bureaucracy and the replication of principal-agent effects throughout the various organisational layers.

Much academic research on corporate entrepreneuring within MNEs recommends a significant amount of autonomy and comprehensive business mandates be granted to subsidiaries, subject often to subsidiary capabilities, in order to allow for the driving of entrepreneurial activity primarily by subsidiary management (e.g. Birkinshaw, 1995; Birkinshaw, 1997; Birkinshaw, Hood, and Young, 2005). The cases here, however, suggest a somewhat passive entity management which is urged to entrepreneurial action by direct orders from higher organisational levels (i.e. by corporate and divisional management). This may be linked to circumstances within Siemens whereby the key elements of vision, mission, and strategy of the entities – and especially human resource aspects like employee selection, promotion mechanisms, and incentive structures, recognition, and rewards – are defined 'top down'. From a practical perspective, in the Siemens Fire Safety context at the time of our study, various measures to strengthen the entrepreneurial 'predisposition' of management and the willingness of key staff to 'get in the driving seat' are first necessary before expecting more autonomy or the award of comprehensive business mandates. As outlined previously, however, existing organisational antecedents may well prove critical – even unrecognised – impediments, and thereby undermine this potential.

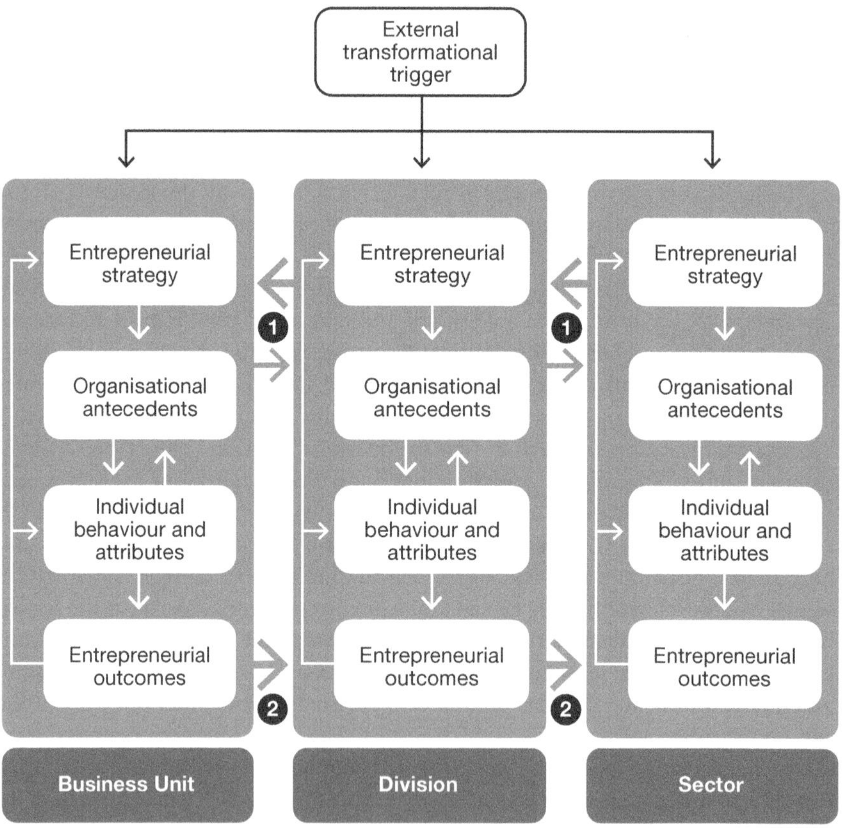

Figure 7.3 Drivers of CE throughout layers of a conglomerate MNE

Challenges and recommendations for managerial entrepreneurship

The previous discussion of the array of organisational, individual, and contextual factors interacting to sustain inertia in low levels of corporate entrepreneuring within Siemens Fire Safety points to the need for a multifaceted approach to redress this inertia. Indeed, as shown in Figure 7.2, several key initiatives were emerging at the time of our study, including a reworked corporate vision and strategy, the Siemens-wide SMART initiative, new subsidiary and expert certification processes, and a new collaboration model between headquarters and subsidiaries. These new initiatives are an important part of 'managerial entrepreneurship' in Siemens AG.

As described in Chapter 1, managerial entrepreneurship is the system of firm-specific managerial processes that enhances knowledge generation, coordination, and exploitation within the organisation to foster corporate entrepreneurship. It may include a range of systems, structures, and processes (e.g. planning systems, reporting structures, team-building initiatives, and HRM policies and activities). Formal managerial entrepreneurship is directed by decision makers, while informal managerial entrepreneurship arises through the discretionary efforts of employees. Recognising the key role of people throughout the organisation in corporate entrepreneuring, the first column of Table 7.1 describes human resource management activities that constitute managerial entrepreneurship.[3] The second column describes related activities, policies, or procedures within Siemens Fire Safety that either support or impede corporate entrepreneuring. The third column summarises specific recommendations to foster CE in the context of Siemens Fire Safety arising from the findings of the case studies.

Of course, just as corporate entrepreneuring in Siemens exhibits stability (including inertia in low levels of CE), there was also considerable flux at the time of our study, with significant moves for change afoot within Siemens AG. For example, the regional cluster organisations introduced in 2008 (see Chapter 4) were dismantled by the new CEO, Joe Kaeser, in 2013. Instead, countries that are most important for Siemens – based on their business volume and growth prospects – were to report directly to the four Managing Board members responsible for each sector. Smaller countries were to report directly to these 'lead countries', which accounted for more than 85 per cent of Siemens' revenue (Siemens Press Release, 2013). This decision to eliminate a layer in the global management structure was intended to "put the power back in the hands of country managers" and to make Siemens "more agile and competitive" (Boston, 2013). The restructuring was described as being in response to internal criticism that the regional cluster structure had caused extra bureaucracy and a blurring in lines of authority (Bryant, 2013), which was a drag on decision-making (Boston, 2013). Notably, our research had highlighted that problems around indecisiveness and a lack of ownership and accountability were faced by Siemens – at least in the Fire Safety business unit – well before and irrespective of the regional cluster structure being introduced (see, in particular, Chapters 5 and 6). Within organisations, meanings of events and actions are in constant flux, with interpretations evolving in the face of new knowledge or changed interests. Corporate entrepreneuring itself is an *ongoing* accomplishment involving constant search, creation, renewal, and innovation. Thus, research findings and specific recommendations for corporate entrepreneuring are inevitably situated in time and space.

The false promise of universal best practices

When seeking to foster corporate entrepreneuring, a key implication of our findings is the importance of analysing a comprehensive set of influential organisational and individual factors, including their interactions within a specific *context*. 'Context' is the set of circumstances surrounding an event or situation that help in its interpretation (McGaughey, 2004). It includes, for example, the set of historical factors, such as key leaders and founding characteristics that have shaped and continue to inform firm operations and strategy; industry characteristics, including the nature of technology, dynamism, and competition; and local country characteristics, such as the contrast between emerging and developed markets, cultural norms, and so on. That is, in seeking to understand continuing low levels of corporate entrepreneurship, interconnected levels of context – both temporal and spatial – and relationships or connections between critical elements need to be discerned.

The importance of a deep understanding context and interactions between the 'cogs and wheels' in an organisation cautions against the false promise of universal 'best practices' as a panacea to organisational woes, and supports a more nuanced understanding of the potential for 'unintended consequences' that could be harmful to organisations when best practices are uncritically applied (Lawrence, Suddaby, and Leca, 2011; McGaughey, 2013; Benner and Tushman, 2015; McGaughey, Kumaraswarmy, and Liesch, 2016). Further, those working within a long established organisation such as Siemens AG are embedded in often taken-for-granted organisational structures, meaning systems and day-to-day activities and routines that enable and constrain individual action, define one's interests, and shape individual identities (Suchman, 1995). This 'taken for grantedness' implies inevitability in actions or permanence in organisational arrangements – people simply do not think to do otherwise. Indeed, through habit and tradition, taken for granted organisational elements and behaviours may become infused with value beyond the requirements at hand (Oliver, 1992; McGaughey, 2007, 2013). This raises an important question when seeking to encourage new individual behaviours for corporate entrepreneuring: when individuals are embedded in largely taken-for-granted organisational structures, processes, and meaning systems, how are they able to envisage new practices and get others to adopt them?[4]

Within Siemens, a strong process orientation in particular was illustrative of taken-for-granted organisational elements that both enable and constrain individual entrepreneurial behaviour. The research showed a high maturity in the formal processes applied throughout Siemens entities in relation to the exploitation of internally derived entrepreneurial opportunities. Furthermore, the Siemens Reference Process House framework is well established as the mandatory reference

Table 7.1 Managerial entrepreneurship in Siemens Fire Safety – impediments, positive elements, and recommendations

Supporting entrepreneurial rents (Chadwick and Dabu 2009)	*Siemens case study findings – positive (✓) and negative (×) impacts on CE*	*Additional recommendations to foster CE in Siemens Fire Safety*
Acquisition. Selection favours workers with a taste for entrepreneurial knowledge sharing. Preference is also given to individuals with requisite entrepreneurial capital, such as social networks or knowledge in specific areas of need. To the degree that spontaneous entrepreneurship is favoured within the firm, hiring decisions can be decentralised and based on locally perceived needs for specific entrepreneurial human capital.	× Hiring decisions for key appointments are centralised and favour internal, German executives (associated with higher levels of risk aversion) due to rotations in top talent career model × CE capabilities (e.g. in corporate venturing, risk taking) are not part of selection criteria in the Siemens Leadership Framework × Process orientation aims at 'person independence', thereby potentially discounting the importance of individual competencies underpinning entrepreneurial initiative and judgement × Famous formula of "11–6–3": with every 11 top talents coming from R&D, there are 6 from purchasing, and only 3 come from product management and sales, reinforcing inward focus	• Selection by whom? Empower local divisions to have greater say in selection for CE • Reduce the expatriation of German (top talent) managers to executive jobs worldwide by giving more weight to the recruitment of candidates representing the local culture • Rework the Siemens Leadership Model to include selection criteria that capture key entrepreneurial characteristics beyond knowledge sharing (e.g. risk taking, decisiveness) • Recognise distinct capabilities required for opportunity exploration and opportunity exploitation, providing dedicated teams with appropriately differentiated selection criteria to foster organisational ambidexterity perceived necessary for CE • Encourage external recruitment within a knowledge domain (e.g. industry), including from competitors, to strengthen infusion and recombinations of knowledge and entrepreneurial alertness • Revisit functional origins of top talents, drawing more on outward-facing functional areas

(*Continued*)

Table 7.1 (Continued)

Supporting entrepreneurial rents (Chadwick and Dabu 2009)	*Siemens case study findings – positive (✓) and negative (×) impacts on CE*	*Additional recommendations to foster CE in Siemens Fire Safety*
Retention. The value of retention varies across workers and circumstances. Turnover can be detrimental to entrepreneurship when valuable knowledge is lost, but it can also substitute new workers with valuable entrepreneurial capital for workers whose entrepreneurial value is negligible or redundant. However, because managerial entrepreneurship has strong firm specificity, retention is generally desirable.	✓ Stable cadre of 'top talent' expatriates transfers knowledge, but. . . × 2–3 year executive stays, reinforced by career model, undermine development of valuable domain knowledge deemed important to successful knowledge recombinations and exploration of entrepreneurial opportunity × Short stays undermine clan communications × Short stays promote short-term orientation to performance management, thereby undermining the long-term orientation needed for CE	• Retention enhances development of deep domain knowledge and clan networks • Duration in an assignment or role should enable measurement of outcomes over a longer time horizon to capture CE outcomes; that is, a longer-term orientation is required. However, definitions of 'long-term' are specific to industry product life-cycles. • Extend the average periods of service of executives from three to five years by adaptations of the top talent programme and delegation rules
Training. Because the focus is on innovation, training [. . .] focuses on interpersonal skills and group processes that facilitate workers' ability to aggregate their localised knowledge into entrepreneurial innovations.	✓ Siemens Leadership Framework builds social capital among units. Junior executives have mentorship with senior executives across units × Cultural sensitivity has a low profile in the leadership framework × Primarily inward focussed – understanding of transfer of key elements in external environment (e.g. customer needs and relationships) not developed	• Training required to develop skills in not only aggregating local (domain) knowledge, but also effectively acquiring it • Cross-cultural training that facilitates inter-cultural team work is essential to enhance the potential to identify and recombine knowledge acquired across national borders into new configurations, especially in the case of international mergers and acquisitions by MNEs • Add required entrepreneurial capabilities and adapt the reference job profiles within the Siemens Leadership Framework

(*Continued*)

Table 7.1 (Continued)

Supporting entrepreneurial rents (Chadwick and Dabu 2009)	*Siemens case study findings – positive (✓) and negative (×) impacts on CE*	*Additional recommendations to foster CE in Siemens Fire Safety*
		• Include coaching/ mentoring for entrepreneurial ideas and subsequent endeavours of top talents in the role definitions of superiors.
Motivation. Because innovation cannot be foreseen by management, motivation in entrepreneurial rents favours practices that build up incentives for workers to exercise discretionary effort in entrepreneurship, rewarding outcomes rather than conformity to management-specified processes. Motivation is often in the form of ownership.	✓ Recognition through subsidiary and expert certification is an important form of reward that grants autonomy and thus increases motivation × Policy of exclusive sales rights curtails entrepreneurial initiatives and discretionary effort × Pioneering values and innovation is limited to technology markets in strategy of "One Siemens" × Disconnect between pioneering vision and strategies of entities (FS division and business units) at lower levels × Performance measures over short time horizon, perceived to undermine the building of new business sustainable in the longer term × Risk-averse culture with low levels of forgiveness for failure, little discretion/ empowerment, and a lack of decisiveness are perceived, undermining motivation ? Incentives to share information	• Ownership of entrepreneurial endeavours is key, but challenges arise for what this may mean in a conglomerate MNE as opposed to an independent entity • Extend established mechanism of round tables to assess the overall entrepreneurial behaviour based on the levels defined in the adapted capability profiles • Develop organisational culture that displays a tolerance for failure and entrepreneurial risk, linked to incentive structures • Identify appropriate KPIs including, for example, a 'filling level' of the innovation pipeline for senior managers • Measure outcomes over a longer time horizon to capture entrepreneurial/ business-building outcomes and to provide disincentives for overly self-interested 'career-making' • Expand existing tools 'Top+ awards' and '3i' towards new business venturing endeavours

(*Continued*)

Table 7.1 (Continued)

Supporting entrepreneurial rents (Chadwick and Dabu 2009)	*Siemens case study findings – positive (✓) and negative (×) impacts on CE*	*Additional recommendations to foster CE in Siemens Fire Safety*
		• Stronger support for new ideas by means of invested time (e.g. 'open door policy' of executives), a more positive attitude towards new business ideas of employees, and employee inclusion in management discussion of updated business strategy • Define slack time for the development of entrepreneurial ideas and respective business proposals – specifically by function and length of service of employees – by additions in job profiles and yearly targets. • Allow the usage of sabbatical days for entrepreneurial activities within the firm, or training. • Empower managers and employees through clear decisions on goals and respective appointments of goal owners
Coordination/ deployment. Entrepreneurial rents also require complex and idiosyncratic coordination and deployment mechanisms, but these concern the generation and exploitation of knowledge held by the unique community of actors constituting the firm.	✓ Development of process definitions that align employees' behaviours with objectives of the firm, seeking to reduce 'person dependence' ✓ Processes aligned to and supporting the exploitation of technical innovations (strong inward focus), but. . .	• Develop distinct teams for opportunity identification and exploitation (see acquisition and selection criteria above). That is, there may be different communities and clan structures within the firm

(*Continued*)

Table 7.1 (Continued)

Supporting entrepreneurial rents (Chadwick and Dabu 2009)	*Siemens case study findings – positive (✓) and negative (×) impacts on CE*	*Additional recommendations to foster CE in Siemens Fire Safety*
	× Processes not aligned to customers or external knowledge acquisition, leading to poor exploration and failure to transfer knowledge of customer networks and knowledge (Outward focus lacking) ✓ Ad hoc initiatives to set up explorative teams outside formal processes through 'clans' ✓ New collaboration model, yet to be fully implemented, may reduce complexity and facilitate coordination involving diverse actors and units across national borders	• Further foster the domain-specific Building Technologies working groups and expand the approach to the Building Technologies business units as part of the organisational design. Use certification levels granted to subsidiary entities and subsidiary experts to define clan membership in such working groups • Develop process definitions to support leveraging knowledge possessed and opportunities identified by those *outside* the firm • Define an entrepreneurial process within the existing Management Process definition, emphasising opportunity recognition and thereby fostering entrepreneurial alertness • Define related process activities and standardised result formats for the investigation and reporting of these potential new business fields and derived business plans • Strengthen implementation of the new collaboration model to reduce complexity and facilitate coordination involving diverse actors and units across national borders

(*Continued*)

Table 7.1 (Continued)

Supporting entrepreneurial rents (Chadwick and Dabu 2009)	*Siemens case study findings – positive (✓) and negative (×) impacts on CE*	*Additional recommendations to foster CE in Siemens Fire Safety*
		• Strengthen and further develop the concept of Building Technologies as a globally distributed systems house, harmonised with the concepts and targets of the SMART initiative • Keep strategy definitions simple with 'use-cases' to clarify task roles, required competencies, and responsibilities

to be used when defining content, ownership, and interconnection of activities within Siemens AG. This process orientation is underpinned by the firm's history and culture and sustained by a growing pressure to apply such defined processes in compliance to industry standards and customer requirements. Hence, in reviewing Table 7.1 it is not surprising that – despite the perceived impediments of the process orientation to corporate entrepreneuring – numerous recommendations of working within and adapting aspects of this enduring process orientation were advocated in relation to explorative activities ranging from, for example, a lighter touch in process definitions and their application (e.g. in the SP new setup and SMART initiative) to further developing and rolling out process definitions (e.g. the development of the process management definition to explicitly support corporate entrepreneuring with an outward focus). Proposed revisions in the Siemens Leadership Framework that identify appropriate host-country or host-region nationals for executive positions may not only help foster local entrepreneurship, but also introduce new ways of thinking and doing things. Indeed, such employees may be less susceptible to the blinding potential of the taken-for-grantedness of 'the Siemens way'.

What we can learn, and where next?

The importance of context, connections among critical elements and vital feedback loops, and the extent to which individuals are embedded within organisational structures or 'systems of meaning' heightens the value of in-depth qualitative case studies for better understanding of corporate entrepreneuring in MNEs, and more generally. This is not to suggest that quantitative studies ignore context completely, simply that it is typically ascribed a secondary or minor role in the search for empirical generalisability and more universal truth conditions. Indeed, the notion of context is always relevant when different sets of data or examples are being compared and one is interested in identifying and explaining similarities and differences (Hodder, 1994; McGaughey, 2007). Without context, there is no meaning (Bateson, 1978). In contrast to most quantitative approaches, though, in-depth, qualitative case studies undertaken in real time and in retrospect (such as in our study) allow the pursuit of more complex and emergent interactions, with unexpected findings more readily explored and diverse perspectives captured. Indeed, through verbatim quoting case studies are able to portray the equivocality of meaning and multiple interpretations so common in organisational settings, and inevitable in MNEs that span national borders and diverse social, economic, political, and cultural contexts. Case studies thus typically offer a greater degree of 'verisimilitude' (or *vraisemblance*). Verisimilitude speaks to how lifelike an account or the presentation of findings is taken to be, with coherence and plausibility essential features of this. It reflects the ability of a case study to draw the reader closely into the world captured in the account (Adler and Adler, 1994). But what can we learn from a single case study of the Fire Safety business unit? How can we generalise the findings of this study to aid our understanding of other instances of corporate entrepreneuring?

Proponents of qualitative case studies typically recognise the human capacity for generalisation. The art is, according to Wolcott (1994, p. 113) to portray the case at hand "so well that readers themselves make the generalisations for us". As discussed in Chapter 1, Stake (1978, p. 6) calls this "naturalistic generalisation" and argues that case studies are a natural basis for generalisation "arrived at by [readers] recognising the similarities of objects and issues in and out of context and by *sensing* the natural covariations of happenings". In discerning *patterns* of behaviour from observed *instances*, we have the capacity to generalise within a case (Wolcott, 1999), but also to other instances. Naturalistic generalisations thus draw on the tacit knowledge of readers based on their experience: as readers recognise essential similarities between cases or situations, they establish the basis for naturalistic generalisations. Generalisation is, therefore, not to populations, but within a case and to similar cases: "To generalise in this way is to be both intuitive and empirical, not idiotic" (Stake, 1978, p. 6).

Qualitative case studies of corporate entrepreneuring can thus convey meaning to diverse readers in a way to which other forms of scientific research and writing are less able (McGaughey, 2006; Amberg and McGaughey, 2016). Published case studies are also one of the best ways for aspiring or practicing managers to develop judgement and analytical skills, as they display 'real-world' complexity and multiple perspectives (Weil, Oyelere, and Rainsburg, 2004; Culpin and Scott, 2012; Gill 2014), often pulling together theory and practice (Weil, Oyelere, Yeoh, and Firer, 2001). Yet what we learn is also very much dependent on who we are. Naturalisitic generalisations draw on prior experience and knowledge. As discussed in Chapter 1, readers may well each take away different insights from this book or reach different conclusions, according to their own unique biographies. Similarly, what resonates may change over time as new experiences and expectations for the future are created and drawn upon in reflections or re-readings of the Siemens case study. As discussed in Chapter 1, reading is an 'event in time' (Rosenblatt, 1978).

Where next? As a scholarly field of inquiry, corporate entrepreneurship has evolved significantly over the past 40 years (Kuratko, Hornsby, and Hayton, 2015). As Bloodgood, Hornsby, Burkemper, and Sarooghi (2015) observe, however, progress has been limited in introducing the dynamic complexity present in corporate entrepreneuring, such as that which we observed in Siemens Fire Safety. This may in part be because of a tendency among some university-based academics to focus on a limited number of variables in the theoretical models they test and abstract theorisations rather than to try to capture the complex 'lived experience' of managers and employees. It may also be due to a tendency towards engagement in fieldwork and analysis as either consultants for organisations who are 'clients', or as investigators where organisations, their executives, and employees are the 'subjects of study' who must be kept at arms' length to ensure the 'rigour' of the research in the pursuit of 'scientific' knowledge (Kieser and Leiner, 2009). Management, international business, and entrepreneurship as fields of academic inquiry have tended to favour rigour over relevance (Bartunek and Rynes, 2010; Pearce and Huang, 2012; Doh, 2015; Frank and Landström, 2016). Relatedly, Rynes, Bartunek, and Daft (2001) point to a substantial body of evidence suggesting that executives generally do not turn to academics or academic research findings when devising organisational strategies and practices.

This often perceived gap between rigour and relevance and debate over whether the divide is insurmountable dates back many decades, at least to the 1950s (for an historical review, see Gulati, 2007), and has not abated (see Fincham and Clark, 2009; Hodgkinson and Rousseau, 2009; Kieser and Leiner, 2009; Thorpe, Eden, Bessant, and Ellwood, 2011; Bartunek and Rynes, 2014). In particular, recent calls for more phenomenon-based research in management and international business (Von Krogh, Rossi-Lamastra, and Haefliger, 2012; Doh, 2015, 2016) – that is, "any research that takes as a principal focus the ability to accurately and insightfully inform a real-world phenomenon or phenomena" (Doh, 2015, p. 609) – are reflective of a concern to produce and disseminate research with 'real-world' implications (Thorpe et al., 2011). They are also a reminder that the "duty of intellectuals in society is to make a difference" (Pettigrew, 2001, p. 61). Gulati (2007) thus suggests academics should rely more on managerial sensibility to shape research questions, with researchers discovering through interactions with managers what is of importance to them.

Yet 'making a difference' does not mean that scholars should simply pursue those questions that practitioners *think* are important for them. As Weick (2001, p. 71) observes, the "much lamented 'relevance gap' is as much a product of practitioners wedded to gurus and fads as it is of academics wedded to abstractions and fundamentals". Weick (2001, p. 72) elaborates: "Practitioners want the big picture. Gurus, training, best practices and other vocational activities may temporarily supply it. But the big picture has a quality of sham relevance. More relevant is what the best of academia offers, namely 'the big story'". Rigour and relevance need not be in opposition – as though one community exists in a 'real world' and the other does not – but can create a 'positive sum world' when academic and practice-oriented 'ways of knowing and being' are mutually respected and seen as complements. That is, a world where valuable knowledge is *co*-produced through mutual learning and mutual engagement. It is not always easy, but it *is* immensely rewarding. An important future direction in the scholarship of corporate entrepreneurship is to further foster such collaborations.

Notes

1 See also http://www.siemens.com/annual/10/_pdf/Siemens_AR2010_One Siemens.pdf, last accessed 2011-02-02
2 Energy Savings Performance Contracting was developed in the 1980s in the United States to foster energy saving mechanisms. In 1992 US Congress authorised federal agencies to utilise pay from savings contracts under ESPC legislation. Source: http://www.siemensgovt.com/cap_oep_energys_savings.html, last accessed 2011-01-23
3 Elements of this table are drawn from J. Amberg and S.L. McGaughey (2016), Human resource activities and corporate entrepreneurship in a multinational enterprise, *The International Journal of Human Resource Management*. DOI: 10.1080/09585192.2016.1192051
4 See related discussions of 'embedded agency' (DiMaggio and Powell, 1991; Holm, 1995; Seo and Creed, 2002; Lawrence and Suddaby, 2006; Garud, Hardy, and Maquire, 2007; McGaughey, 2013; McGaughey, Kumaraswarmy, and Liesch, 2016), in which a 'middle ground' is sought. That is, while the agency of individuals is not unconstrained, nor is the taken-for-grantedness of some organisational elements all constraining.

References

Adler, P. A. and Adler, P. (1994). Observational techniques. In Denzin, N. K. and Lincoln, Y. S. (Eds.), *Handbook of qualitative research*. Thousand Oaks, CA: Sage, pp. 377–392.

Amberg, J. and McGaughey, S. L. (2016). Human resource activities and corporate entrepreneurship in a multinational enterprise. *The International Journal of Human Resource Management, 6*, 1–35. DOI: 10.1080/09585192.2016.1192051

Audretsch, D., Lehmann, E. and Plummer, L. (2009). Agency and governance in strategic entrepreneurship. *Entrepreneurship Theory and Practice, 33*, 149–166.

Bartunek, J. M. and Rynes, S. L. (2010). The construction and contributions of "implications for practice": What's in them and what might they offer? *Academy of Management Learning and Education, 9*(1), 100–117.

Bartunek, J. M. and Rynes, S. L. (2014). Academics and practitioners are alike and unalike: The paradoxes of academic–practitioner relationships. *Journal of Management, 40*(5), 1181–1201.

Bateson, G. (1978). The pattern which connects. *Coevolution Quarterly*, Summer, 5–15.

Baum, J. R., Edwin, A. L. and Ken, G. S. (2001). A multidimensional model of venture growth. *Academy of Management Journal, 44*, 292–303.

Baum, J. R. and Locke, E. A. (2004). The relationship of entrepreneurial traits, skill, and motivation to subsequent venture growth. *Journal of Applied Psychology, 89*, 587–598.

Behrens, J. and Patzelt, H. (2016). Corporate entrepreneurship managers' project terminations: Integrating portfolio-level, individual-level, and firm-level effects. *Entrepreneurship Theory and Practice, 40*(4), 815–842. DOI: 10.1111/etap.12147

Benner, M. J. and Tushman, M. L. (2015). Exploitation, exploration and process management: The productivity dilemma revisited ten years later. *Academy of Management Review, 40*(4), 497–514.

Birkinshaw, J. (1995). Encouraging entrepreneurial activity in multinational corporations. *Business Horizons, 38*, 32–38.

Birkinshaw, J. (1997) Entrepreneurship in multinational corporations: The characteristics of subsidiary initiatives. *Strategic Management Journal, 18*, 207–229.

Birkinshaw, J. and Hood, N. (1998). Multinational subsidiary evolution: Capability and charter change in foreign-owned subsidiary companies. *The Academy of Management Review, 23*(4), 773–795.

Birkinshaw, J., Hood, N. and Young, S. (2005). Subsidiary entrepreneurship, internal and external competitive forces, and subsidiary performance. *International Business Review, 14*, 227–248.

Bloodgood, J. M., Hornsby, J. S., Burkemper, A. C. and Sarooghi, H. (2015). A system dynamics perspective of corporate entrepreneurship. *Small Business Economics, 45*(2), 383–402.

Boston, W. (2013). Siemens CEO, breaking from past, puts new power in hands of country heads. *Wall Street Journal*, 17 October. Available at: http://www.wsj.com/articles/SB10001424052702304864504579141663820674216

Bryant, C. (2013). New Siemens chief shakes-up regional clusters: Attempt to cut bureaucracy and close profitability gap with rivals. *Financial Times*, 18 October, Berlin. Available at: https://www.ft.com/content/433d56ba-3743-11e3-9603-00144feab7de

Clandinin, D. J. and Connelly, F. M. (2000). *Narrative inquiry: Experience and story in qualitative research.* San Francisco, CA: Jossey-Bass.

Covin, J. G. and Slevin, D. P. (1991). A conceptual model of entrepreneurship as firm behavior. *Entrepreneurship Theory and Practice, 16*, 7–25.

Culpin, V. and Scott, H. (2012). The effectiveness of a live case study approach: Increasing knowledge and understanding of 'hard' versus 'soft' skills in executive education. *Management Learning, 43*(5), 565–577.

De Geus, A. (1997). *The living company.* Boston: Longview Publishing.

Doh, J. P. (2015). From the editor: Why we need phenomenon-based research in international business. *Journal of World Business, 50*(4), 609–611.

Doh, J. P. (2016). The world of global business 1965–2015: Perspectives on the 50th anniversary issue of the Journal of World Business: Introduction to the special issue. *Journal of World Business, 51*(1), 1–5.

Fincham, R. and Clark, T. (2009). Introduction: Can we bridge the rigour- relevance gap? *Journal of Management Studies, 46*(3), 510–515.

Foster, W. M., Suddaby, R., Minkus, A. and Wiebe, E. (2011). History as social memory assets: The example of Tim Hortons. *Management and Organizational History, 6*(1), 101–120.

Frank, H. and Landström, H. (2016). What makes entrepreneurship research interesting? Reflections on strategies to overcome the rigour–relevance gap. *Entrepreneurship and Regional Development, 28*(1–2), 51–75.

Garud, R., Hardy, C. and Maguire, S. (2007). Institutional entrepreneurship as embedded agency: An introduction to the special issue. *Organisation Studies, 28*(7), 957–969.

Gill, T. G. (2014). The complexity and the case method. *Management Decision, 52*(9), 1564–1590.

Glykas, M. M. (2011). Effort based performance measurement in business process management. *Knowledge and Process Management, 18*(1), 10–33.

Gulati, R. (2007). Tent poles, tribalism and boundary spanning: The rigor-relevance debate in management research. *Academy of Management Journal, 50*(4), 775–782.

Guth, W. D. and Ginsberg, A. (1990). Corporate entrepreneurship. *Strategic Management Journal, 11*, 297–308.

Heinonen, J. and Toivonen, J. (2007). Approaching a deeper understanding of corporate entrepreneurship – focusing on co-evolutionary processes. *Journal of Enterprising Culture, 15*, 165–186.

Hodder, I. (1994). The interpretation of documents and material culture. In Denzin, N. K. and Lincoln, Y. S. (Eds.), *Handbook of qualitative research*. Thousand Oaks, CA: Sage, pp. 393–402.

Hodgkinson, G. P. and Rousseau, D. (2009). Bridging the rigour-relevance gap in management research: It's already happening! *Journal of Management Studies, 46*(3), 354–346.

Holm, P. (1995). The dynamics of institutionalization: Transformation processes in Norwegian fisheries. *Administrative Science Quarterly, 40*, 398–422.

Hornsby, J. S., Kuratko, D. F. and Zahra, S. A. (2002). Middle managers' perception of the internal environment for corporate entrepreneurship: Assessing a measurement scale. *Journal of Business Venturing, 17*, 253–273.

Ireland, R., Covin, J. and Kuratko, D. (2009). Conceptualizing corporate entrepreneurship strategy. *Entrepreneurship Theory and Practice, 33*(1), 19–46.

Kaya, N. (2006). The impact of human resource management practices and corporate entrepreneurship on firm performance: Evidence from Turkish firms. *International Journal of Human Resource Management, 17*(12), 2074–2090.

Kieser, A. and Leiner, L. (2009). Why the rigour-relevance gap in management research is unbridgeable. *Journal of Management Studies, 46*(3), 516–533.

Kirzner, I. M. (2009). The alert and creative entrepreneur: A clarification. *Small Business Economics, 32*(2), 145–152.

Kohlbacher, M. (2010). The effects of process orientation: A literature review. *Business Process Management Journal, 16*(1), 135–152.

Kohlbacher, M. and Gruenwald, S. (2011). Process orientation: Conceptualization and measurement. *Business Process Management Journal, 17*(2), 267–283.

Kohlbacher, M. and Reijers, H. A. (2013). The effects of process-oriented organizational design on firm performance. *Business Process Management Journal, 19*(2), 245–262.

Kuratko, D. F., Hornsby, J. S. and Goldsby, M. G. (2004). Sustaining corporate entrepreneurship: Modelling perceived implementation and outcome comparisons at organizational and individual levels. *International Journal of Entrepreneurship and Innovation Management, 5*(2), 77–90.

Kuratko, D. F., Hornsby, J. S. and Hayton, J. (2015). Corporate entrepreneurship: The innovative challenge for a new global economic reality. *Small Business Economics, 45*, 245–253.

Kuratko, D. F., Ireland, R. D., Covin, J. G. and Hornsby, J. S. (2005). A model of middle-level managers' entrepreneurial behavior. *Entrepreneurship Theory and Practice, 29*, 699–716.

Lawrence, T. B. and Suddaby, R. (2006). Institutions and institutional work In Clegg, S., Hardy, C., Lawrence, T. B. and Nord, W. R. (Eds.), *Handbook of organizational studies (2d edition)*. London: Sage, pp. 215–254.

Lawrence, T. B., Suddaby, R. and Leca, B. (2009). *Institutional work: Actors and agency in institutional studies of organizations*. Cambridge, UK: Cambridge University Press.

Lawrence, T. B., Suddaby, R. and Leca, B. (2011). Institutional work: Refocusing institutional studies of organization. *Journal of Management Inquiry, 20*(1), 52–58.

Lumpkin, G. T. and Dess, G. G. (1996). Clarifying the entrepreneurial orientation construct and linking it to performance. *Academy of Management Review, 21*, 135–172.

Martin, J. (1995). The style and structure of "cultures in organizations: Three perspectives". *Organization Science, 6*, 230–232.

McGaughey, S. L. (2004). 'Writing it up': The challenges of representation in qualitative research. In Piekarri, R. and Welch, C. (Eds.), *Handbook of qualitative research methods for international business*. Cheltenham, UK: Edward Elgar, pp. 529–550.

McGaughey, S. L. (2006). Reading as a method of inquiry in IB: Re-presentations of the 'born global'. *Management International Review*, Special Issue on Qualitative Methods in International Business, *46*(4), 461–480.

McGaughey, S. L. (2007). *Narratives of internationalisation: Legitimacy, standards and portfolio entrepreneurs*. Cheltenham, UK: Edward Elgar.

McGaughey, S. L. (2013). Institutional entrepreneurship in North American lightning protection standards: Rhetorical history and unintended consequences of failure. *Business History, 55*(1), 73–97.

McGaughey, S. L., Kumaraswarmy, A. and Liesch, P. W. (2016). Institutions, entrepreneurship and co-evolution in international business. *Journal of World Business, 51*, 871–881. http://dx.doi.org/10.1016/j.jwb.2016.07.003

Miller, D. (1986). Configurations of strategy and structure: Towards a synthesis. *Strategic Management Journal, 7*, 233–249.

Miller, D. (1996). Configurations revisited. *Strategic Management Journal, 17*, 505–512.

Morris, M. H., Kuratko, D. F. and Covin, J. G. (2008). *Corporate entrepreneurship and innovation*. Mason, OH: South Western Cengage Learning.

Munn, N. D. (1992). The cultural anthropology of time: A critical essay. *Annual Review of Anthropology, 21*, 93–123.

Narayanan, V. K., Yang, Y. and Zahra, S. A. (2009). Corporate venturing and value creation: A review and proposed framework. *Research Policy, 38*, 58–76.

Nason, R. S., McKelvie, A. and Lumpkin, G. T. (2015). The role of organizational size in the heterogeneous nature of corporate entrepreneurship. *Small Business Economics, 45*(2), 279–304.

Oliver, C. (1992). The antecedents of deinstitutionalization. *Organisation Studies, 13*(4), 563–588.

Paterson, S. L. and Brock, D. M. (2002). The development of subsidiary-management research: Review and theoretical analysis. *International Business Review, 11*, 139–163.

Pearce, J. L. and Huang, L. (2012). The decreasing value of our research to management education. *Academy of Management Learning and Education, 11*, 247–262.

Pettigrew, A. M. (2001). Management research after modernism. *British Journal of Management, 12*(s1), 61–70.
Richardson, L. (1990). *Writing strategies: Reaching diverse audiences* (Qualitative Research Methods No. 21). Newbury Park, CA: Sage.
Rosenblatt, L. M. (1978). *The reader, the text, the poem: The transactional theory of the literary work.* Carbondale, IL: Southern Illinois University Press.
Rynes, S. L., Bartunek, J. M. and Daft, R. L. (2001). Across the great divide: Knowledge creation and transfer between practitioners and academics. *Academy of Management Journal, 44*(2), 340–355.
Seo, M-G. and Creed, W. E. D. (2002). Institutional contradictions, praxis, and institutional change: A dialectical perspective. *Academy of Management Review, 27*(2), 222–247.
Shleifer, A. and Vishny, R. W. (1997). A survey of corporate governance. *The Journal of Finance, 52*, 737.
Siemens Press Release. (2013). *Siemens to realign regional organization and strengthen corporate units.* 17 October, Berlin. Available at: http://www.siemens.com/press/en/pressrelease/?press=/en/pressrelease/2013/corporate/axx20131003.htm&content[]=CC&content[]=Corp
Stake, R. E. (1978). The case study method in social inquiry. *Educational Researcher, 7*(2), 5–8.
Suchman, M. (1995). Managing legitimacy: Strategic and institutional approaches. *Academy of Management Review, 20*, 571–611.
Suddaby, R. and Greenwood, R. (2005). Rhetorical strategies of legitimacy. *Administrative Science Quarterly, 50*, 35–67.
Tang, G., Wei, L-Q., Snape, E. and Ng, Y. C. (2015). How effective human resource management promotes corporate entrepreneurship: Evidence from China. *The International Journal of Human Resource Management, 26*(12), 1586–1601.
Thorpe, R., Eden, C., Bessant, J. and Ellwood, P. (2011). Rigour, relevance and reward: Introducing the knowledge translation value-chain. *British Journal of Management, 22*, 420–431.
Von Krogh, G., Rossi-Lamastra, C. and Haefliger, S. (2012). Phenomenon-based research in management and organisation science: When is it rigorous and does it matter? *Long Range Planning, 45*(4), 277–298.
Weick, K. E. (2001). Gapping the relevance bridge: Fashions meet fundamentals in management research. *British Journal of Management, 12*(special issues), 71–75.
Weil, S., Oyelere, P. and Rainsburg, E. (2004). The usefulness of case studies in developing core competencies in a professional accounting programme: A New Zealand case study. *Accounting Education, 13*(2), 139–169.
Weil, S., Oyelere, P., Yeoh, J. and Firer, C. (2001). A study of students' perceptions of the usefulness of case studies for the development of finance and accounting-related skills and knowledge. *Accounting Education, 10*(2), 123–146.
Wolcott, H. F. (1994). *Transforming qualitative data.* Thousand Oaks, CA: Sage.
Wolcott, H. F. (1999). *Ethnography: A way of seeing.* Walnut Creek, CA: AltaMira Press.

Index

Page numbers in *italic* format indicate figures and tables.

For Product Safety Concerns and Information please contact our EU representative GPSR@taylorandfrancis.com Taylor & Francis Verlag GmbH, Kaufingerstraße 24, 80331 München, Germany